AF662893

BUSINESS ESSENTIAL
MARKETING AND PROMOTION

BUSINESS ESSENTIAL
MARKETING AND PROMOTION

Ajay Kumar Sharma

RANDOM
RANDOM PUBLICATIONS
NEW DELHI - 110 002 (INDIA)

Business Essential: Marketing and Promotion

ISBN 978-93-51117-17-9

Published in 2015 in India by

RANDOM PUBLICATIONS

4376-A/4B, Gali Murari Lal, Ansari Road
New Delhi-110 002
Phone: +9111-43580356, 23289044
E-mail: randomexports@gmail.com; sales@randompublications.com;
info@randompublications.com

Reprint 2021

Type Setting by: Friends Media, Delhi-110089
Digitally Printed at : Replika Press Pvt. Ltd.

Preface

Marketing is the science of choosing target markets through market analysis and market segmentation, as well as understanding consumer behaviour and providing superior customer value. From a societal point of view, marketing is the link between a society's material requirements and its economic patterns of response. Marketing satisfies these needs and wants through exchange processes and building long term relationships.

Promotion is one of the market mix elements or features, and a term used frequently in marketing. The marketing mix includes the four P's: price, product, promotion, and place. Promotion refers to raising customer awareness of a product or brand, generating sales, and creating brand loyalty. Promotion is also found in the specification of five promotional mix or promotional plan. These elements are personal selling, advertising, sales promotion, direct marketing, and publicity. A promotional mix specifies how much attention to pay to each of the five subcategories, and how much money to budget for each. A promotional plan can have a wide range of objectives, including: sales increases, new product acceptance, creation of brand equity, positioning, competitive retaliations, or creation of a corporate image. Fundamentally, there are three basic objectives of promotion. There are different ways to promote a product in different areas of media. Promoters use internet advertisements, special events, endorsements, and newspapers to advertise their product. Many times with the purchase of a product there is an incentive like discounts (i.e., coupons), free items, or a contest. This method is used to increase the sales of a given product. The term "promotion" is usually an "in" expression used internally by the marketing company, but not normally to the public or the market - phrases like "special offer" are more common. An example of a fully integrated, long-term, and a large-scale promotion are My Coke Rewards and Pepsi Stuff. The UK version of My Coke Rewards is Coke Zone. Promotions are also held in physical environments at special events such as concerts, festivals, trade shows, and in the field such as in grocery or department stores. Interactions in the field (i.e., grocery and department stores), allow customers to purchase the brand or product immediately. The interactions among the brand and the customer are performed by brand ambassadors or promotional models that represent the products and brands in physical environments. Brand ambassadors or promotional models are hired by marketing companies that are hired by the brand to represent the product and/or service. Person-to-person interaction, as opposed to media-to-person involvement, establishes connections that add another dimension to promotion. Building a community through promoting goods and services can lead to brand loyalty. Promotion can be done by different media, namely print media which includes Newspaper and magazines, Electronic media which includes radio and television, Digital media which includes internet, social networking and social media sites and lastly outdoor media which includes banner ads, OOH (out of home). Digital media is a modern way of brands interacting with consumers as it releases news, information and advertising from the technological limits of print and broadcast infrastructures.

This straightforward, practical book cuts through the morass of marketing theory to reveal the practical steps that small businesses can take to achieve the success.

I thank all members of my team who have helped in the preparation of the book. My special thanks go to "Random Publications" who have published the book.

— *Ajay Kumar Sharma*

Contents

Chapter 1

A Strategic Management Framework for Collaborative Product Development

Introduction

Global market competition and globalization of operations are forcing manufacturing companies to develop new high quality products at an increased speed and reduced cost.

Clark and Fujimoto [1991] observed that intensive, frequent, and bidirectional communication and information sharing are two important strategies for a successful and competitive product development process. However, this strategy proved difficult to implement within a global environment due to several factors discussed in McDonough et al. [1999].

On another front, Electronic-business is also influencing dramatically the ways these companies share and manage their information during Product Development (PD).

Rapid advancements of information technologies and computer networking offer new possibilities for a geographically dispersed team to work concurrently on development projects without the need for co-location. These above phenomena signal a new era in PD management practice, where companies are out sourcing more and more pieces of their PD process.

This leads to a complex and distributed development process requiring companies not only to share and exchange information with suppliers but also knowledge, methods, and tools.

Level Collaboration Type

Examples

1. Information sharing and management E-mail, data files, PIM.
2. Knowledge sharing and management Expert systems, Internet.
3. Collaboration architecture.

Structure, Roadmaps, Common Tools

Most advances in IT solutions for PD have focused on information management and data sharing. However, knowledge capturing and management is still a big challenge. The information and knowledge requirements needed in today's business have dramaticly increased. Tomiyama [1996] has emphasized the importance of knowledge as a core issue in engineering research. The core issue of concurrent engineering is sharing information and knowledge during distributed product development.

Beyond well-known communication, organizational and technological problems, which concurrent engineering addresses, we must focus more on knowledge as a source of added value. By intensively using product life cycle knowledge in an integrated manner, we can generate more added value including innovation, longer life, higher reliability and robustness, more flexibility, and cheaper life cycle cost. However, a good and widely accepted, methodology for information and knowledge management in product development does not exist. Consequently, there is an urgent need for a structured framework that facilitates the implementation and execution of collaborative and distributed PD Processes.

Many researchers have worked on this problem, which resulted in the development of several architectural frameworks and models for a distributed, collaborative PD. In what follows we will discuss the most relevant to our proposed framework. Hameri and Nihtila [1997] described a case study where geographically distributed product development teams utilized the World Wide Web (WWW) to share engineering information and data ranging form meeting minutes to 3D models and prototype test results. Their analysis suggested that the WWW can provide the needed functionality and flexibility required for supporting the communication needs of large distributed PD projects. Riitahuhta and Andreasen have suggested for this purpose a paradigm called Dynamic Modularization [1999].

Pahng et al. [1998] proposed an object oriented framework where a large design problem is modelled through the interaction of several distributed modules. Each module represents a specific aspect or concern in the development process and can encapsulate engineering models and software applications. The interaction between the modules is implemented in a "publish" and "subscribe" approach. The major advantage that this framework offered is the ability for the distributed modules (that contain data and tools) to interact and communicate over the network.

The Design Roadmap (DR) framework described by Park and Cutkosky [1999] is a process-oriented model of PD, which enables computer supported collaboration among distributed development teams. The DR framework is built on a directed graph description of the development process, where each node, in the graph, represents an activity, and arcs represent a precedence relationship between the activities. These graphs represent design process templates, which can be reused within their framework.

The framework proposed in this paper differs from the above literature in its focus. While these frameworks, except for the DR framework, concentrate on the engineering aspects of product development, our framework is concerned with the management aspect of a distributed PD process. Also, in a way similar to the DR framework, we adopt a process oriented view of the PD process in order to facilitate the management of the distributed teams.

The rest of the article proceeds as follows. In the next, section we present the basic conceptual framework for distributed and collaborative PD processes. In Section 3, we discuss one possible application scenario. Then, we illustrate the proposed framework with a case study in Section 4. Our future research direction in this project is described in Section 5. Finally, we present a summary and our conclusions in Section 6.2. The Proposed Strategic Management Framework In this paper we take a process-oriented view of the development process similar to the one described in Park and Cutkosky [1999].

We start this section by defining a process, as used within our framework, and show that this definition is used within the proposed framework. We define a process as a roadmap or recipe for change. Processes do not execute in vacuum. That is, they operate on something to change its state and they require the use of tools to facilitate this change. A strategic process is a collaborative process that either requires a model (i.e. information) or a tool form an entity outside its own organizational boundary or is a process that triggers another process outside its own organization.

One of the most important features of the proposed collaborative environment is the definition of a consistent and universal set of strategic processes. They are collaborative blueprints (i.e. templates, recipes, or roadmaps) describing all necessary and required interactions between the distributed entities involved in the PD process.

Systems and tools normally differ from one company to another, but the common IT Infrastructure enables the collaboration by enforcing that the right people are interacting with each others through a common (i.e. standard) process, while eliminating unnecessary interactions. A collaborative blueprint can simply be a binary matrix highlighting the existence of a relationship (This is also known as a Design Structure Matrix (DSM) as discussed elaborately in Eppinger et al. (1994)). Each "X" in the DSM is linked/mapped to a set of tools in the tools layer and models from the models layer.

The execution of a process augments the state of a model and the augmented new model is saved as a new revision of the earlier model.

These blueprints can be attained through several brainstorming sessions that include experts from different organizations involved in the execution of the process. Alternatively these templates can be obtained through a benchmarking effort.

Enterprises should decide on common information logistics and build a set of common strategic processes. This allows for the standardization of cooperative processes and finding out the similarities and differences in their modelling practices and use of tools. Finally, a collaborative IT Infrastructure should be designed and implemented around the established strategic processes to make this cooperation possible through the whole product/service life cycle.

The proposed management framework has a layered architecture. The layers are: strategic processes layer, models layer, tools layer, and physical layer. Distributed development teams react to the changes in the business environment, which sits on top of the framework as depicted, by interacting through the framework. The business environment plays a critical role in shaping and determining the processes that should be included in the strategic processes layer. The elements in the business environment are usually uncertain and outside the control of any development participant. For example, the strategic process used to formulate a new product platform includes uncertain elements, form the business environment, such as available technologies and competition.

The tools, models, and physical layers facilitate and support the execution of collaborative processes that are included in the strategic processes layer. The strategic processes layer provides templates for a set of predefined processes applicable to a specific PD project. Processes can be added or deleted from this layer as necessary and as PD practices evolve within the collaboration with time.

The models layer contains consistent and up-to-date product, process, project, and organizational information. These models can range from simple Excel files to complex 3D solid models. The utilization of standard collaborative processes (defined in the processes layer) and a common tool set (as defined in the tools layer) allow these models to become a common language between development participants. There is no confusion to where a model is used, for what purpose, and with which tool.

The tools layer provides development participants with a consistent set of tools utilized during the executing of collaborative processes. These tools are accessible on demand to the whole development community. Tools might include CAD software (i.e. CATIA), PDM (i.e. metaphase), ERP (i.e. SAP), simulation, supply chain management and decision support tools to name a few. Again note that tools that should be included in this layer are dependent of a specific development environment. Finally, the tools layer would eliminate the need for duplication of tools within the development community.

The physical layer facilitates communication, information sharing, tools sharing, and ties up the distributed databases. Security issues are also addressed at this layer. This layer can simply be a computer network with a standard protocol for distributed computing such as CORBA.

An Application Scenario

The application scenario presented in this article describes a distributed product development process with value added R&D service providers. Information technology offers the possibility to use community solutions for the PD partners allowing better groupware environment and use of common models and tools. Approval of semantic issues by all partners is an important part of starting this collaborative partnership.

One of the most important decisions is the architecture of the common IT Infrastructure, which enables and manages the desired collaboration between customers, knowledge brokers, and knowledge providers. The main supplier is normally running the broker service for the customer and facilitates the information flows, knowledge management and acquisition/availability of models and tools. Knowledge providers are usually the second and third tier suppliers that provide the required tools, models, or even communication infrastructure.

Within this proposed environment, it is possible to have multi-tiered brokering structure. That is, a supplier that acts as a knowledge provider, at a certain level of the PD brokering hierarchy, can act also as knowledge broker, at a lower level of the hierarchy. This process cascades down the PD supply chain until all PD participants (i.e. suppliers) are included. This multi-tiered brokering structure facilitates the PD collaboration processes in a consistent and easy to manage process. The multi-tier brokering concept is based on networked competence. Clusters of organizations collaborate with each other by using a common framework to deliver independent elements of value that grow with the number of participating organizations.

Case Study: R&D Support Network

The case study is an "R&D support network" that provides information and knowledge management services in a networked environment. The R&D Support Network is an information and knowledge brokering system that has been created in Finland during the national technology program "Improving the Efficiency of Product Development, RAPID" [RAPID, WWW]. It is used in business chain for linking value added service networks to support individual enterprises as describe. The R&D Support Network is a source of information and knowledge and is used as broker service environment offering a work space for the whole supply chain and customer network.

The goal of the R&D Support Network is to support Small and Medium size Enterprises (SMEs) in their product development activities and in the creation of partnerships and support networks. The ultimate goal is to support virtual enterprises working together in the various product development phases, using same methodologies, semantics and process as well as project models and supporting tools.

Common semantics, methodologies, models and tools, which are updated by R&D Support Network, are accessible on demand to the whole development community. R& D Support Networks are functioning as application service provider (ASP). R&D Support networks need a conceptual strategic management framework to act as a backbone for information and operation sharing and management.

Users in the network can be categorized in different groups:

- *End users:* these are enterprises who are looking for information, knowledge or business opportunities.
- *Brokers:* these are agents that can provoke, collect and manage information and services.
- Information and knowledge providers: these are entities that own the information and knowledge (i.e. processes, models, and/ or tools) which becomes available to customers through the broker services. Users of the service may often be mixture of above mentioned groups.

The main process provided by the R&D Support Network is a flexible and modular relationship and partnership management. It has been used in to facilitate the collaboration between various enterprises and academic organizations. Interested companies plug-in (i.e. subscribe) into R&D Support Broker Service whenever they need to build up a cooperation network/project. How supplier 1 uses the R&D Support Network to construct the second tier brokering system, which ties the second tier suppliers into the partnership network. The R&D Support Network allows companies to have access to capabilities (i.e. processes, models, and tools) of many information and knowledge providers.

Independence and trust in this type of community service is very important. The collaborative working process should be based on well-defined internal knowledge and processes based on the companies' own core competencies. After the competencies have been defined, efforts will be directed towards how to change the culture, processes and technology to support the new way of working.

Future Research

The long-range vision, of this research, is that value networks will grow up as dynamic markets in which valued knowledge is traded by value added service providers. Value added service providers and services would be searched according to agent based methodology. A strategic management framework is an important part of this scenario. We conjecture that the IT Infrastructure for a virtual enterprise has four specific value-added service layers separated based on the strategic management framework: IT Broker service layer, Infrastructure service layer, Information and Communication Technology (ICT) service layer, specialized service layer. System management is based on the proposed conceptual framework and it supports the start up and running of broker services or virtual businesses. It gives the necessary backbone and guidelines for strategy development and management concepts (portfolio management etc.). Networking methodologies and usable tools are restored and downloadable (ASP) from that part of the IT Framework.

Broker Service Layer categorizes various kinds of broker services. Infrastructure Service Layer supports partners to use common semantics and metadata base. ICT Service Layer allows partners to do actual distributed work in global network. Specialized Service Layer links specialized tools (e.g. web based project management or documentation tools), which are restored in distributed databases, to be used through ICT service layer by all partners of the whole virtual enterprise.

Owner-managers and the Practice of Strategic Management

The language of strategy and strategic management is recontextualizing the practice of management in many parts of the modern business world. This amounts to a wholesale change in the belief systems of managers. It involves managers in weaving into their existing beliefs and values various beliefs about strategy and strategic plans. Strategy, which may be formally defined as strategic objectives (or strategic direction) plus strategic plan for how to achieve the objectives, is itself a set of beliefs about how a firm can be successful or more successful. But there are also beliefs about the desirability of strategic management as a practice and the use of strategic management processes and tools.

This recontextualization of management has been accompanied by academic inquiry into the benefits of plans. For example, a number of empirical studies of small firms have attempted to correlate the presence of planning behaviour and business performance. Schwenk and Shrader (1993) in a meta analysis of existing studies concluded that, on balance, planning was positively linked to growth.

Much public policy in the UK and Europe also subscribes to the view that there are benefits of planning, not only for start-ups and for new businesses, but also for encouraging innovation in small businesses. Managers who use strategic planning are assumed to be more likely to achieve optimal management and development of their businesses. This public policy assumption has been reflected in the growth of a vast array of help and education for small firms' managers on how to do planning, that is provided by a variety of means including Government-supported services and agencies, private consultancy firms, private companies with training courses aimed at small business managers, programmes on small business management at Business Schools and business courses in Colleges and universities.

Despite this diverse range of support and educational activity for strategic business planning and strategic behaviour, there are critical voices regarding the efficacy of such behaviour. One voice has been particularly effective in raising doubts about conventional ideas and beliefs about strategic planning—this is Mintzberg (1979). He has sought to offer an empirical picture of the nature of reality in small entrepreneurial firms and in so doing has presented an anti-planners view of the small business. Mintzberg (1979: 306) characterized the small business as follows:

'Typically, it had little or no technostructure, few support staffers, a loose division of labour, minimal differentiation among its units, and a small managerial hierarchy. Little of its behaviour is formalized, and it makes minimal use of planning, training, and liaison devices. It is above all, organic'. As far as we can see he tends to subscribe to the following theses about small entrepreneurial firms:

(1) A written strategic plan has no explanatory power in respect of their behaviour because personal strategic visions rather than written strategic plans determine actual strategy.

(2) The small entrepreneurial firm develops a strategy that is deliberate and often an extrapolation of the chief executive's personality.

(3) The decision making of a small entrepreneurial firm is often intuitive and thus its success rests on reality confirming its intuitions about the opportunities that exist (and that it seeks to exploit by virtue of its flexibility).

(4) There is a persisting need for strategy based on personal vision and control and thus a persisting need for small entrepreneurial firms.

Mintzberg's particular take on the way these organizations work can end up appearing to justify their management practices as congruent with some true essence of an entrepreneurial personality possessed by some individuals and as compatible with the human nature of its employees who may develop, according to him, solid identification with the business. An important point about this Mintzbergian brand of anti-planning theory is that it is not interested in coming up with suggestions for improvement or reform of small business management. It is largely content with criticizing formal strategic plans. Also, it is hot concerned with making practical detailed comparisons with other forms of entrepreneurial firm that may be defined by their interest in innovation rather than by their flexibility and risk-taking propensity.

The sorts of sceptical doubts raised by Mintzberg about the role of strategic planning in small entrepreneurial firms seem well justified since so few small businesses use strategic planning. Consequently, exhorting the 'average' manager of a small business to transcend their current informal style of management and adopt the formal methods of strategic analysis and strategy formulation may seem utopian. On the other hand, if anti-planners point to deficiencies in strategic planning, or even inconsistencies of strategic planning behaviour with the culture of small business management, they offer small business managers no prospect of handling the direction of their businesses in any way other than the personal, visionary, and arbitrary manner identified by, say, Mintzberg (1979).

Is there a way out of this barren choice of either support for strategic planning or support for an anti-planning approach? One possibility is to follow Mintzberg's example of studying the actions and language of management in small business. This is to focus on 'how things happen in practice', and do so in a way that appreciates future possibilities for change as small business management culture is reformed and evolves through practising managers dealing with the world they are experiencing.

In the next section the methodology, conceptual framework and sample are discussed. This then prepares the ground for a discussion of managers in small businesses and what they know of the vocabulary of strategic management and what they do in terms of strategic management practice. This then is followed by an analysis of the functionality of the vocabularies and practice of strategic management. The final section offers conclusions and a reconsideration of management culture and practice in small businesses.

Methodology, Conceptual Framework, and Sample

Research into small business broadly falls within two methodological camps, one based on quantitative approaches and one on qualitative. There is another smaller camp that attempts with varying degrees of success to combine both in an attempt to square the methodological circle. The approach in this article falls squarely into the quantitative camp. Consequently, the faults and limitations associated with a quantitative approach have to be accepted. On the positive side, this work can be used by other future work as a benchmark to measure changes over time (with due regard for sampling decisions).

It also has the merit of allowing us to generate hypotheses that can be tested. Its relative lack of interpretative power at the level of detailed explanation can be taken up in studies using a more qualitative approach. The conceptual framework for this study is very simple. First, we assume that a range of processes can produce in managers of small firms knowledge of strategic tools and can lead to such managers valuing the results of applying the tools. These processes could include taking part in Business School programmes, employing consultants as management developers, attending short courses provided by business support agencies, and reading business books.

The result of these processes could mean that the managers of small firms are increasingly embracing the new vocabulary of strategic management. If managers are aware of strategic tools and value them, they may use the tools to make judgements. The next step is for managers to apply these judgements to decision making. In other words, we have moved to the stage at which managers' practices evolve as well as their vocabularies. It is also assumed that the results of using tools and applying them to decision making can lead to feedback loops that modify knowledge of these tools and the value placed on their use. Finally, it is envisaged that the use of such tools can lead to better management strategies (objectives and plans). Alternatively the benefits may show up as improved business performance through enhanced management effectiveness without necessarily being directly mediated by a strategic plan.

The intentions behind this study can be related to this conceptual framework. The first intention was to describe what strategic tools the respondents had heard about. The second intention was to examine what use, if any, they made of them. The third intention was to see if these areas of knowledge and practice had any survival or performance value. So, we were interested in determining the knowledge of strategic tools held by managers in small firms not simply to map or describe the diffusion of strategic management vocabulary but also to investigate whether such a vocabulary had any merit for managers as a way of negotiating and interacting with the business world.

The survey questions used various strategic management terms that we evaluated as commonly found in books on strategy. Many, if not all of these terms are themselves open to differing interpretations. We cannot claim that the terms we used were understood in the same way by the respondents as by us. In all likelihood others in the field of strategy would disagree with our definitions anyhow. This is not an easy problem to work around. We looked at several books on strategy, including Johnson and Scholes (1999), Joyce and Woods (2001), and Hussey (1998), and picked out a range of strategic tools mentioned. We did not attempt to use every single tool we came across or make an assessment of how useful the tools were.

We did not seek to establish an inter-subjective understanding of the various strategic management terms with survey respondents. The approach we took was to use the specialized vocabulary and not to interpret it or define it for the respondents. We did this because we wanted to test the extent to which the specialized vocabulary had been transmitted to managers in small businesses. (Neither were we testing to what extent respondents used a range of strategic tools, but did so without naming them in the specialized vocabulary, or used them in an unconscious way).

We wanted a representative sample of businesses within London. We purchased from Electronic Yellow Pages a random sample based on their database of 2500 firms within the M25. We aimed to interview at least 500 senior managers who were able to answer questions on the firm's strategy and related issues. From the list of 2500, every fifth firm was contacted by telephone by one of the team of three interviewers who had extensive experience of this type of work. The interviewer asked to speak to a senior manager or for smaller firms the owner-manager. They then checked that they were able to answer detailed questions on the firm's strategy. If a firm refused to participate the next firm on the list was then contacted. We approached over 700 firms and screened out those respondents who were unable or unwilling to answer questions about the firm's strategy. The telephone interview lasted about 20 minutes. A range of questions about the strategy and strategic tools used in the firm was asked. In all 513 firms were interviewed. Our use of experienced interviewers possibly helped to achieve the high response rate—in excess of 85 percent. As the sample frame was ordered randomly, selecting every fifth firm on the list (or the next one if there was a refusal) ensured that the firms that were interviewed were selected at random. Looking at the firms that were contacted but not interviewed, no systematic bias was detected in terms of size or sector compared to those that were.

The respondents were drawn from three main groups, owner-managers (25 %), partner/director (34%), and manager/supervisor (33%). The owner—managers were considered by us to be of special interest for two reasons. First, it might be assumed that owner-managers often play a distinctively central role in the management of their business, so their abilities and personality could be critical for business performance. This central role could mean they tend to carry a disproportionate share of the responsibility for planning and strategic behaviour as against those who describe themselves as partner/directors or manager/supervisors. Second, we wondered if they might be different from other managers due to acculturation processes. Several researchers have round that in terms of thinking about and resolving business problems, owner-managers use intuition more, whereas other managers favour a more structured and logical approach. It was our intention when analysing the data to probe for differences of vocabulary and practice between the owner-managers and other managers.

Analysis: Vocabulary of Strategic Management

As stated above, the first intention behind the analysis was to describe what strategic tools the respondents had heard about. The results are for all 513 firms irrespective of firm size as measured by employment.

The difference between owner-managers and other managers in respect of their knowledge of strategic management terms is fairly pronounced. The owner-managers appear to have a poorer strategic management vocabulary. For the best-known terms—such as market research and cost benefit analysis—there was little difference between the two groups of managers. But a more substantial difference is observed for the more esoteric terms, especially terms such as scenario planning, gap analysis, and core competency analysis. Perhaps there is a size effect at work? In fact from the data it is clear that, if we analyse just those respondents in firms employing between 1 and 5 employees, owner-managers have still heard of fewer strategic tools than other managers. This might mean that owner-managers have not found it useful to learn about strategic management tools. It may, alternatively, be that they have been less exposed to such techniques.

From Knowledge to Management Practice—Using Strategic Tools

Based on our conceptual framework, it might be expected that the use of strategic tools is more common among groups of managers that have a richer strategic management vocabulary than among groups of managers that have a poorer vocabulary. Since the owner-managers had a poorer knowledge of strategic tools, it might be expected that fewer of them would report using strategic tools than their counterparts in other management positions. So it proved to be. Thus, in the smallest firms with less than 6 employees, owner-managers on average used 1.4 tools compared to 2.3 for other managers (F statistic 6.294, significance 0.014).

As in the case of having knowledge of strategic tools, there seemed to be a size effect in respect of the use of such tools. The use of tools in the smallest firms, it might be noted that managers in firms employing 50 employees or more used 4.8 tools on average.

The Value of Strategic Management

Having a wider vocabulary of strategic management is linked to extent of use of strategic tools. Owner-managers who had heard of strategic tools were just as likely as their counterparts who had heard of them to use them. So, the issue would seem to be that of owner-managers having a poorer vocabulary. Why? One answer is that people in other management positions are often in slightly bigger firms and so may find strategic management to be helpful in dealing with this larger environment and its associated management tasks. If this is right it should be found that owner-managers and other managers are no different when size of firm is controlled. The empirical evidence, data from respondents in firms with rive or less employees is displayed. When firm size was controlled at rive or less employees, among respondents who had heard of strategic tools, the proportion of owner-managers not using them was much the same as the proportion of other managers.

Arguably the nature of management challenges and tasks varies from one context to another, including the size context. If this is right, then managers can be understood to develop strategic management practices that work for them, and the bigger the firm the more evidently does experience teach that they work. The corollary of this is that we might predict that, on the whole, if managers have hot developed such practices it is because their current ones are seen as serving them well. They should, in principle, experience no lack of expertise. For expertise is a function of the managers' need to handle their situation and tasks, hot a function of some ideal standard of knowledge and practices imposed from outside of their experience.

A comparison of owner-managers and other managers did hot reveal any difference in perception that a lack of expertise was interfering with the firm's strategic planning. It was found for both groups that those respondents who used the fewest number of tools were the least likely to say it was lack of expertise that was interfering with their strategic planning effort. The data for the whole sample and shows a pronounced tendency for those respondents reporting less tools being used to be also those reporting that lack of expertise was not interfering with strategic planning. At this point in the analysis we seem to have ended up in confirming the anti-planners' view that small businesses are ill suited to strategic planning. We have, it appears, justified the absence of strategic planning in large parts of the small firm sector.

Comparisons and Contradictory Evidence

There is, however, some contradictory evidence on the value of strategic tools. A concrete comparison of owner-managers and other managers in terms of the growth record of their businesses suggested that the use of tools did confer advantages to businesses. The evidence for this is as follows.

First, respondents were asked to describe the current health of their business. They could identify it as ranging from growing rapidly, through healthy and growing, stable, and finally declining. Out of the 41 firms that described themselves as rapidly growing only three respondents were owner-managers. Of the 28 declining firms 15 respondents were owner-managers. There was a statistically significant association between firm performance and respondent. It seems that owner-managers were more likely to be in firms that were declining and less likely than other managers to be able to report a growth record. Second, the use of strategic tools was correlated with the performance of the business. On average, rapid growers used 3.75 tools compared with only 1.00 for the decliners. Interestingly the healthy and growing group used 2.36 and the stable group 1.75. This was significant (F = 3.490, at 0.017 level of significance).

Third, owner-managers used typically 1.38 tools as against 2.34 for the other managers (F = 6.294, 0.013 level of significance).

We suggest that this analysis is consistent with the idea that the use of strategic management tools causes growth. Hence, owner-managers are less likely to be in firms that are growing because they do not make use of strategic management tools. It is also consistent with a very different analysis: owner-managers are more prone to be in firms that are declining and are thus not under the same pressure from their environments to use strategic management tools needed to cope with more dynamic growth issues. The informal practices that stood the firm in good stead in the past are now seen to be less relevant and a more 'professional' approach is called for. So the adoption of the vocabulary and use of the tools is not a cause of the improved performance but a consequence of it. Further as the firm grows the owner-manager starts to recruit managers who have had previous exposure to strategic management tools and naturally use them in managing the firm's strategy. As the firm begins to acquire the tools.

Enhancing Organisational Performance through Strategic Management

Strategic management is a disciplined approach utilizing the principles and process of management to identify the corporate objective or mission of any business. It determines an appropriate target to satisfy the objective, recognize existing opportunities and constraints in the environment, and device a rational practical way by which objective can be achieved.

Strategic management is both the process and philosophy for determining and controlling the organizational relationship in its dynamic environment. As a process, it attempts to define approaches and techniques to assist management adapt to the dynamic of today, through the use of objectives and strategies. Strategic management endeavours to achieve effective and efficient programs to accomplish the organization's mission. As a philosophy, it changes how manager looks at competitors, customers, markets and even the organization itself. Its objective is to stimulate management's awareness of the strategic implication of environmental events and internal decision.

Lawrence and William (1988) defined strategic management as a stream of decisions and actions, which leads to the development of an effective strategy or strategies to help achieve corporate objectives. The strategic management process is the way in which strategists determine objectives and make strategic decisions.Strategic management's main focus is the achievement of organizational goals taking into consideration the internal and external environmental factors. Porter (1985) argues that the essence of formulating comprehensive strategy is relating a company to its environment. Strategic management permits the systematic management of change. It enables organization to purposefully mobilize resources towards a desired future.

Chandler (1962) also posited that any effective successful strategy is dependent on structure, thus to achieve any effective economic performance the organization needs to alter its structure. The objective of this paper is to examine the conceptual and theoretical approach of strategic management on the performance of business organization.

The objectives of the paper are:

i. To examine the importance and relevance of strategic management in an organization.
ii. To examine the effectiveness of strategic management.
iii. To see how strategic management influence performance of the business organization.

Literature Review/Theoretical Framework

Strategy is the determination of the basic term goals and objectives of an enterprise, and the adoption of course of action and the allocation of resources necessary for carrying out those goals Chandler (1962).

In Chandler definition of strategy he attempts to view that strategy is as much as about defining goals and objectives as it is about providing the means for achieving them.

Ansoff and McDonnell (1990) also separate goal setting (concerned with ends) from strategy (concerned with means). On the subject of strategic management they provide the following definition:

Strategic management is a systematic approach for managing strategic change, which consists of the following:

a. Positioning of the firm through strategy and capability planning.
b. Real-time strategic response through issue management.
c. Systematic management of resistance during strategic implementation.

Strategy and market positions are necessary to set directions for a firm and to outsmart competitors or at least enable it to overcome threatening environment. A good strategy when adequately implemented can ensure a topmost position for the weakest firm among other superior competitors, but without good strategies.

Strategic planning if well conceptualized and implemented with an organization should result in strategic management. Strategic management treats strategic thinking as a pervasive concept for running a business organization and regards strategic planning as an instrument around which all other control system budgeting, information, reward and organization can be integrated. Strategic planning specifically entails the allocation of resources to programmed activities in such a way as to achieve a set of business goals in a dynamic competitive environment. Glueck and Jauch (1984) posited that strategic management as a steam of decisions and actions that lead to the development od effective strategies to help achieve corporate objectives.

Mintzberg (1991) sees strategy as 5 P's – plans, ploys, patterns, position and perspective. He describes a plan as 'some sort of consciously intended course of action'. In this situation organizations are expected to decide what they want to do and how they intend to achieve it. Failure of many organizations in recent time has been attributed to poor plan. A ploy is a sub-set of a plan, and is a strategy in the sense of a strategies (i.e. a ruse or trick designed to put a rival company off the sent by disguising the real intention of the company).

Mintzberg (1991) describes pattern as the consistent behaviour and processes that emerge from strategic thinking, due to intended or unintended actions. He sees plans and ploys as deliberate strategy use by an organization, but considers pattern as emergent strategies. According to Mintzberg position is acceptable location for the organization in an environment. In business organization position boils down to its product market position in its chosen market. This is what Nigeria Bottling Company (NBC) has been using over other any soft drink industry. Perspective is looking inside the organization. Any of business organization with high degree of perspective approach will have management that have shared view and vision and make a positive impact on the environment where it operates.

Strategy is needed to focus effort and promote coordination of activities. Without strategy an organization becomes bunch of individuals, hence strategy is required to ensure collective actions and concentration of efforts towards achieving organizational plans and objective.

Johnson and Scholes (1993) view corporate strategy from cultural perspective, they described it as a strategy based on the experiences, assumptions and beliefs of management overtime and which may eventually permeate the whole organization.

Henceforth, strategy can help in defining an organization to both insiders and outsiders. Strategy as plan, ploy pattern, position and perspectives defines the organization by providing proper understanding of the organization to the people and a way of differentiating it from others. One needs to understand that a clearly defined strategy that will lead to enthusiasm among various stakeholders – shareholders, suppliers, creditors, customers, promoter and employees as a result promote commitment that will enhance better performance of business organization.

Strategy provides consistency and stability. It deals with irregularity in behaviour and reduces uncertainty about the operation of an organization. It resist changes thereby ensuring consistency which gives a sense of being in control to the management and relief from the anxiety created by complexity. This does not mean a static or stationary situation but rather it implies an efficient response to the environment to ensure stability and continual domination or retention of market leadership by the business organization involved. This assists the organization to focus its resources and exploit its opportunities, skill and knowledge to the fullest. Strategy is a broad based formular for how business is going to compete, that is, what its goal should be, and what policies will be needed to carryout these goals.

An organization strategic management has its ultimate objective in the development of its corporate values, managerial capabilities, organizational responsibilities and operational decision making at all hierarchical levels and across all business and functional lines of authority. According to Child (1972) strategic decision making is seen as a crucial part of the process by which organization adapt to their environments. It is argued that those decision that actually succeed in creating or changing organizations do so via complex iterative process, which strategy theorists subsume under the concept of strategy implementation.

Importance of Strategic Planning

The importance of strategic planning in any business organization can not be overemphasized. Most of the organizations recently recognized the role of strategic planning to the long range growth and survival of their business organization. Most of the managers have observed that by specifically defining the mission of their organization they are better able to give it direction and focus its activities.

Some Nigerian Business Organizations are without formal plans or where there are formal plans they do operate without adhering to them. Some argued that the market place changes so fast for a plan to be useful. All business organizations are heading somewhere but unfortunately some do not know where they are going, then any road will lead them there.

This therefore emphasizes the need for organizations to utilize strategic planning concepts. Planning remains the key to organization success because absence of proper planning could lead to confusion and unethical practices. However, despite the importance of strategic planning many organizations still fail to plan, hence planning to fail.

In recent times, the study of strategic management is being given much attention Lambo (1986) studies bank portfolio management examining profit maximization and accommodation principle models in Nigeria commercial banks. Adeyemi (1992) who established that there is a positive correlation between strategic management and organizational performance in some Nigeria banks also carried out another study.

It is worthy of note that whatever conclusions are made, it has been empirically stated that the success or failure of strategic planning is determined by a number of components which include the environment, organization structure and strategic decision making. According to Ansoff (1979), when these three components are properly matched, the performance of any organization is optimized.

Lorange (1979) posited that the importance of strategic planning is to accomplish a sufficient process of innovation to support and enhance the planning process. He further argues that effective strategic planning does not have to be elaborate or complicated but must be logical and focused on strategic decisions to be undertaken.

Effectiveness of Strategic Management

Alli (1992) gives the characteristics of an effective strategic management as follows:

a. Clear direction and purpose.
b. Objectives, goals, and strategic consistency.
c. Continuous monitoring of internal and external (environment).
d. Integration of operating budget and profit plans with strategic plan.
e. Continuous monitoring of progress with revision of plan and programs as appropriate.
f. Creation of strategic atmosphere that foresters a team spirit.
g. Commitment of necessary resources and the development of system to provide necessary management information.

Basically, there are three major perspectives of studying strategic management effectiveness in literature.

Firstly, uses of goal centred approach to assess organizational effectiveness. In this situation, individual organization seeks to analyse the extent of fulfilment of important planning objectives. Cameron and Whitton (1983), King (1987) and Steiner (1979) also support this.

Secondly, specific capabilities to develop a 'generic view' if system capabilities as stated by Lorange (1979) a generic capability required of every formal strategic planning system is the ability to encourage both creativity and control.

In this perspective, creativity and control are used here not as opposite objective but as requisite properties of an effective planning system. The third perspective traditionally examines the role and impact of corporate planning on organizational effectiveness. Although, the link may be a little bit difficult however, there are strong arguments that the ultimate test of the system's effectiveness and justification for its existence is the impact on organizational performance.

Methodology

For this study the researcher designed questionnaire and was administered to the First Bank of Nigeria, Plc. Ilorin Branch. The researcher administered thirty-five questionnaires, which was divided into two parts. This first part contained demographic characteristics of the respondents while the second part was used to tap information on how strategic management enhances organization performance.

The researcher was able to retrieved twenty-nine questionnaires from the respondents. This represents eighty-three per cent (83%) rate. The respondents for the study were randomly selected and stratified into male and female. The collected data were analysed descriptively.

Analysis and Discussion

The first part of the questionnaire which is on demographic characteristic of the respondents revealed that 72.4% of the sample were male while 27.6% of the respondents were female. This shows that majority of the respondents interviewed are male. The ages of the respondents were between 21 to 50, although about 62.1% of the respondents fall within 31-40 age bracket. While only 13.8% were between 41-50 age group.

The study also revealed that 75.9% of the respondents were married while 24.1% were still single. About 44.8% of the respondents have spent above 11 years with the organisation. This shows that information was collected from the well-experienced personnel from the organisation, and this is an indication of the reliability of the information obtained.

Table: *Demographic characteristics of the respondents*

Sex	*frequency*	*percentage*
Male	21	72.4
Female	8	27.6
Total	**29**	**100**
Age	***frequency***	***percentage***
Under 21	-	-
21-30	7	24.1
31-40	18	62.1
41-50	4	13.8
Total	**29**	**100**

Length of service	*frequency*	*percentage*
1-5 yrs	6	20.7
6-10 yrs	13	44.8
11-15 yrs	5	17.2
16-above	5	17.2
Total	**29**	**100**

Education qualification	*frequency*	*percentage*
WASC/GCE	2	6.9
NCE/OND	1	3.4
HND/B.Sc./B.A.	16	55.2
M.Sc./MBA/MPA	10	34.5
Total	**29**	**100**

Table 2: Staff responses on the adoption of strategic management by their organisation

Variables	*Frequency*	*Percentage*
Strongly agree	9	31.0
Agree	15	51.7
Disagree	3	10.3
Strongly disagree	-	-
Undecided	2	6.9
Total	**29**	**100**

Source: researcher findings.

Table 3: Adoption of strategic management has enhanced the organisation performance.

Variables	*Frequency*	*Percentage*
Strongly agree	15	51.7
Agree	11	37.9
Disagree	2	6.9
Strongly disagree	1	3.4
Undecided	-	-
Total	**29**	**100**

Source: researcher findings.

The table 2 above shows that the responses of the respondents as regards to the adoption of strategic management in their organisation. 31.0% of the people interviewed strongly agreed while 51.7% also agreed that their organisation is fully adopted strategic management in its operation. Although, about 10.3% of the respondents disagreed that their operation has not fully adopted strategic management in their operation.

The study also revealed that 51.7% and 37.9% of the respondents strongly agreed and agreed respectively that adoption of strategic management has enhanced the organisation performance. This shows that management recognition of strategic management has enabled it to make a sound decision, which has enhanced its successful operation in its environment.

However, 10.3% of the respondents disagreed with that position, according to them their organisation performance was due to other factors, which is outside the scope of this paper. It was also revealed from the study that strategic planning in the organization is occasionally handled by the consultant, and also done at the top management level.

Conclusion and Summary

This paper examines the enhancement of Organisational performance through strategic management: conceptual theoretical and approach. In recent times world economy has witnessed a lot of dynamism and challenges.

Therefore, there is need to take longer perspectives of operations so as to ensure that available resources are purposely harnessed for the optimal direction of the affairs of the business organizations.

An enhancement of business organization performance through strategic management will depend on management's recognition of the following functions: setting objectives, establishing policies with which to work towards objectives, assign responsibilities and provide for coordinated action, selecting and developing key personnel, helping them adjust to change, motivating and stimulating them to think creatively and measuring progress and evaluating results.

Strategic management allows an organization to make its decisions based on long-range forecast and not on the spur of the moment reaction. It also allows the establishment to make action at an early stage of new trend and consider the lead-time for effective management.

Ansoff et al (1979) studies ninety-three large firms, all of which have made acquisition between 1946 and 1965 and their financial and sales measure. They found that managers were able to predict outcomes better than non-planners.

The business organizations should adopt a competitive position, which will allow them to defend themselves against any forces in the industry environment. Harmnermesh (1993) proposed three broad generic strategies which if adopted by business organization will enable it to compete in a given business and position itself among it's competitors.

These strategies are: overall cost leadership (achieve lower cost than competitors; differentiation (creating something unique and superior) and focus that is, selecting a particular buyer group or segment of the market as the basis for competition.

In order to achieve better performance, business organizations need to take bold step of adopting strategic management in their various organizations. Knowing fully well that the level and intensity of the competition between the organizations is fast increasing as the level of business organizations and individual.

In meeting the current challenges by the business organizations call for application of better and more meaningful strategic management which would transcend all categories of worker within the business organization.

Strategic Management

Strategic management is the process of specifying an organization's objectives, developing policies and plans to achieve these objectives, and allocating resources so as to implement the plans. It is the highest level of managerial activity, usually performed by the company's Chief Executive Officer (CEO) and executive team.

It provides overall direction to the whole enterprise. An organization's strategy must be appropriate for an organizations resources, circumstances, and objectives. The process involves matching the companies' strategic advantages to the business environment the organization faces. One objective of an overall corporate strategy is to put the organization into a position to carry out its mission effectively and efficiently. A good corporate strategy should integrate an organization's goals, policies, and action sequences (tactics) into a cohesive whole.

Strategy Formulation and Implementation

Strategic management can be seen as a combination of strategy formulation and strategy implementation. Strategy formulation involves:

- Doing a situation analysis: both internal and external; both micro-environmental and macro-environmental.

- Concurrent with this assessment, objectives are set. This involves crafting vision statements (long term), mission statements (medium term), overall corporate objectives (both financial and strategic), strategic business unit objectives (both financial and strategic), and tactical objectives.
- These objectives should, in the light of the situation analysis, suggest a strategic plan. The plan provides the details of how to obtain these goals.
- This three-step strategy formation process is sometimes referred to as determining where you are now, determining where you want to go, and then determining how to get there.

  These three questions are the essence of strategic planning.

Strategy implementation involves:

- Allocation of sufficient resources (financial, personnel, time, computer system support)
- Establishing a chain of command or some alternative structure (such as cross functional teams)
- Assigning responsibility of specific tasks or processes to specific individuals or groups
- It also involves managing the process. This includes monitoring results, comparing to benchmarks and best practices, evaluating the efficacy and efficiency of the process, controlling for variances, and making adjustments to the process as necessary.
- When implementing specific programs, this involves acquiring the requisite resources, developing the process, training, process testing, documentation, and integration with (and/or conversion from) legacy processes.

Strategy formation and implementation is an on-going, never-ending, integrated process requiring continuous reassessment and reformation. Strategic management is dynamic. It involves a complex pattern of actions and reactions.

It is partially planned and partially unplanned. Strategy is both planned and emergent, dynamic, and interactive.

Some people (such as Andy Grove at Intel) feel that there are critical points at which a strategy must take a new direction in order to be in step with a changing business environment.

These critical points of change are called strategic inflection points.

The Strategy Hierarchy

In most (large) corporations there are several levels of strategy. Strategic management is the highest in the sense that it is the broadest, applying to all parts of the firm. It gives direction to corporate values, corporate culture, corporate goals, and corporate missions. Under this broad corporate strategy there are often functional or business unit strategies.

Functional strategies include marketing strategies, new product development strategies, human resource strategies, financial strategies, legal strategies, and information technology management strategies. The emphasis is on short and medium term plans and is limited to the domain of each department's functional responsibility. Each functional department attempts to do its part in meeting overall corporate objectives, and hence to some extent their strategies are derived from broader corporate strategies.

Many companies feel that a functional organizational structure is not an efficient way to organize activities so they have reengineered according to processes or strategic business units (called SBU's).

A strategic business unit is a semi-autonomous unit within an organization. It is usually responsible for it's own budgeting, new product decisions, hiring decisions, and price setting. An SBU is treated as an internal profit centre by corporate headquarters. Each SBU is responsible for developing it's business strategies, that must be in tune with broader corporate strategies.

The "lowest" level of strategy is operational strategy. It is very narrow in focus and deals with day-to-day operational activities such as scheduling criteria.

It must operate within a budget but is not at liberty to adjust or create that budget. Operational level strategy was encouraged by Peter Drucker in his theory of management by objectives (MBO). Operational level strategies are informed by business level strategies which, in turn, are informed by corporate level strategies.

Since the turn of the millennium, there has been a tendency in some firms to revert to a simpler strategic structure.

This is being driven by information technology. It is felt that knowledge management systems should be used to share information and create common goals. Strategic divisions are thought to hamper this process.

Dual Strategies

Strategic management operates on several time scales. Short term strategies involve planning and managing for the present. Long term strategies involve preparing for and pre-empting the future.

Marketing strategist, Derek Abell (1993), has suggested that understanding this dual nature of strategic management is the least understood part of the process. He claims that balancing the temporal aspects of strategic planning requires the use of dual strategies simultaneously.

Establishing Strategic Intent: Vision, Mission, Objectives and Goals

Defining Your Strategic Intent

Any successful business—large or small—didn't achieve success on good ideas alone. Succeeding in the business world requires what professors Gary Hamel and C.K. Prahalad term "strategic intent." Strategic intent, they explain, is a business' long-term, far-reaching goal. In order to determine your business' strategic intent, you must not only consider what you want in the next five or ten years, but what you want to accomplish in a 50 year time frame.

For example, decades ago, Coca-Cola's strategic intent was for there to be a Coke within the reach of every human being on the planet. This seemed like a crazy idea at the time, but think about how prevalent Coke products are these days. By setting a developing a vision of the future and developing long-term goals, Coca-Cola made enormous strides in developing their brand. The main tenets of strategic intent planning are direction, discovery and destiny.

- Sense of Direction includes an understanding about the long-term market or competitive position that a firm aims to build over the next decade. Your sense of direction should be a view of the future that conveys a unifying and personalizing sense of direction.
- Sense of Discovery. Your strategic intent should retain a sense of discovery and excitement about the future. This helps create a competitively unique outlook and gives employees the opportunity to explore new competitive territory.
- Sense of Destiny. Strategic intent has an emotional edge to it and it should be a goal that both you and your employees perceive as inherently worthwhile.

But strategic intent is not just a concept; it's also a three-step process.

- Set the Strategic Intent (having all three characteristics stated above).
- Set the Challenges: find appropriate challenges and communicate them to the entire work force. These challenges are the means to get into the Strategic Intent. (For example: Suppose the Strategic Intent of Google is: Allow end users to access all of the information of the Internet with the click of a mouse. A strategic challenge could be: Come up with a search engine capable of producing accurate search results.)
- Empowerment of the Strategic Intent: The strategic intent works best when everyone is invested in its goals. Managers and business owners should keep in mind the "wisdom of the anthill" and challenge traditional downward communications styles.

Defining your strategic intent clarifies objectives for both you and your employees. By setting out your strategic intent, you make clear your company's goals and help set the path for future successes.

Chapter 2

Pursuing Product Differentiation and Cost Leadership Strategies

For years management scholars have debated whether firms can simultaneously pursue cost leadership and product differentiation. Students often ask the same question. One question that usually arises in discussions of product differentiation is: When a store advertises its low prices like Wal-Mart does, is that evidence of a cost leadership strategy or is that evidence of a product differentiation strategy? The answer is: Yes.

Most firms' strategies contain elements of both cost leadership and product differentiation. But, in the vast majority of firms one is clearly emphasized over the other. The relatively few firms that can effectively pursue both strategies are in an enviable position indeed. Anecdotal evidence suggests that firms that are able to simultaneously pursue both strategies started out with a sharp focus on one and in time were able to pursue the other as well. Conversely, anecdotal evidence also suggests that some firms that have tried to do both and failed weren't really achieving one before they started to pursue the other. Here are some quick examples from the discount retail market and the auto industry:

Wal-Mart started out with a sharp focus on cost leadership. This strategy allowed them to gain market share and become very profitable. In time, the firm could afford to advertise heavily to convince customers that they had the low price. Always. This heavy advertising is indicative of a product differentiation strategy. It is also interesting to note that local store managers, although obligated to follow fairly strict guidelines, are able to carry items of local interest that are not part of the national buying program. Toyota developed a manufacturing system that drove costs to a minimum. Toyota recognized that they could achieve low manufacturing costs and very high quality simultaneously with their system. Most American consumers initially viewed Toyota as a low cost alternative to higher priced American cars. In time, Toyota began to differentiate its products on quality. Its Lexus line is very much a differentiated product that is manufactured at a very competitive cost among luxury car makers.

Mercedes developed a strong reputation for high quality cars. For many years, cost was not a critical issue for Mercedes. The introduction of car lines like the Lexus and the rising popularity of SUVs has forced Mercedes to focus more on cost. In other words, Mercedes is being forced to be concerned about cost. It remains to be seen if Mercedes will become competitive on cost or if Mercedes will further differentiate its cars on quality. Some industry analysts worry that Mercedes may hurt its reputation for quality if it tries to focus on cost too much.

Ford very successfully introduced the Taurus as described above. However, in 1996 Ford tried to move the Taurus up market. Other car makers had imitated many of the Taurus' most distinguishing features. Ford tried to differentiate the Taurus with even more 'rounding' of the body. The sticker price was raised about $2,500. This attempt to differentiate the Taurus was a failure. Many customers turned to the Toyota Camry and the Honda Accord. By 1996 the Taurus wasn't a cost leader and it wasn't highly differentiated. It seems to have become stuck in the middle.

K-Mart tried to differentiate itself by moving upscale in the mid-1990s. Having realized it couldn't compete with Wal-Mart on price, K-Mart seems to have decided to adopt a level of differentiation. Celebrities such as Kathy Ireland and Martha Stewart were used to try to generate more sales in clothing and household goods, respectively. Stores were remodeled.

Many were converted to "Big K" stores. Several years of financial performance, including a bankruptcy, suggest that this attempt at differentiation did not work. K-Mart seems to have tried to abandon cost leadership in favour of differentiation. In the end, it seems to have become stuck in the middle.

International Implementation of Product Differentiation

When a firm contemplates entering an international market, one of the main questions to be answered is: How much must the products and/or services of the focal firm be modified for the foreign market?

The answer to this question depends primarily on two issues. First, the degree of necessary modification depends on whether the product or service in question lends itself to standardization across national boundaries. Second, the degree of modification depends on how similar the tastes and preferences of the foreign customers are to the tastes and preferences of customers in the firm's domestic market.

If a global standard exists for a product or service, then local tastes and preferences are not a major concern. This is often the case with electronics and high technology products. Such a situation calls for what is known as a global international expansion strategy. Firms using this strategy rely on centralized decision making and strive for efficiencies from being able to produce at global volumes. The business functions remain centralized at headquarters. In many ways, the logic of the global strategy is similar to the cost leadership strategy. Historically, Japanese companies like Sony and Hitachi have been successful with global strategies.

On the other hand, if a product does not have a global standard and there are significant differences in local tastes and preferences from country to country, then what is known as a multi-domestic strategy is used. This strategy consists of replicating business functions in multiple countries as needed. For example, a firm using this strategy might establish marketing and finance organizations in each country where it operates. The implementation of this strategy is similar to the implementation of a product differentiation strategy in that managers and employees are given great latitude in responding to local tastes and preferences. Historically, European companies like Phillips, Siemens, and Unilever have been successful using the multi-domestic strategy. A hybrid of these two approaches, known as the transnational strategy, has been suggested as a way to exploit the benefits of both the global and multi-domestic strategies. The basic idea behind this strategy is that the local knowledge gleaned from *multi-domestic* operations can be transferred around the world through a *global* network of coordinated reporting relationships.

Summary of Product Differentiation

The main points from this discussion that students need to understand are:

1) successful product differentiation means that customers have a preference for the focal firm's products and/or services
2) customers' preferences will lead them to pay a premium price for the focal firm's products and/or services

3) there are many possible bases of differentiation—in fact, almost anything could be a base of differentiation
4) product differentiation may lead to competitive advantage if the base of differentiation meets the VRIO criteria
5) the value of a base of differentiation can be manifest by limiting a threat and/or exploiting an opportunity in the external environment
6) some bases of differentiation are easy to duplicate, some may be costly to duplicate, and some are usually costly to duplicate
7) a successful product differentiation strategy depends on the appropriate implementation of the strategy with respect to organizational structure, management controls, and compensation policies
8) firms can simultaneously pursue both cost leadership and product differentiation strategies but it is difficult to do.

Non-price Competition

Non-price competition is a marketing strategy "in which one firm tries to distinguish its product or service from competing products on the basis of attributes like design and workmanship" (McConnell-Brue, 2002, p. 437-438). The firm can also distinguish its product offering through quality of service, extensive distribution, customer focus, or any other sustainable competitive advantage other than price. It can be contrasted with price competition, which is where a company tries to distinguish its product or service from competing products on the basis of low price. Non-price competition typically involves promotional expenditures, (such as advertising, selling staff, sales promotions, coupons, special orders, or free gifts), marketing research, new product development, and brand management costs. Firms will engage in non-price competition, in spite of the additional costs involved, because it is usually more profitable than selling for a lower price, and avoids the risk of a price war. Although any company can use a non-price competition strategy, it is most common among oligopolies and monopolistic competition, because firms can be extremely competitive.

Marketing

Marketing is the process associated with promoting for sale goods or services. It is considered a "social and managerial process by which individuals and groups obtain what they need and want through creating and exchanging products and values with others." It is an integrated process through which companies create value for customers and build strong customer relationships in order to capture value from customers in return. Marketing is used to create the customer, to keep the customer and to satisfy the customer. With the customer as the focus of its activities, it can be concluded that *marketing management* is one of the major components of business management. The evolution of marketing was caused due to mature markets and overcapacities in the last decades.

Companies then shifted the focus from production more to the customer in order to stay profitable. The term *marketing concept* holds that achieving organisational goals depends on knowing the needs and wants of target markets and delivering the desired satisfactions. It proposes that in order to satisfy its organizational objectives, an organization should anticipate the needs and wants of consumers and satisfy these more effectively than competitors.

Further Definitions

Marketing is defined by the American Marketing Association as *"the activity, set of institutions, and processes for creating, communicating, delivering, and exchanging offerings that have value for customers, clients, partners, and society at large."* The term developed from the original meaning which referred literally to going to a market to buy or sell goods or services. Seen from a systems point of view, sales process engineering views marketing as *"a set of processes that are interconnected and interdependent with other functions, whose methods can be improved using a variety of relatively new approaches."*

The Chartered Institute of Marketing defines marketing as *"the management process responsible for identifying, anticipating and satisfying customer requirements profitably."* A different concept is the *value-based marketing* which states the role of marketing to contribute to increasing shareholder value. In this context, marketing is defined as *"the management process that seeks to maximise returns to shareholders by developing relationships with valued customers and creating a competitive advantage."*

Marketing practice tended to be seen as a creative industry in the past, which included advertising, distribution and selling. However, because the academic study of marketing makes extensive use of social sciences, psychology, sociology, mathematics, economics, anthropology and neuroscience, the profession is now widely recognized as a science, allowing numerous universities to offer Master-of-Science (MSc) programmes. The overall process starts with marketing research and goes through market segmentation, business planning and execution, ending with pre and post-sales promotional activities. It is also related to many of the creative arts. The marketing literature is also adept at re-inventing itself and its vocabulary according to the times and the culture.

Organizational Orientation

In this sense, a firm's marketing department is often seen as of prime importance within the functional level of an organization. Information from an organization's marketing department would be used to guide the actions of other departments within the firm. As an example, a marketing department could ascertain (via marketing research) that consumers desired a new type of product, or a new usage for an existing product. With this in mind, the marketing department would inform the R&D department to create a prototype of a product/ service based on consumers' new desires. The production department would then start to manufacture the product, while the marketing department would focus on the promotion, distribution, pricing, etc. of the product. Additionally, a firm's finance department would be consulted, with respect to securing appropriate funding for the development, production and promotion of the product.

Inter-departmental conflicts may occur, should a firm adhere to the marketing orientation. Production may oppose the installation, support and servicing of new capital stock, which may be needed to manufacture a new product. Finance may oppose the required capital expenditure, since it could undermine a healthy cash flow for the organization.

Mutually Beneficial Exchange

A further marketing orientation is the focus on a *mutually beneficial exchange*. In a transaction in the market economy, a firm gains revenue, which thus leads to more profits/market share/sales. A consumer on the other hand gains the satisfaction of a need/want, utility, reliability and value for money from the purchase of a product or service. As no one has to buy goods from any one supplier in the market economy, firms must entice consumers to buy goods with contemporary marketing ideals.

Herd Behaviour

Herd behaviour in marketing is used to explain the dependencies of customers' mutual behaviour. *The Economist* reported a recent conference in Rome on the subject of the simulation of adaptive human behaviour. It shared mechanisms to increase impulse buying and get people "to buy more by playing on the herd instinct."

The basic idea is that people will buy more of products that are seen to be popular, and several feedback mechanisms to get product popularity information to consumers are mentioned, including smart card technology and the use of Radio Frequency Identification Tag technology. A "swarm-moves" model was introduced by a Florida Institute of Technology researcher, which is appealing to supermarkets because it can "increase sales without the need to give people discounts." Other recent studies on the "power of social influence" include an "artificial music market in which some 14,000 people downloaded previously unknown songs" (Columbia University, New York); a Japanese chain of convenience stores which orders its products based on "sales data from department stores and research companies;" a Massachusetts company exploiting knowledge of social networking to improve sales; and online retailers who are increasingly informing consumers about "which products are popular with like-minded consumers" (e.g., Amazon, eBay).

Further Orientations

- An emerging area of study and practice concerns *internal marketing*, or how employees are trained and managed to deliver the brand in a way that positively impacts the acquisition and retention of customers, see also *employer branding.*
- *Diffusion of innovations* research explores how and why people adopt new products, services and ideas.
- With consumers' eroding attention span and willingness to give time to advertising messages, marketers are turning to forms of *permission marketing* such as *branded content, custom media* and *reality marketing.*

Marketing Research

Marketing research involves conducting research to support marketing activities, and the statistical interpretation of data into information. This information is then used by managers to plan marketing activities, gauge the nature of a firm's marketing environment, attain information from suppliers, etc. Marketing researchers use statistical methods (such as quantitative research, qualitative research, hypothesis tests, Chi-squared tests, linear regression, correlation co-efficients, frequency distributions, Poisson and Binomial distributions, etc.) to interpret their findings and convert data into information. The marketing research process spans a number of stages including the definition of a problem, development of a research plan, collecting and interpretation of data and disseminating information formally in form of a report.

A distinction should be made between *marketing research* and *market research.* Market research pertains to research in a given market. As an example, a firm may conduct research in a target market, after selecting a suitable market segment. In contrast, marketing research relates to all research conducted within marketing. Thus, market research is a subset of marketing research.

Marketing Environment

The term *marketing environment* relates to all of the factors (whether internal, external, direct or indirect) that affect a firm's marketing decision-making or planning and is subject of the marketing research. A firm's marketing environment consists of two main areas, which are:

Macro Environment

On the macro environment a firm holds only little control. It consists of a variety of external factors that manifest on a large (or macro) scale. These are typically economic, social, political or technological phenomena. A common method of assessing a firm's macro-environment is via a PESTLE (Political, Economic, Social, Technological, Legal, Ecological) analysis. Within a PESTLE analysis, a firm would analyse national political issues, culture and climate, key macroeconomic conditions, health and indicators (such as economic growth, inflation, unemployment, etc.), social trends/attitudes, and the nature of technology's impact on its society and the business processes within the society.

Micro Environment

A firm holds a greater amount (though not necessarily total) control of the micro environment. It comprises factors pertinent to the firm itself, or stakeholders closely connected with the firm or company. A firm's micro environment typically spans:

- Customers/consumers
- Employees
- Suppliers
- The Media.

By contrast to the macro environment, an organization holds a greater degree of control over these factors.

Market Segmentation

Market segmentation pertains to the division of a market of consumers into persons with similar needs and wants. As an example, if using Kellogg's cereals in this instance, Frosties are marketed to children. Crunchy Nut Cornflakes are marketed to adults. Both goods aforementioned denote two products which are marketed to two distinct groups of persons, both with like needs, traits, and wants.

The purpose for market segmentation is conducted for two main issues. First, a segmentation allows a better allocation of a firm's finite resources. A firm only possesses a certain amount of resources. Accordingly, it must make choices (and appreciate the related costs) in servicing specific groups of consumers. Furthermore the diversified tastes of the contemporary Western consumers can be served better. With more diversity in the tastes of modern consumers, firms are taking noting the benefit of servicing a multiplicity of new markets. Market segmentation can be defined in terms of the *STP* acronym, meaning *Segment, Target* and *Position.*

Segment

Segmentation involves the initial splitting up of consumers into persons of like needs/wants/tastes. Four commonly used criteria are used for segmentation, which include:

- Geographical (e.g. country, region, city, town, etc.)
- Psychographic (i.e. personality traits or character traits which influence consumer behaviour)
- Demographic (e.g. age, gender, socio-economic class, etc.)
- Behavioural (e.g. brand loyalty, usage rate, etc.).

Target

Once a segment has been identified, a firm must ascertain whether the segment is beneficial for them to service. The *DAMP* acronym, meaning *Discernible, Accessible, Measurable* and *Profitable,* are used as criteria to gauge the viability of a target market. DAMP is explained in further detail below:

- Discernable-How a segment can be differentiated from other segments.
- Accessible-How a segment can be accessed via Marketing Communications produced by a firm.
- Measurable-Can the segment be quantified and its size determined?
- Profitable-Can a sufficient return on investment be attained from a segment's servicing?

The next step in the targeting process is the level of differentiation involved in a segment serving. Three modes of differentiation exist, which are commonly applied by firms. These are:

- Undifferentiated-Where a company produces a like product for all of a market segment.
- Differentiated-In which a firm produced slight modifications of a product within a segment.
- Niche-In which an organisation forges a product to satisfy a specialised target market.

Position

Positioning concerns how to position a product in the minds of consumers. A firm often performs this by producing a perceptual map, which denotes products produced in its industry according to how consumers perceive their price and quality. From a product's placing on the map, a firm would tailor its marketing communications to suit meld with the product's perception among consumers.

Marketing Information System

A *marketing information system (MKIS)* is an information system that is commonly used by marketing management to analyse and view information pertaining to marketing activities. As the label suggests, an MKIS is a computer-based information system therefore used to input, store, process and output marketing information. An MKIS spans four subset components, which are detailed below:

Marketing Intelligence System

This sub-system stores information gathered from a firm's marketing intelligence activities. Marketing intelligence consists of actions a firm would undertake within its own market or industry, geared towards information existing within its markets. This can be obtained via communication with suppliers, consumers or other bodies within a market.

Internal Processes System

The internal processes system catalogues all internal marketing processes within a firm.

Marketing Research System

This section of the overall system contains data from a firm's marketing research activities.

Analytical System

The analytical system is the only sub-system which does not store data or information. It's function is to analyse and process data from the other three systems, into reliable, timely and relevant information for the perusal and use of marketing management.

Types of Marketing Research

Marketing research, as a sub-set aspect of marketing activities, can be divided into the following parts:

- Primary research (also known as field research), which involves the conduction and compilation of research for the purpose is was intended.
- Secondary research (also referred to as desk research), is initially conducted for one purpose, but often used to support another purpose or end goal.

By these definitions, an example of primary research would be market research conducted into health foods, which is used *solely* to ascertain the needs/wants of the target market for health foods. Secondary research, again according to the above definition, would be research pertaining to health foods, but used by a firm wishing to develop an unrelated product.

Primary research is often expensive to prepare, collect and interpret from data to information. Nonetheless, while secondary research is relatively inexpensive, it often can become outdated and outmoded, given it is used for a purpose other than for which is was intended.

Primary research can also be broken down into quantitative research and qualitative research, which as the labels suggest, pertain to numerical and non-numerical research methods, techniques. The appropriateness of each mode of research depends on whether data can be quantified (quantitative research), or whether subjective, non-numeric or abstract concepts are required to be studied (qualitative research).

Marketing Planning

The area of *marketing planning* involves forging a plan for a firm's marketing activities. A marketing plan can also pertain to a specific product, as well as to an organisation's overall marketing strategy. Generally speaking, an organisation's marketing planning process is derived from its overall business strategy. Thus, when top management are devising the firm's strategic direction or mission, the intended marketing activities are incorporated into this plan. Within the overall strategic marketing plan, the marketing planning process contains the following stages:

- Mission statement
- Corporate objectives-These are the broad-based objectives resulting from the firm's mission statement.
- Marketing audit-a marketing audit is an audit of all marketing processes within a firm. It's purpose is to highlight which areas require improvement, and which ones require modification, prior to the establishment of the marketing plan.
- SWOT analysis
- Assumptions arising from the marketing audit and SWOT analysis
- Marketing objectives derived from the assumptions
- An estimation of the expected results of the objectives
- Identification of alternative plans or mixes
- Budgeting for the marketing plan
- A first-year implementation program.

There are several levels of marketing objectives within an organization. As stated previously, the senior management of a firm would formulate a general business strategy for a firm. However, this general business strategy would be interpreted and implemented in different contexts throughout the firm.

Corporate

Corporate marketing objectives are typically broad-based in nature, and pertain to the general vision of the firm in the short, medium or long-term. As an example, if one pictures a group of companies (or a conglomerate), top management may state that sales for the group should increase by 25% over a ten year period.

Strategic Business Unit

An SBU is an autonomous entity within a firm, which produces a unique product/service. It could be a single product, a product line, or a subsidiary of a larger group of companies. The SBU would embrace the corporate strategy, and attune it to its own particular industry.

For instance, an SBU may partake in the sports goods industry. It thus would ascertain how it would attain additional sales of sports goods, in order to satisfy the overall business strategy.

Functional

The functional level relates to departments within the SBUs, such as marketing, finance, HR, production, etc. The functional level would adopt the SBU's strategy and determine how to accomplish the SBU's own objectives in its market.

To use the example of the sports goods industry again, the marketing department would draw up marketing plans, strategies and communications to help the SBU achieve its marketing aims.

Product Life Cycle

The Product Life Cycle or *PLC* is a tool used by marketing managers to gauge the progress of a product, especially relating to sales or revenue accrued over time. The PLC is based on a few key assumptions, including that a given product would possess an *introduction, growth, maturity* and *decline* stage. Furthermore it is assumed that no product lasts perpetually on the market. Last but not least a firm must employ differing strategies, according to where a product is on the PLC.

Introduction

In this stage, a product is launched onto the market. To stimulate growth of sales/revenue, use of advertising may be high, in order to heighten awareness of the product in question.

Growth

The product's sales/revenue is increasing, which may stimulate more marketing communications to sustain sales. More entrants enter into the market, to reap the apparent high profits that the industry is producing.

Maturity

A product's sales start to level off, and an increasing number of entrants to a market produce price falls for the product. Firms may utilise sales promotions to raise sales.

Decline

Demand for a good begins to taper off, and the firm may opt to discontinue manufacture of the product. This is so, if revenue for the product comes from efficiency savings in production, over actual sales of a good/service. However, if a product services a niche market, or is complementary to another product, it may continue manufacture of the product, despite a low level of sales/revenue being accrued.

Marketing Strategy

The field of marketing strategy encompasses the strategy involved in the management of a given product.

A given firm may hold numerous products in the marketplace, spanning numerous and sometimes wholly unrelated industries. Accordingly, a plan is required in order to manage effectively such products. Such decisions consist of the following decisions:

- Should we (,i.e. the firm) enter a market/industry?
- Should we increase funding for our product(s)?
- Should we maintain funding for our product(s)?
- Should we divest or cease production of our product(s)?

Evidently, a company needs to weigh up and ascertain how to utilise effectively its finite resources. As an example, a start-up car manufacturing firm would face little success, should it attempt to rival immediately Toyota, Ford, Nissan or any other large global car maker. Moreover, a product, may be reaching the end of its life-cycle.

Thus, the issue of divest, or a ceasing of production may be made. With regard to the aforesaid questions, each scenario requires a unique marketing strategy to be employed. Below are listed some prominent marketing strategy models, which seek to propose means to answer the preceding questions.

Ansoff Matrix

The Ansoff Matrix was devised by Igor Ansoff, a Russian-born American pioneer of strategic planning.

Ansoff proposed his Matrix, as a means of identifying how a firm should market its product in differing scenarios. The labels are listed below:

- X-axis
- Existing markets
- Existing products
- Y-axis
- New markets
- New products.

Four quadrants can then be determined, which are:

- Market penetration
- Diversification
- Market development
- Product Development.

Each aforesaid category provides a unique marketing scenario, in which Ansoff denoted a given strategy.

Marketing mix

In the early 1960s, Professor Neil Borden at Harvard Business School identified a number of company performance actions that can influence the consumer decision to purchase goods or services. Borden suggested that all those actions of the company represented a "Marketing Mix". Professor E. Jerome McCarthy, at the Michigan State University in the early 1960s, suggested that the Marketing Mix contained 4 elements product, price, place and promotion.

Product

The product aspects of marketing deal with the specifications of the actual goods or services, and how it relates to the end-user's needs and wants. The scope of a product generally includes supporting elements such as warranties, guarantees, and support.

Pricing

This refers to the process of setting a price for a product, including discounts. The price need not be monetary; it can simply be what is exchanged for the product or services, e.g. time, energy, or attention. Methods of setting prices optimally are in the domain of pricing science. A number of modes of pricing techniques exist, which span:

- Elasticities (whether Price Elasticity of Demand, Cross Elasticity of Demand, or Income Elasticity of Demand)
- Market skimming pricing
- Market penetration pricing.

Elasticities are a microeconomic concept, which gauges how elastic demand is for a given good/service. In a marketing context, its usefulness relates to the suitable level at which a product can be priced, in accordance with price, a product's complements and substitutes, and the level of income a consumer possesses.

Market skimming pertains to firm releasing a good in a "first to market" scenario. As an example, picture a company which releases a new type of personal media playing system. It may set the good at an initially high level, but reduce it over time, once the level of demand gradually rises. Market skimming is best operable within a first to market scenario, since there would be few competitors within the company's industry. This pricing strategy is also best implemented within a market of high entry barriers (such as a monopoly or an oligopoly). This is so since the high barriers to entry discourage competitors into the industry for the product.

Market penetration concerns pricing policies for late entrants to a market. As another example, a company could release a product into a market years after it is initially introduced, but at an artificially low price in order to stimulate demand. The result of such a pricing strategy would be to draw consumers from competitors and into purchasing its own product. Market penetration, in contrast to market skimming, best functions within a market form with low barriers to entry (such as perfect competition or monopolistic competition). Low barriers to entry facilitates a company's ability to sell goods at a price lower than its market clearing point.

Placement (or Distribution)

This refers to how the product gets to the customer; for example, point-of-sale placement or retailing. This third P has also sometimes been called *Place*, referring to the channel by which a product or service is sold (e.g. online vs. retail), which geographic region or industry, to which segment (young adults, families, business people), etc. also referring to how the environment in which the product is sold in can affect sales.

Promotion

This includes advertising, sales promotion, including promotional education, publicity, and personal selling. Branding refers to the various methods of promoting the product, brand, or company. These four elements are often referred to as the marketing mix, which a marketer can use to craft a marketing plan. The four Ps model is most useful when marketing low value consumer products. Industrial products, services, high value consumer products require adjustments to this model. Services marketing must account for the unique nature of services.

Industrial or B2B marketing must account for the long term contractual agreements that are typical in supply chain transactions. Relationship marketing attempts to do this by looking at marketing from a long term relationship perspective rather than individual transactions. As a counter to this, Morgan, in *Riding the Waves of Change* (Jossey-Bass, 1988), suggests that one of the greatest limitations of the 4 Ps approach "is that it unconsciously emphasizes the inside–out view (looking from the company outwards), whereas the essence of marketing should be the outside–in approach". In order to recognize the different aspects of selling services, as opposed to Products, a further three Ps were added to make a range of *Seven Ps* for service industries:

- Process-the way in which orders are handled, customers are satisfied and the service is delivered.
- Physical Evidence-is tangible evidence of the service customers will receive (for example a holiday brochure).
- People-the people meeting and dealing with the customers.

As markets have become more satisfied, the 7 Ps have become relevant to those companies selling products, as well as those solely involved with services: customers now differentiate between sellers of goods by the service they receive in the process from the people involved.

Some authors cite a further P-Packaging-this is thought by many to be part of Product, but in certain markets (Japan, China for example) and with certain products (perfume, cosmetics) the packaging of a product has a greater importance-maybe even than the product itself.

Marketing Communications

Marketing communications is defined by actions a firm takes to communicate with end-users, consumers and external parties. A simple definition of marketing communication is *"the means by which a supplier of goods, services, values and/or ideas represent themselves to their target audience with the goal of stimulating dialog leading to better commercial or other relationships". Marcoms* is a frequently used short-form for marketing communications. Marketing communications can be seen as a part of the promotional mix, as the exact nature of how to apply marketing communications depends on the nature of the product in question.

Accordingly, a given product would require a unique communications mix, in order to convey successfully information to consumers. Some products may require a stronger emphasis on personal sales, while others may need more focus on advertising. The process in which the differing modes of marketing communications are complemented and synthesised is called *integrated marketing communications (IMC).*

It is used in order to create a single and coherent marketing communications process. As an example, a firm can advertise the existence of a sales promotion, via a newspaper, magazine, TV, radio, etc. The same promotion can also be communicated via direct marketing, or personal selling. The aim of IMC is to lessen confusion among a product's target market, and to lessen cost for the firm. Several different subsets of marketing communications can be distinguished.

Personal Selling

Oral presentation given by a salesperson who approaches individuals or a group of potential customers. Personal selling is often used in business to business (,i.e. "B2B") settings, in addition to business to consumer (,i.e. "B2C") scenarios in which a personal and face to face medium is required for the communication of the product.

In B2B situations, personal selling is preferred if the product is technical in nature. Personal selling can compose of the use of presentations, in order to convey the benefits of a firm's good/service. In B2C settings, personal selling is utilised if the product requires to be tailored to the unique needs of an individual. Examples of this include car (and other vehicle) sales, financial services (such as insurance or investment), etc. Personal selling involves the following points:

- Live, interactive relationship
- Personal interest
- Attention and response
- Interesting presentation
- Clear and thorough.

Sales Promotion

Short-term incentives to encourage buying of products.

- Instant appeal
- Anxiety to sell.

An example is coupons or a sale. People are given an incentive to buy, but this does not build customer loyalty or encourage future repeat buys. A major drawback of sales promotion is that it is easily copied by competition. It cannot be used as a sustainable source of differentiation. Sales promotions are typically used to heighten sales/revenue, especially if a firm holds dead/excess stock, or if the market for a product has matured.

Public Relations

Public Relations (or PR, as an acronym) is the use of media tools by a firm in order to promote goodwill from an organization to a target market segment, or other consumers of a firm's good/service. PR stems from the fact that a firm cannot seek to antagonize or inflame its market base, due to incurring a lessened demand for its good/service. Organizations undertake PR in order to assure consumers, and to forestall negative perceptions towards it. PR can span:

- Interviews
- Speeches/Presentations
- Corporate literature, such as financial statements, brochures, etc.

Publicity

Publicity involves attaining space in media, without having to pay directly for such coverage. As an example, an organization may have the launch of a new product covered by a newspaper or TV news segment. This benefits the firm in question since it is making consumers aware of its product, without necessarily paying a newspaper or television station to cover the event.

Advertising

Advertising occurs when a firm directly pays a media channel to publicize its product. Common examples of this include TV and radio adverts, billboards, branding, sponsorship, etc.

Direct Marketing

Direct marketing is a process where a firm uses communication channels to attain and retain consumers for its product. It is a comparatively new mode of marketing communications (when compared with forms such as advertising, sales promotions, personal selling, etc.) Direct marketing involves carefully seeking out persons within a target market, and communicating to them about the nature of a product. This process is signified by brochures sent via the mail, e-mails from companies, etc. It can also constitute the use of telemarketing, in order to communicate with a target market.

International Marketing

International marketing can be defined as the application of marketing strategies, planning and activities to external or foreign markets. International marketing is of consequence to firms which operate in countries and territories other than their home country or the country in which they are registered in and have their head office.

The factors influencing international marketing are culture, political and legal factors, a country's level of economic development and the mode of involvement in foreign markets. The reasons why a firm would engage in international markets are numerous, including:

- Maturity within domestic markets
- To increase general market share, sales or revenue.

Culture

Social norms, attitudes towards buying foreign goods, and the working practices of foreign markets are all cultural factors when opting to invest in foreign markets. Social norms affect business practices, since social norms are one factor in the demand for a product.

A company marketing pork would experience less sales in an Islamic country, than it would in China (which is the world's largest consumer of pork). In Western societies, sexuality and sexual topics are often used in marketing communications (such as advertising, for instance). However, in a comparatively more conservative society (such as India for instance) social attitudes may shun the use of sexual topics to advertise products.

Political and Legal Factors

The following political/legal factors are of bearing in international marketing:

- Government attitude to business
- The level of governmental regulations, red-tape and bureaucracy
- Monetary regulations
- Political stability.

Not all governments are as open to foreign investment as others, nor are all governments equally favourable to business. Typically, a firm may opt to invest in an economy in which the government is more inclined to support business activity in a country. In other words, the "business-friendliness" of a foreign government is paramount in this instance.

Additionally, some economies are more "liberal" and less regulated, by comparison to other economies. Excessive regulations can be a hindrance on a firm, since they contribute to additional costs to a firm. Conversely, regulations can aid in assisting firms, by easing the path of doing business. A firm seeking to invest in foreign markets must gauge the regulatory arrangement of the economy it is looking to invest in. Monetary regulations, akin to the above points, can hinder the ability to do business. A high level of monetary regulations can hamper foreign investment within an economy.

Lastly, the political stability of a country is also a key factor in foreign investment decisions. Nation-states experiencing continual coup-d'etat can appear unattractive to invest in, since the continual changes in political system can compound the inherent risk in investing.

Typically, a firm would opt to invest in a country which had a stable mode of government, in which handovers of power were peaceful and non-violent. Even if a country is not a liberal democracy, the level of political stability within a country may supersede the political system (or, more accurately, the perceived immorality of a government's policies/constitutional structure) of a given nation-state.

Level of Economic Development

The level of economic development of an economy can affect foreign investment decisions. Within the field of developmental economics, differing modes of economic development can be identified. These are:

- Developing economy
- Newly-Industrialised country
- Industrialised country (also known as a developed country, advanced economy or first world economy).

A developing economy has a comparatively low general living standard (as defined by material lifestyle/level of material possession). Moreover, a developing economy may also be at subsistence level, or possess a large share of its Gross Domestic Product in primary industries. Accordingly, a developing country would not be a profitable market for high-end consumer goods, or fast-moving consumer goods commonly found in developed/advanced economies. Exports of machinery (related to the extraction and processing of raw materials) may be viable for a developing economy, due to primary industries possessing a large share of national income.

A newly-industrialised economy is an economy which has experienced high recent economic growth, and thus has experienced a rise in general living standards. Coupled with the rapid economic growth, the emergence of a middle class leads to the development of a consumerist culture in the society. A newly-industrialised economy would consequently possess a small general demand for high-end consumer goods, but not to the extent of an advanced economy. A newly-industralised economy may export manufactured goods to other countries, and often possess secondary sector industries as a high percentage of its economic output.

An industrialised economy is typically identified via a high Gross Domestic Product per capita, a high United Nations Human Development Index rating and a high level of tertiary/quaternary/ quinary sector industries in the context of its national income. Thus, the high general living standard denotes the highest generalised demand for goods and services within all modes of economic development. Commonly, developed/advanced economies are high exporters of high-tech manufactured goods, as well as service sector products (such as financial services, for instance).

Green Marketing

Green marketing can be defined as the marketing of products which are environmentally sound. The notion of green marketing is a comparatively new one within general marketing thought, as it has chiefly grown in acceptance since the 1990s. Nonetheless, as a contemporary branch of marketing thought, it can be seen as one of the fastest growing areas of marketing principles.

The rationale for the devising and emergence of green marketing is thus:

- A higher quantity of persons willing and able to buy green products.
- Heightened awareness among consumers, concerning the potentially negative aspects of global climate change.

Green marketers thus target persons who are more environmentally conscious. The segmentation and market research processes of numerous firms denote that the target market for green products has grown widely in numerous years. Accordingly, green marketers are willing to supply what persons are willing and able to buy. It can also be stated that green products are often more expensive than "non-green" products, due perhaps to higher production costs. Nevertheless, green consumers are typically willing to pay higher prices, as a means of doing their part to safeguard the environment of the planet Earth.

Some drawbacks of green marketing are thus:

- The ideal of "green washing"
- Disputes and contention surrounding the exact meaning of a green product

Green washing pertains to when a firm misleadingly produces a product, with ostensible green characteristics, which is not actually environmentally sound. In addition to evident ethical issues concerning deceit, such conduct can undermine an organisation's drive to be deemed a "green" company. Accordingly, a firm must be sincere in its efforts to be environmentally sound, regarding its environmental practices and policies. Moreover, the extent and nature of a green product can be a moot point.

To some, a product must be wholly green to be viewed as green. To others, a product may only possess a reduction in environmentally harmful inputs to be worthy of being labelled green. Nonetheless, a firm can enhance its green marketing efforts if it persuades consumers that the purchase of green products can enhance environmental protection.

Buying Behaviour

A marketing firm, in the course of its operations, must ascertain the nature of buying behaviour, if it is to market properly its product. In order to entice and persuade a consumer to buy a product, the psychological/behavioural process of how a given product is purchased.

Buying behaviour consists of two prime strands, namely being consumer (B2C) behaviour and organisational/industrial behaviour (B2B).

B2C Buying Behaviour

This mode of behaviour concerns consumers, in the purchase of a given product. The B2C buying process is as thus:

- Need/want recognition
- Information search
- Search for alternatives (to satisfy need/want)
- Purchase decision
- Post-purchase evaluation.

As an example, if one pictures a pair of sneakers, the desire for a pair of sneakers would be followed by an information search on available types/ brands. This may include perusing media outlets, but most commonly consists of information gathered from family and friends. If the information search is insufficient, the consumer may search for alternative means to satisfy the need/want. In this case, this may be buying leather shoes, sandals, etc. The purchase decision is then made, in which the consumer actually buys the product.

Following this stage, a post-purchase evaluation is often conducted, comprising an appraisal of the value/utility brought by the purchase of the sneakers. If the value/utility is high, then a repeat purchase may be bought. This could then develop into consumer loyalty, for the firm producing the pair of sneakers.

B2B buying Behaviour

B2B buying behaviour relates to organisational/industrial buying behaviour. B2C and B2B behaviour are not exact, as similarities and differences exist. Some of the key differences are listed below:

- Consumer behaviour
- Low in monetary value
- Low in volume/mass
- Swift purchase
- Transaction marketing-based
- Single buying instances
- Number of consumer is higher
- Individual/market-based demand
- Organisational behaviour
- High in monetary value
- High in volume/mass
- Lengthy purchase process
- Relationship marketing-based
- Multiple buying instances
- Number of consumers is lesser
- Demand is consumer derived (in that firms purchase goods to ultimately meet consumer demand) .

The organisational buying process is thush:

- Problem recognition
- Need description
- Product specification
- Supplier search
- Proposal solicitation
- Supplier selection
- Order routine specification
- Supplier performance review.

In a straight rebuy, the fourth, fifth and sixth stages are omitted. In a modified rebuy scenario, the fifth and sixth stages are precluded. In a new buy, all aforementioned stages are conducted.

The Decision Making Unit (DMU)

The DMU, in other terms, can be labelled as the Purchasing or Procurement departments of an organisation Accordingly, it is responsible for the purchasing of organisational items and assets. The persons comprising a DMU are as thus:

- Gatekeepers
- Users
- Buyers
- Decision Makers
- Influencers
- Initiators.

Areas of Marketing Specialization

- Agricultural marketing
- Article marketing
- Cause marketing
- Communal marketing
- Business marketing
- Database marketing
- Digital marketing
- Direct marketing
- Engagement marketing
- Ethical marketing
- Evangelism marketing
- Experiential marketing Global marketing
- Guerrilla marketing
- Integrated marketing
- International marketing
- Internet marketing
- Industrial marketing
- Macromarketing
- Mobile marketing
- Multichannel marketing
- Permission marketing
- Political marketing
- Product marketing
- Proximity marketing
- Public marketing

- Reality marketing
- Referral marketing
- Relationship marketing
- Reverse marketing
- Search engine marketing
- Shopper marketing
- Social media marketing
- Trade marketing
- Value-based marketing
- Wholesale marketing.

Market Segment

A market segment is a group of people or organizations sharing one or more characteristics that cause them to have similar product and/or service needs. A true market segment meets all of the following criteria: it is distinct from other segments (different segments have different needs), it is homogeneous within the segment (exhibits common needs); it responds similarly to a market stimulus, and it can be reached by a market intervention. The term is also used when consumers with identical product and/or service needs are divided up into groups so they can be charged different amounts. These can broadly be viewed as 'positive' and 'negative' applications of the same idea, splitting up the market into smaller groups.

"Positive" Market Segmentation

Market segmenting is dividing market into groups of individual with similar wants or needs that a company divides the market into distinct groups who have distinct needs, wants, behaviour or who might want different products & services.

Broadly, markets can be divided according to a number of general criteria, such as by industry or public versus private although industrial market segmentation is quite different from consumer market segmentation, both have similar objectives. All of these methods of segmentation are merely proxies for true segments, which don't always fit into convenient demographic boundaries. Consumer-based market segmentation can be performed on a *product specific* basis, to provide a close match between specific products and individuals.

However, a number of generic market segment systems also exist, e.g. the Nielsen Claritas PRIZM system provides a broad segmentation of the population of the United States based on the statistical analysis of household and geodemographic data. The process of segmentation is distinct from targeting (choosing which segments to address) and positioning (designing an appropriate marketing mix for each segment).

The overall intent is to identify groups of similar customers and potential customers; to prioritize the groups to address; to understand their behaviour; and to respond with appropriate marketing strategies that satisfy the different preferences of each chosen segment. Revenues are thus improved. Improved segmentation can lead to significantly improved marketing effectiveness. Distinct segments can have different industry structures and thus have higher or lower attractiveness (Michael Porter). With the right segmentation, the right lists can be purchased, advertising results can be improved and customer satisfaction can be increased leading to better reputation.

Successful Segmentation

Successful segmentation requires the following

- homogeneity within the segment
- heterogeneity between segments
- segments are measurable and substantial
- segments are differentiable
- segments are accessible and actionable
- target segment is large enough to be profitable.

Variables Used for Segmentation

- Geographic variables.
  - region of the world or country, East, West, South, North, Central, coastal, hilly, etc.
  - county size: Metropolitan Cities, small cities, towns.
  - Density of Area Urban, Semi-urban, Rural.
  - climate Hot, Cold, Humid, Rainy.
- Demographic variables.
  - age.
  - gender Male and Female.
  - family size.
  - family life cycle: young children, empty nest, etc.
  - education Primary, High School, Secondary, College, Universities.

    - income.
    - occupation.
    - socioeconomic status.
    - religion.
    - nationality/race (ethnic marketing).
    - language.
- Psychographic variables.
    - personality.
    - lifestyle.
    - value.
    - attitude.
- Behavioural variables.
    - benefit sought.
    - product usage rate.
    - brand loyalty.
    - product end use.
    - readiness-to-buy stage.
    - buying centre.
    - profitability.
    - income status.
- Technological segmentation variables.
    - motivations.
    - usage patterns.
    - attitudes about technology.
    - fundamental values.
    - lifestyle perspective.
    - standard of living.
    - profit is there in business from the existing clients.

When numerous variables are combined to give an in-depth understanding of a segment, this is referred to as depth segmentation. When enough information is combined to create a clear picture of a typical member of a segment, this is referred to as a buyer profile.

When the profile is limited to demographic variables it is called a demographic profile (typically shortened to "a demographic"). A statistical technique commonly used in determining a profile is cluster analysis.

Other techniques used to identify segments are algorithms such as CHAID and regression-based CHAID and discriminant analysis. Alternatively, segments can be modelled directly from consumer preferences via discrete choice methodologies such as choice-based conjoint and MaxDiff.

Top-Down and Bottom-Up

George S. Day (1980) describes model of segmentation as the top-down approach: *You start with the total population and divide it into segments.* He also identified an alternative model which he called the bottom-up approach. In this approach, you start with a single customer and build on that profile.

This typically requires the use of customer relationship management software or a database of some kind. Profiles of existing customers are created and analysed. Various demographic, behavioural, and psychographic patterns are built up using techniques such as cluster analysis.

This process is sometimes called database marketing or micro-marketing. Its use is most appropriate in highly fragmented markets. McKenna (1988) claims that this approach treats every customer as a "micromajority". Pine (1993) used the bottom-up approach in what he called "segment of one marketing". Through this process mass customization is possible.

Creating a market segment will allow you to set yourself apart from other competitors.

Using Segmentation in Customer Retention

Segmentation is commonly used by organizations to improve their customer retention programs and help ensure that they are.

- Focused on retaining their most profitable customers
- Employing those tactics most likely to retain these customers

The basic approach to retention-based segmentation is that a company tags each of its active customers with 3 values:

Tag #1: Is this Customer at high risk of Canceling the Company's Service? (Or Becoming a non-user)

One of the most common indicators of high-risk customers is a drop off in usage of the company's service. For example, in the credit card industry this could be signaled through a customer's decline in spending on his card.

Tag #2: Is this Customer worth Retaining?

This determination boils down to whether the post-retention profit generated from the customer is predicted to be greater than the cost incurred to retain the customer.

Tag #3: What Retention Tactics Should be used to retain this Customer?

For customers who are deemed "save-worthy", it's essential for the company to know which save tactics are most likely to be successful. Tactics commonly used range from providing "special" customer discounts to sending customers communications that reinforce the value proposition of the given service.

Process for Tagging Customers

The basic approach to tagging customers is to utilize historical retention data to make predictions about active customers regarding:

- Whether they are at high risk of canceling their service.
- Whether they are profitable to retain.
- What retention tactics are likely to be most effective.

The idea is to match up active customers with customers from historic retention data who share similar attributes.

Using the theory that "birds of a feather flock together", the approach is based on the assumption that active customers will have similar retention outcomes as those of their comparable predecessors.

From a technical perspective, the segmentation process is commonly performed using a combination of predictive analytics and cluster analysis.

Product Management

Product management is an organizational lifecycle function within a company dealing with the planning or marketing of a product or products at all stages of the product lifecycle.

Product management (inbound focused) and product marketing (outbound focused) are different yet complementary efforts with the objective of maximizing sales revenues, market share, and profit margins. The role of product management spans many activities from strategic to tactical and varies based on the organizational structure of the company.

Product management can be a function separate on its own or a member of marketing or engineering. While involved with the entire product lifecycle, product management's main focus is on driving new product development. According to the Product Development and Management Association (PDMA), superior and differentiated new products-ones that deliver unique benefits and superior value to the customer-is the number one driver of success and product profitability.

Aspects of Product Management

Depending on the company size and history, product management has a variety of functions and roles. Sometimes there is a product manager, and sometimes the role of product manager is held by others. Frequently there is Profit and Loss (P&L) responsibility as a key metric for evaluating product manager performance. In some companies, the product management function is the hub of many other activities around the product. In others, it is one of many things that need to happen to bring a product to market. Product management often serves an interdisciplinary role, bridging gaps within the company between teams of different expertise, most notably between engineering-oriented teams and business-oriented teams. For example product managers often translate business objectives set for a product by Marketing or Sales into engineering requirements. Conversely they may work to explain the capabilities and limitations of the finished product back to Marketing and Sales.

Product Planning

- Identifying new product candidates.
- Gathering market requirements.
- Determine business-case and feasibility.
- Scooping and defining new products at high level.
- Evangelizing new products within the company.
- Building product roadmaps, particularly Technology roadmaps.
- Product Life Cycle considerations.
- Product differentiation.
- Detailed Product planning.

Product Marketing

- Product positioning and outbound messaging.
- Promoting the product externally with press, customers, and partners.
- Bringing new products to market.
- Monitoring the competition.
- more detail on Product marketing.

Brand

A brand is a name or trademark connected with a product or producer. Brands have become increasingly important components of culture and the economy, now being described as "cultural accessories and personal philosophies".

Concepts

Some people distinguish the psychological aspect of a brand from the experiential aspect. The experiential aspect consists of the sum of all points of contact with the brand and is known as the brand experience. The psychological aspect, sometimes referred to as the brand image, is a symbolic construct created within the minds of people and consists of all the information and expectations associated with a product or service.

People engaged in branding seek to develop or align the expectations behind the brand experience, creating the impression that a brand associated with a product or service has certain qualities or characteristics that make it special or unique. A brand is therefore one of the most valuable elements in an advertising theme, as it demonstrates what the brand owner is able to offer in the marketplace. The art of creating and maintaining a brand is called brand management. Orientation of the whole organisation towards its brand is called integrated marketing.

Careful brand management, supported by a cleverly crafted advertising campaign, can be highly successful in convincing consumers to pay remarkably high prices for products which are inherently extremely cheap to make. This concept, known as creating value, essentially consists of manipulating the projected image of the product so that the consumer sees the product as being worth the amount that the advertiser wants him/her to see, rather than a more logical valuation that comprises an aggregate of the cost of raw materials, plus the cost of manufacture, plus the cost of distribution.

Modern value-creation branding-and-advertising campaigns are highly successful at inducing consumers to pay, for example, 50 dollars for a T-shirt that cost a mere 50 cents to make, or 5 dollars for a box of breakfast cereal that contains a few cents' worth of wheat. Brands should be seen as more than the difference between the actual cost of a product and its selling price-they represent the sum of all valuable qualities of a product to the consumer. There are many intangibles involved in business, intangibles left wholly from the income statement and balance sheet which determine how a business is perceived. The learned skill of a knowledge worker, the type of metal working, the type of stitch: all may be without an 'accounting cost' but for those who truly know the product, for it is these people the company should wish to find and keep, the difference is incomparable. Failing to recognize these assets that a business, any business, can create and maintain will set an enterprise at a serious disadvantage.

A brand which is widely known in the marketplace acquires brand recognition. When brand recognition builds up to a point where a brand enjoys a critical mass of positive sentiment in the marketplace, it is said to have achieved brand franchise. One goal in brand recognition is the identification of a brand without the name of the company present. For example, Disney has been successful at branding with their particular script font (originally created for Walt Disney's "signature" logo), which it used in the logo for go.com. Consumers may look on branding as an important value added aspect of products or services, as it often serves to denote a certain attractive quality or characteristic. From the perspective of brand owners, branded products or services also command higher prices. Where two products resemble each other, but one of the products has no associated branding (such as a generic, store-branded product), people may often select the more expensive branded product on the basis of the quality of the brand or the reputation of the brand owner.

Brand Name

The brand name is quite often used interchangeably within "brand", although it is more correctly used to specifically denote written or spoken linguistic elements of any product. In this context a "brand name" constitutes a type of trademark, if the brand name exclusively identifies the brand owner as the commercial source of products or services. A brand owner may seek to protect proprietary rights in relation to a brand name through trademark registration. Advertising spokespersons have also become part of some brands, for example: Mr. Whipple of Charmin toilet tissue and Tony the Tiger of Kellogg's.

Brand names will fall into one of three spectrums of use- Descriptive, Associative or Freestanding.

Descriptive brand names assist in describing the distinguishable selling point(s) of the product to the customer (eg Snap, Crackle and Pop or Bitter Lemon). Associative brand names provide the customer with an associated word for what the product promises to do or be (e.g. Walkman, Sensodyne or Natrel). Finally, Freestanding brand names have no links or ties to either descriptions or associations of use. (eg

Mars Bar or Pantene) The act of associating a product or service with a brand has become part of pop culture. Most products have some kind of brand identity, from common table salt to designer jeans. A brandnomer is a brand name that has colloquially become a generic term for a product or service, such as Band-Aid or Kleenex, which are often used to describe any kind of adhesive bandage or any kind of facial tissue respectively.

Brand Identity

A product identity, or brand image are typically the attributes one associates with a brand, how the brand owner wants the consumer to perceive the brand-and by extension the branded company, organization, product or service. The brand owner will seek to bridge the gap between the brand image and the brand identity. Effective brand names build a connection between the brand personality as it is perceived by the target audience and the actual product/service. The brand name should be conceptually on target with the product/service (what the company stands for). Furthermore, the brand name should be on target with the brand demographic. Typically, sustainable brand names are easy to remember, transcend trends and have positive connotations. Brand identity is fundamental to consumer recognition and symbolizes the brand's differentiation from competitors.

Brand identity is what the owner wants to communicate to its potential consumers. However, over time, a products brand identity may acquire (evolve), gaining new attributes from consumer perspective but not necessarily from the marketing communications an owner percolates to targeted consumers. Therefore, brand associations become handy to check the consumer's perception of the brand.

Brand identity needs to focus on authentic qualities-real characteristics of the value and brand promise being provided and sustained by organisational and/or production characteristics.

Brand Parity

Brand parity is the perception of the customers that all brands are equivalent.

Branding Approaches

Company Name

Often, especially in the industrial sector, it is just the company's name which is promoted (leading to one of the most powerful statements of "branding"; the saying, before the company's downgrading, "No one ever got fired for buying IBM").

In this case a very strong brand name (or company name) is made the vehicle for a range of products (for example, Mercedes-Benz or Black & Decker) or even a range of subsidiary brands (such as Cadbury Dairy Milk, Cadbury Flake or Cadbury Fingers in the United States).

Individual Branding

Each brand has a separate name (such as Seven-Up, Kool-Aid or Nivea Sun (Beiersdorf)), which may even compete against other brands from the same company (for example, Persil, Omo, Surf and Lynx are all owned by Unilever).

Attitude Branding and Iconic Brands

Attitude branding is the choice to represent a larger feeling, which is not necessarily connected with the product or consumption of the product at all. Marketing labelled as attitude branding include that of Nike, Starbucks, The Body Shop, Safeway, and Apple Inc.. In the 2000 book *No Logo*, Naomi Klein describes attitude branding as a "fetish strategy". "A great brand raises the bar — it adds a greater sense of purpose to the experience, whether it's the challenge to do your best in sports and fitness, or the affirmation that the cup of coffee you're drinking really matters."-Howard Schultz (president, CEO, and chairman of Starbucks)

Iconic brands are defined as having aspects that contribute to consumer's self-expression and personal identity. Brands whose value to consumers comes primarily from having identity value comes are said to be "identity brands". Some of these brands have such a strong identity that they become more or less "cultural icons" which makes them iconic brands. Examples of iconic brands are: Apple Inc., Nike and Harley Davidson. Many iconic brands include almost ritual-like behaviour when buying and consuming the products. There are four key elements to creating iconic brands (Holt 2004):

1. "Necessary conditions"-The performance of the product must at least be ok preferably with a reputation of having good quality.
2. "Myth-making"-A meaningful story-telling fabricated by cultural "insiders". These must be seen as legitimate and respected by consumers for stories to be accepted.
3. "Cultural contradictions"-Some kind of mismatch between prevailing ideology and emergent undercurrents in society. In other words a difference with the way consumers are and how they some times wish they were.

4. "The cultural brand management process"-Actively engaging in the myth-making process making sure the brand maintains its position as an icon.

"No-brand" Branding

Recently a number of companies have successfully pursued "No-Brand" strategies, examples include the Japanese company Muji, which means "No label" in English (from !qpSo,ÁT – "Mujirushi Ryohin" – literally, "No brand quality goods"). Although there is a distinct Muji brand, Muji products are not branded. This no-brand strategy means that little is spent on advertisement or classical marketing and Muji's success is attributed to the word-of-mouth, a simple shopping experience and the anti-brand movement. "No brand" branding is actually branding as the brand is made conspicous through its absence.

Derived Brands

In this case the supplier of a key component, used by a number of suppliers of the end-product, may wish to guarantee its own position by promoting that component as a brand in its own right. The most frequently quoted example is Intel, which secures its position in the PC market with the slogan "Intel Inside".

Brand Extension

The existing strong brand name can be used as a vehicle for new or modified products; for example, many fashion and designer companies extended brands into fragrances, shoes and accessories, home textile, home decor, luggage, (sun-) glasses, furniture, hotels, etc.

Mars extended its brand to ice cream, Caterpillar to shoes and watches, Michelin to a restaurant guide, Adidas and Puma to personal hygiene. Dunlop extended its brand from tires to other rubber products such as shoes, golf balls, tennis racquets and adhesives. There is a difference between brand extension and line extension. When Coca-Cola launched "Diet Coke" and "Cherry Coke" they stayed within the originating product category: non-alcoholic carbonated beverages. Procter & Gamble (P&G) did likewise extending its strong lines (such as Fairy Soap) into neighbouring products (Fairy Liquid and Fairy Automatic) within the same category, dish washing detergents.

Multi-brands

Alternatively, in a market that is fragmented amongst a number of brands a supplier can choose deliberately to launch totally new brands in apparent competition with its own existing strong brand (and often with identical product characteristics); simply to soak up some of the share of the market which will in any case go to minor brands. The rationale is that having 3 out of 12 brands in such a market will give a greater overall share than having 1 out of 10 (even if much of the share of these new brands is taken from the existing one). In its most extreme manifestation, a supplier pioneering a new market which it believes will be particularly attractive may choose immediately to launch a second brand in competition with its first, in order to pre-empt others entering the market.

Individual brand names naturally allow greater flexibility by permitting a variety of different products, of differing quality, to be sold without confusing the consumer's perception of what business the company is in or diluting higher quality products.

Once again, Procter & Gamble is a leading exponent of this philosophy, running as many as ten detergent brands in the US market. This also increases the total number of "facings" it receives on supermarket shelves. Sara Lee, on the other hand, uses it to keep the very different parts of the business separate — from Sara Lee cakes through Kiwi polishes to L'Eggs pantyhose. In the hotel business, Marriott uses the name Fairfield Inns for its budget chain (and Ramada uses Rodeway for its own cheaper hotels). Cannibalization is a particular problem of a "multibrand" approach, in which the new brand takes business away from an established one which the organization also owns. This may be acceptable (indeed to be expected) if there is a net gain overall. Alternatively, it may be the price the organization is willing to pay for shifting its position in the market; the new product being one stage in this process.

Own Brands and Generics

With the emergence of strong retailers the "own brand", a retailer's own branded product (or service), also emerged as a major factor in the marketplace. Where the retailer has a particularly strong identity (such as Marks & Spencer in the UK clothing sector) this "own brand" may be able to compete against even the strongest brand leaders, and may outperform those products that are not otherwise strongly branded.

Concerns were raised that such "own brands" might displace all other brands (as they have done in Marks & Spencer outlets), but the evidence is that — at least in supermarkets and department stores — consumers generally expect to see on display something over 50 percent (and preferably over 60 percent) of brands other than those of the retailer. Indeed, even the strongest own brands in the UK rarely achieve better than third place in the overall market. This means that strong independent brands (such as Kellogg's and Heinz), which have maintained their marketing investments, are likely to continue their strong performance.

More than 50 per cent of UK FMCG brand leaders have held their position for more than two decades, although it is arguable that those which have switched their budgets to "buy space" in the retailers may be more exposed.

The strength of the retailers has, perhaps, been seen more in the pressure they have been able to exert on the owners of even the strongest brands (and in particular on the owners of the weaker third and fourth brands). Relationship marketing has been applied most often to meet the wishes of such large customers (and indeed has been demanded by them as recognition of their buying power). Some of the more active marketers have now also switched to 'category marketing'- in which they take into account all the needs of a retailer in a product category rather than more narrowly focusing on their own brand.

At the same time, probably as an outgrowth of consumerism, "generic" (that is, effectively unbranded) goods have also emerged. These made a positive virtue of saving the cost of almost all marketing activities; emphasizing the lack of advertising and, especially, the plain packaging (which was, however, often simply a vehicle for a different kind of image). It would appear that the penetration of such generic products peaked in the early 1980s, and most consumers still appear to be looking for the qualities that the conventional brand provides.

History

Although connected with the history of trademarks and including earlier examples which could be deemed "protobrands" (such as the marketing puns of the "Vesuvinum" wine jars found at Pompeii), brands in the field of mass-marketing originated in the 19th century with the advent of packaged goods. Industrialization moved the production of many household items, such as soap, from local communities to centralized factories. When shipping their items, the factories would literally brand their logo or insignia on the barrels used, extending the meaning of "brand" to that of trademark.

Bass & Company, the British brewery, claims their red triangle brand was the world's first trademark. Lyle's Golden Syrup makes a similar claim, having been named as Britain's oldest brand, with its green and gold packaging having remained almost unchanged since 1885.

Cattle were branded long before this; the term "maverick", originally meaning an unbranded calf, comes from Texas rancher Samuel Augustus Maverick who, following the American Civil War, decided that since all other cattle were branded, his would be identified by having no markings at all.

Factories established during the Industrial Revolution, generating mass-produced goods and needed to sell their products to a wider market, to a customer base familiar only with local goods. It quickly became apparent that a generic package of soap had difficulty competing with familiar, local products.

The packaged goods manufacturers needed to convince the market that the public could place just as much trust in the non-local product. Campbell soup, Coca-Cola, Juicy Fruit gum, Aunt Jemima, and Quaker Oats were among the first products to be 'branded', in an effort to increase the consumer's familiarity with their products. Many brands of that era, such as Uncle Ben's rice and Kellogg's breakfast cereal furnish illustrations of the problem.

Around 1900, James Walter Thompson published a house ad explaining trademark advertising. This was an early commercial explanation of what we now know as branding. Companies soon adopted slogans, mascots, and jingles which began to appear on radio and early television. By the 1940s, manufacturers began to recognize the way in which consumers were developing relationships with their brands in a social/psychological/anthropological sense.

From there, manufacturers quickly learned to build their brand's identity and personality, such as youthfulness, fun or luxury. This began the practice we now know as "branding" today, where the consumers buy "the brand" instead of the product. This trend continued to the 1980s, and is now quantified in concepts such as brand value and brand equity.

Naomi Klein has described this development as "brand equity mania". In 1988, for example, Philip Morris purchased Kraft for six times what the company was worth on paper; it was felt that what they really purchased was its brand name.

Marlboro Friday: April 2, 1993-marked by some as the death of the brand-the day Philip Morris declared that they were to cut the price of Marlboro cigarettes by 20%, in order to compete with bargain cigarettes.

Marlboro cigarettes were notorious at the time for their heavy advertising campaigns, and well-nuanced brand image. In response to the announcement Wall street stocks nose-dived for a large number of 'branded' companies: Heinz, Coca Cola, Quaker Oats, PepsiCo. Many thought the event signalled the beginning of a trend towards "brand blindness" (Klein 13), questioning the power of "brand value".

Country of Origin

Country of origin (often abbreviated to COO), is the country of manufacture, production, or growth where an article or product comes from. There are differing rules of origin under various national laws and international treaties.

Country of Origin as a Marketing Strategy

From a marketing perspective, "country of origin" gives a way to differentiate the product from the competitors.

Research shows (Josiassen and Harzing, 2008, European Management Review) that the country of origin has an impact on the willingness to buy a product, and studies (Shimp and Sharma, 1987, Journal of International Business Studies) have shown that consumers may tend to have a relative preference to products from their own country or may tend to have a relative preference for or aversion to certain products that originate from certain countries.

The effect of country of origin is however debated (Usunier, 2006, European Management Review) as studies (e.g. Chao, 2001, Journal of Advertising) have shown that the origin of design (for instance Apple computers or Nike shoes) can be more important than the country of origin.

Non-specific Country of Origin Labeling

While many products made within the European Union carry the country of origin label or marking "Made in EU" or "Made in EC", some non-EU manufacturers in Europe and some others outside the continent of Europe use vaguer markings, such as "Made in Europe" (made anywhere else in Europe, but not in the EU or EC; this may constitute any country geographically close to Europe or the EU that also wishes to be in) or "Made for Europe" (made anywhere else in the world, but not in Europe or the European Union).

These practices could lead to consumer deception, whereby a buyer not proficient in English may come to believe from looking at the label that the non-EU product he is interested in is made in the EU.

Country of Origin Contextual Importance for Consumer Choice

Consumers tend to utilize the country of origin more when they are less involved and less familiar (Josiassen et al., 2008, International Marketing Review).

Consumers further tend to use country of origin more as a decision tool when they consider luxury products (Piron, 2000, Journal of Consumer Marketing).

Country of Origin in International Trade

When shipping products from one country to another, the products may have to be marked with country of origin, and the country of origin will generally be required to be indicated in the export/import documents and governmental submissions.

Country of origin will affect its admissibility, the rate of duty, its entitlement to special duty or trade preference programs, antidumping, and government procurement.

Today, many products are an outcome of a large number of parts and pieces that come from many different countries, and that may then be assembled together in a third country. In these cases, it's hard to know exactly what is the country of origin, and different rules apply as to how to determine their "correct" country of origin.

Generally, articles only change their country of origin if the work or material added to an article in the second country constitutes a substantial transformation, or, the article changes its name, tariff code, character or use (for instance from wheel to car). Value added in the second country may also be an issue.

Country of Origin in Movie and Television Production

The International Federation of Film Archives defines the country of origin as the country of the principal offices of the production company or individual by whom the moving image work was made. No consistent reference or definition exists.

Sources include the item itself, accompanying material (e.g. scripts, shot lists, production records, publicity material, inventory lists, synopses etc.), the container (if not an integral part of the piece), or other sources (standard and special moving image reference tools). In law, definitions of "country of origin" and related terms are defined differently in different jurisdictions.

Europe, Canada, and the United States have different definitions for a variety of reasons, including tax treatment, advertising regulations, distribution; even within the European Union, different member states have different legislation. As a result, an individual work can have multiple countries as its "country of origin", and may even have different countries recognized as originating places for the purpose of different legal jurisdictions.

Under copyright law in the United States and other signatories of the Berne Convention, "country of origin" is defined in an inclusive way to ensure the protection of intellectual rights of writers and creators.

Marketing Plan

A marketing plan is a written document that details the necessary actions to achieve one or more marketing objectives. It can be for a product or service, a brand, or a product line. Marketing plans cover between one and five years. A marketing plan may be part of an overall business plan. Solid marketing strategy is the foundation of a well-written marketing plan. While a marketing plan contains a list of actions, a marketing plan without a sound strategic foundation is of little use.

The Marketing Planning Process

The marketing process model based on the publications of Philip Kotler. It consists of 5 steps, beginning with the market & environment research. After fixing the targets and setting the strategies, they will be realised by the marketing mix in step 4. The last step in the process is the marketing controlling.

In most organizations, "strategic planning" is an annual process, typically covering just the year ahead. Occasionally, a few organizations may look at a practical plan which stretches three or more years ahead.

To be most effective, the plan has to be formalized, usually in written form, as a formal "marketing plan." The essence of the process is that it moves from the general to the specific; from the overall objectives of the organization down to the individual action plan for a part of one marketing program. It is also an interactive process, so that the draft output of each stage is checked to see what impact it has on the earlier stages-and is amended..

Marketing Planning Aims and Objectives

Behind the corporate objectives, which in themselves offer the main context for the marketing plan, will lay the "corporate mission"; which in turn provides the context for these corporate objectives. In a sales-oriented organization, marketing planning function designs incentive pay plans to not only motivate and reward frontline staff fairly but also to align marketing activities with corporate mission.

This "corporate mission" can be thought of as a definition of what the organization is; of what it does: "Our business is ...". This definition should not be too narrow, or it will constrict the development of the organization; a too rigorous concentration on the view that "We are in the business of making meat-scales," as IBM was during the early 1900s, might have limited its subsequent development into other areas. On the other hand, it should not be too wide or it will become meaningless; "We want to make a profit" is not too helpful in developing specific plans.

Abell suggested that the definition should cover three dimensions: "customer groups" to be served, "customer needs" to be served, and "technologies" to be utilized. Thus, the definition of IBM's "corporate mission" in the 1990s. might well have been: "We are in the business of handling accounting information for the larger US organizations [customer group] by means of punched cards [technology]."

Perhaps the most important factor in successful marketing is the "corporate vision." Surprisingly, it is largely neglected by marketing textbooks; although not by the popular exponents of corporate strategy-indeed, it was perhaps the main theme of the book by Peters and Waterman, in the form of their "Superordinate Goals." "In Search of Excellence" said: "Nothing drives progress like the imagination. The idea precedes the deed."

If the organization in general, and its chief executive in particular, has a strong vision of where its future lies, then there is a good chance that the organization will achieve a strong position in its markets (and attain that future).

This will be not least because its strategies will be consistent; and will be supported by its staff at all levels. In this context, all of IBM's marketing activities were underpinned by its philosophy of "customer service"; a vision originally promoted by the charismatic Watson dynasty. The emphasis at this stage is on obtaining a complete and accurate picture.

A "traditional"-albeit product-based-format for a "brand reference book" (or, indeed, a "marketing facts book") was suggested by Godley more than three decades ago:

1. Financial data—Facts for this section will come from management accounting, costing and finance sections.

2. Product data—From production, research and development.
3. Sales and distribution data-Sales, packaging, distribution sections.
4. Advertising, sales promotion, merchandising data-Information from these departments.
5. Market data and miscellany-From market research, who would in most cases act as a source for this information. His sources of data, however, assume the resources of a very large organization. In most organizations they would be obtained from a much smaller set of people (and not a few of them would be generated by the marketing manager alone).

It is apparent that a marketing audit can be a complex process, but the aim is simple: *"it is only to identify those existing (external and internal) factors which will have a significant impact on the future plans of the company."*

It is clear that the basic material to be input to the marketing audit should be comprehensive. Accordingly, the best approach is to accumulate this material continuously, as and when it becomes available; since this avoids the otherwise heavy workload involved in collecting it as part of the regular, typically annual, planning process itself-when time is usually at a premium.

Even so, the first task of this *annual* process should be to check that the material held in the current *facts book* or *facts files* actually *is* comprehensive and accurate, and can form a sound basis for the marketing audit itself. The structure of the facts book will be designed to match the specific needs of the organization, but one simple format-suggested by Malcolm McDonald-may be applicable in many cases. This splits the material into three groups:

1. Review of the marketing environment. A study of the organization's markets, customers, competitors and the overall economic, political, cultural and technical environment; covering developing trends, as well as the current situation.
2. Review of the detailed marketing activity. A study of the company's marketing mix; in terms of the 7 Ps.
3. Review of the marketing system. A study of the marketing organization, marketing research systems and the current marketing objectives and strategies. The last of these is too frequently ignored. The marketing system itself needs to be regularly questioned, because the validity of the whole

marketing plan is reliant upon the accuracy of the input from this system, and 'garbage in, garbage out' applies with a vengeance.

- Portfolio planning. In addition, the coordinated planning of the individual products and services can contribute towards the balanced portfolio.
- 80:20 rule. To achieve the maximum impact, the marketing plan must be clear, concise and simple. It needs to concentrate on the 20 percent of products or services, and on the 20 percent of customers, which will account for 80 percent of the volume and 80 percent of the profit.
- 7 P's: Product, Place, Price and Promotion, Physical Environment, People, Process. The 7 P's can sometimes divert attention from the customer, but the framework they offer can be very useful in building the action plans.

It is only at this stage (of deciding the marketing objectives) that the active part of the marketing planning process begins'. This next stage in marketing planning is indeed the key to the whole marketing process. The "marketing objectives" state just where the company intends to be; at some specific time in the future. James Quinn succinctly defined objectives in general as: *Goals (or objectives) state what is to be achieved and when results are to be accomplished, but they do not state 'how' the results are to be achieved.* They typically relate to what products (or services) will be where in what markets (and must be realistically based on customer behaviour in those markets). They are essentially about the match between those "products" and "markets." Objectives for pricing, distribution, advertising and so on are at a lower level, and should not be confused with marketing objectives.

They are part of the marketing strategy needed to achieve marketing objectives. To be most effective, objectives should be capable of measurement and therefore "quantifiable." This measurement may be in terms of sales volume, money value, market share, percentage penetration of distribution outlets and so on. An example of such a measurable marketing objective might be "to enter the market with product Y and capture 10 percent of the market by value within one year." As it is quantified it can, within limits, be unequivocally monitored; and corrective action taken as necessary.

The marketing objectives must usually be based, above all, on the organization's financial objectives; converting these financial measurements into the related marketing measurements. He went on to explain his view of the role of "policies," with which strategy is most often confused: "Policies are rules or guidelines that express the 'limits' within which action should occur." Simplifying somewhat, marketing strategies can be seen as the means, or "game plan," by which marketing objectives will be achieved and, in the framework that we have chosen to use, are generally concerned with the 8 P's. Examples are:

1. Price-The amount of money needed to buy products
2. Product-The actual product
3. Promotion (advertising)-Getting the product known
4. Placement-Where the product is located
5. People-Represent the business
6. Physical environment-The ambiance, mood, or tone of the environment
7. Process-How do people obtain your product
8. Packaging-How the product will be protected.

(Note: At GCSE the 4 P's are Place, Promotion, Product and Price and the "secret" 5th P is Packaging, but which applies only to physical products, not services usually, and mostly those sold to individual consumers).

In principle, these strategies describe how the objectives will be achieved. The 7 P's are a useful framework for deciding how the company's resources will be manipulated (strategically) to achieve the objectives. It should be noted, however, that they are not the only framework, and may divert attention from the real issues. The focus of the strategies must be the objectives to be achieved-not the process of planning itself. Only if it fits the needs of these objectives should you choose, as we have done, to use the framework of the 7 P's. The strategy statement can take the form of a purely verbal description of the strategic options which have been chosen. Alternatively, and perhaps more positively, it might include a structured list of the major options chosen.

One aspect of strategy which is often overlooked is that of "timing." Exactly when it is the best time for each element of the strategy to be implemented is often critical. Taking the right action at the wrong time can sometimes be almost as bad as taking the wrong action at the right time. Timing is, therefore, an essential part of any plan; and should normally appear as a schedule of planned activities. Having completed this crucial stage of the planning process, you will need to re-check the feasibility of your objectives and strategies in terms of the market share, sales, costs, profits and so on which these demand in practice. As in the rest of the marketing discipline, you will need to employ judgment, experience, market research or anything else which helps you to look at your conclusions from all possible angles.

Detailed Plans and Programs

At this stage, you will need to develop your overall marketing strategies into detailed plans and program. Although these detailed plans may cover each of the 7 P's, the focus will vary, depending upon your organization's specific strategies. A product-oriented company will focus its plans for the 7 P's around each of its products. A market or geographically oriented company will concentrate on each market or geographical area. Each will base its plans upon the detailed needs of its customers, and on the strategies chosen to satisfy these needs. Again, the most important element is, indeed, that of the detailed plans; which spell out exactly what programs and individual activities will take place over the period of the plan (usually over the next year). Without these specified-and preferably quantified-activities the plan cannot be monitored, even in terms of success in meeting its objectives. It is these programs and activities which will then constitute the "marketing" of the organization over the period. As a result, these detailed marketing programs are the most important, practical outcome of the whole planning process. These plans therefore be:

- Clear-They should be an unambiguous statement of 'exactly' what is to be done.
- Quantified-The predicted outcome of each activity should be, as far as possible, quantified; so that its performance can be monitored.
- Focused-The temptation to proliferate activities beyond the numbers which can be realistically controlled should be avoided. The 80:20 Rule applies in this context too.
- Realistic-They should be achievable.
- Agreed-Those who are to implement them should be committed to them, and agree that they are achievable. The resulting plans should become a working document which will guide the campaigns taking place throughout the organization over the period of the plan. If the marketing plan is to work, every exception to it (throughout the year) must be questioned; and the lessons learned, to be incorporated in the next year's planning.

Content of the Marketing Plan

A marketing plan for a small business typically includes Small Business Administration Description of competitors, including the level of demand for the product or service and the strengths and weaknesses of competitors

1. Description of the product or service, including special features
2. Marketing budget, including the advertising and promotional plan
3. Description of the business location, including advantages and disadvantages for marketing
4. Pricing strategy
5. Market Segmentation.

Medium-sized and Large Organizations

The main contents of a marketing plan are.

1. Executive Summary.
2. Situational Analysis.
3. Opportunities/Issue Analysis-SWOT Analysis.
4. Objectives.
5. Strategy.
6. Action Program (the operational marketing plan itself for the period under review).
7. Financial Forecast.
8. Controls.

In detail, a Complete Marketing plan Typically Includes:

1. Title page.
2. Executive Summary.
3. Current Situation-Macroenvironment.
    - economy.
    - legal.
    - government.
    - technology.
    - ecological.
    - sociocultural.
    - supply chain.

4. Current Situation-Market Analysis.
   - market definition.
   - market size.
   - market segmentation.
   - industry structure and strategic groupings.
   - Porter 5 forces analysis.
   - competition and market share.
   - competitors' strengths and weaknesses.
   - market trends.
5. Current Situation-Consumer Analysis
   - nature of the buying decision.
   - participants.
   - demographics.
   - psychographics.
   - buyer motivation and expectations.
   - loyalty segments.
6. Current Situation-Internal.
   - company resources.
   - financial.
   - people.
   - time.
   - skills.
   - objectives.
   - mission statement and vision statement.
   - corporate objectives.
   - financial objective.
   - marketing objectives.
   - long term objectives.
   - description of the basic business philosophy.
   - corporate culture.
7. Summary of Situation Analysis.
   - external threats.
   - external opportunities.
   - internal strengths.

- internal weaknesses.
- Critical success factors in the industry.
- our sustainable competitive advantage.

8. Marketing research.
   - information requirements.
   - research methodology.
   - research results.
9. Marketing Strategy-Product.
   - product mix.
   - product strengths and weaknesses.
   - perceptual mapping.
   - product life cycle management and new product development.
   - Brand name, brand image, and brand equity.
   - the augmented product.
   - product portfolio analysis.
   - B.C.G. Analysis.
   - contribution margin analysis.
   - G.E. Multi Factoral analysis.
   - Quality Function Deployment.
10. Marketing Strategy-segmented marketing actions and market share objectives.
    - by product,
    - by customer segment,
    - by geographical market,
    - by distribution channel.
11. Marketing Strategy-Price.
    - pricing objectives.
    - pricing method (eg.: cost plus, demand based, or competitor indexing).
    - pricing strategy (eg.: skimming, or penetration).
    - discounts and allowances.
    - price elasticity and customer sensitivity.
    - price zoning.
    - break even analysis at various prices.

12. Marketing Strategy-promotion.
    - promotional goals.
    - promotional mix.
    - advertising reach, frequency, flights, theme, and media.
    - sales force requirements, techniques, and management.
    - sales promotion.
    - publicity and public relations.
    - electronic promotion (eg.: Web, or telephone).
    - word of mouth marketing (buzz).
    - viral marketing.
13. Marketing Strategy-Distribution.
    - geographical coverage.
    - distribution channels.
    - physical distribution and logistics.
    - electronic distribution.
14. Implementation.
    - personnel requirements.
    - assign responsibilities.
    - give incentives.
    - training on selling methods.
    - financial requirements.
    - management information systems requirements.
    - month-by-month agenda.
    - PERT or critical path analysis.
    - monitoring results and benchmarks.
    - adjustment mechanism.
    - contingencies (What if's).
15. Financial Summary.
    - assumptions.
    - pro-forma monthly income statement.
    - contribution margin analysis.
    - breakeven analysis.
    - Monte Carlo method.
    - ISI: Internet Strategic Intelligence.

16. Scenarios.
    - Prediction of Future Scenarios.
    - Plan of Action for each Scenario.
17. Appendix.
    - pictures and specifications of the new product.
    - results from research already completed.

Measurement of Progress

The final stage of any marketing planning process is to establish targets (or standards) so that progress can be monitored.

Accordingly, it is important to put both quantities and timescales into the marketing objectives (for example, to capture 20 percent by value of the market within two years) and into the corresponding strategies. Changes in the environment mean that the forecasts often have to be changed. Along with these, the related plans may well also need to be changed.

Continuous monitoring of performance, against predetermined targets, represents a most important aspect of this. However, perhaps even more important is the enforced discipline of a regular formal review. Again, as with forecasts, in many cases the best (most realistic) planning cycle will revolve around a quarterly review.

Best of all, at least in terms of the quantifiable aspects of the plans, if not the wealth of backing detail, is probably a quarterly rolling review-planning one full year ahead each new quarter. Of course, this does absorb more planning resource; but it also ensures that the plans embody the latest information, and-with attention focused on them so regularly-forces both the plans and their implementation to be realistic. Plans only have validity if they are actually used to control the progress of a company: their success lies in their implementation, not in the writing'.

Performance Analysis

The most important elements of marketing performance, which are normally tracked, are:

Sales Analysis

Most organizations track their sales results; or, in non-profit organizations for example, the number of clients. The more sophisticated track them in terms of 'sales variance'-the deviation from the target figures-which allows a more immediate picture of deviations to become evident.

'Micro-analysis', which is a nicely pseudo-scientific term for the normal management process of investigating detailed problems, then investigates the individual elements (individual products, sales territories, customers and so on) which are failing to meet targets.

Market Share Analysis

Few organizations track market share though it is often an important metric. Though absolute sales might grow in an expanding market, a firm's share of the market can decrease which bodes ill for future sales when the market starts to drop. Where such market share is tracked, there may be a number of aspects which will be followed:

- overall market share
- segment share-that in the specific, targeted segment
- relative share-in relation to the market leaders
- annual fluctuation rate of market share.

Expense Analysis

The key ratio to watch in this area is usually the 'marketing expense to sales ratio'; although this may be broken down into other elements (advertising to sales, administration to sales, and so on).

Financial Analysis

The "bottom line" of marketing activities should at least in theory, be the net profit (for all except non-profit organizations, where the comparable emphasis may be on remaining within budgeted costs). There are a number of separate performance figures and key ratios which need to be tracked:

- gross contribution<>net profit.
- gross profit<>return on investment.
- net contribution<>profit on sales.

There can be considerable benefit in comparing these figures with those achieved by other organizations (especially those in the same industry); using, for instance, the figures which can be obtained (in the UK) from 'The Centre for Interfirm Comparison'. The most sophisticated use of this approach, however, is typically by those making use of PIMS (Profit Impact of Management Strategies), initiated by the General Electric Company and then developed by Harvard Business School, but now run by the Strategic Planning Institute. The above performance analyses concentrate on the quantitative measures which are directly related to short-term performance. But there are a number of indirect measures, essentially tracking customer attitudes, which can also indicate the organization's performance in terms of its longer-term marketing strengths and may accordingly be even more important indicators. Some useful measures are:

- market research-including customer panels (which are used to track changes over time)
- lost business-the orders which were lost because, for example, the stock was not available or the product did not meet the customer's exact requirements
- customer complaints-how many customers complain about the products or services, or the organization itself, and about what.

Use of Marketing Plans

A formal, written marketing plan is essential; in that it provides an unambiguous reference point for activities throughout the planning period.

However, perhaps the most important benefit of these plans is the planning process itself. This typically offers a unique opportunity, a forum, for information-rich and productively focused discussions between the various managers involved. The plan, together with the associated discussions, then provides an agreed context for their subsequent management activities, even for those not described in the plan itself.

Budgets as Managerial Tools

The classic quantification of a marketing plan appears in the form of budgets. Because these are so rigorously quantified, they are particularly important. They should, thus, represent an unequivocal projection of actions and expected results. What is more, they should be capable of being monitored accurately; and, indeed, performance against budget is the main (regular) management review process.

The purpose of a marketing budget is, thus, to pull together all the revenues and costs involved in marketing into one comprehensive document. It is a managerial tool that balances what is needed to be spent against what can be afforded, and helps make choices about priorities. It is then used in monitoring performance in practice.

The marketing budget is usually the most powerful tool by which you think through the relationship between desired results and available means. Its starting point should be the marketing strategies and plans, which have already been formulated in the marketing plan itself; although, in practice, the two will run in parallel and will interact. At the very least, the rigorous, highly quantified, budgets may cause a rethink of some of the more optimistic elements of the plans.

Mass Customization

Mass customization, in marketing, manufacturing, call centres and management, is the use of flexible computer-aided manufacturing systems to produce custom output. Those systems combine the low unit costs of mass production processes with the flexibility of individual customization.

"Mass Customization" is the new frontier in business competition for both manufacturing and service industries. At its core is a tremendous increase in variety and customization without a corresponding increase in costs. At its limit, it is the mass production of individually customized goods and services. At its best, it provides strategic advantage and economic value.

Mass Customization is the method of "effectively postponing the task of differentiating a product for a specific customer until the latest possible point in the supply network." The concept of mass customization is attributed to Stan Davis in *Future Perfect* and was defined by Tseng & Jiao (2001, p. 685) as "producing goods and services to meet individual customer's needs with near mass production efficiency". Kaplan & Haenlein (2006) concurred, calling it "a strategy that creates value by some form of company-customer interaction at the fabrication and assembly stage of the operations level to create customized products with production cost and monetary price similar to those of mass-produced products".

Implementation

Many implementations of mass customization are operational today, such as software-based product configurators which make it possible to add and/or change functionalities of a core product or to build fully custom enclosures from scratch. This degree of mass customization has only seen limited adoption, however. If an enterprise's marketing department offers individual products (atomic market fragmentation) it doesn't often mean that a product is produced individually, but rather that similar variants of the same mass-produced item are available.

Companies which have succeeded with mass-customization business models tend to supply purely electronic products. However, these are not true "mass customizers" in the original sense, since they do not offer an alternative to mass production of material goods. Service industries are also waking up to the power of a mass customization orientation.

Call centres are leveraging agent-assisted voice technology to build pre-programmed, pre-recorded call flows to handle customers' inquiries. The agent executes the process, varying it only as they need to because of something the customer says or needs, as opposed to varying everything, every time.

Variants

Pine II (1992) described four types of mass customization.

- Collaborative customization-firms talk to individual customers to determine the precise product offering that best serves the customer's needs. This information is then used to specify and manufacture a product that suits that specific customer. For example, some clothing companies will manufacture blue jeans to fit an individual customer.
- Adaptive customization-firms produce a standardized product, but this product is customizable in the hands of the end-user (the customers alter the product themselves)
- Transparent customization-firms provide individual customers with unique products, without explicitly telling them that the products are customized. In this case there is a need to accurately assess customer needs.
- Cosmetic customization-firms produce a standardized physical product, but market it to different customers in unique ways.

He suggested a business model, "the 8.5-figure-path", a process going from invention to mass production to continuous improvement to mass customization and back to invention.

Positioning (Marketing)

In marketing, positioning has come to mean the process by which marketers try to create an image or identity in the minds of their target market for its product, brand, or organization. It is the 'relative competitive comparison' their product occupies in a given market as perceived by the target market.

Re-positioning involves changing the identity of a product, relative to the identity of competing products, in the collective minds of the target market.

De-positioning involves attempting to change the identity of competing products, relative to the identity of your own product, in the collective minds of the target market.

The original work on Positioning was consumer marketing oriented, and was not as much focused on the question relative to competitive products as much as it was focused on cutting through the ambient "noise" and establishing a moment of real contact with the intended recipient.

In the classic example of Avis claiming "No.2, We Try Harder", the point was to say something so shocking (it was by the standards of the day) that it cleared space in your brain and made you forget all about who was #1, and not to make some philosophical point about being "hungry" for business. The growth of high-tech marketing may have had much to do with the shift in definition towards competitive positioning.

Definitions

Although there are different definitions of Positioning, probably the most common is: "A product's position is how potential buyers see the product", and is expressed relative to the position of competitors. Positioning is a concept in marketing which was first popularized by Al Ries and Jack Trout in their bestseller book " Positioning-a battle for your mind".

This differs slightly from the context in which the term was first published in 1969 by Jack Trout in the paper *"Positioning" is a game people play in today's me-too market place"* in the publication *Industrial Marketing*, in which the case is made that the typical consumer is overwhelmed with unwanted advertising, and has a natural tendency to discard all information that does not immediately find a comfortable (and empty) slot in the consumers mind. It was then expanded into their ground-breaking first book, "*Positioning: The Battle for Your Mind*", in which they define Positioning as "an organized system for finding a window in the mind.

It is based on the concept that communication can only take place at the right time and under the right circumstances." (p. 19 of 2001 paperback edition). What most will agree on is that Positioning is something (perception) that happens in the minds of the target market. It is the aggregate perception the market has of a particular company, product or service in relation to their perceptions of the competitors in the same category.

It will happen whether or not a company's management is proactive, reactive or passive about the on-going process of evolving a position. But a company can positively influence the perceptions through enlightened strategic actions.

Product Positioning Process

Generally, the product positioning process involves.

1. Defining the market in which the product or brand will compete (who the relevant buyers are).
2. Identifying the attributes (also called dimensions) that define the product 'space'.
3. Collecting information from a sample of customers about their perceptions of each product on the relevant attributes.
4. Determine each product's share of mind.
5. Determine each product's current location in the product space.
6. Determine the target market's preferred combination of attributes (referred to as an *ideal vector*).
7. Examine the fit between.
    - The position of your product.
    - The position of the ideal vector.
8. Position.

The process is similar for positioning your company's services. Services, however, don't have the physical attributes of products-that is, we can't feel them or touch them or show nice product pictures.

So you need to ask first your customers and then yourself, what value do clients get from my services? How are they better off from doing business with me? Also ask: is there a characteristic that makes my services different?

Write out the value customers derive and the attributes your services offer to create the first draft of your positioning. Test it on people who don't really know what you do or what you sell, watch their facial expressions and listen for their response. When they want to know more because you've piqued their interest and started a conversation, you'll know you're on the right track.

Positioning Concepts

More generally, there are three types of positioning concepts.

1. Functional positions.
    - Solve problems.
    - Provide benefits to customers.
    - Get favourable perception by investors (stock profile) and lenders.

2. Symbolic positions.
   - Self-image enhancement.
   - Ego identification.
   - Belongingness and social meaningfulness.
   - Affective fulfilment.
3. Experiential positions.
   - Provide sensory stimulation.
   - Provide cognitive stimulation.

Measuring the Positioning

Positioning is facilitated by a graphical technique called perceptual mapping, various survey techniques, and statistical techniques like multi dimensional scaling, factor analysis, conjoint analysis, and logit analysis.

Repositioning a Company

In volatile markets, it can be necessary-even urgent-to reposition an entire company, rather than just a product line or brand. Take, for example, when Goldman Sachs and Morgan Stanley suddenly shifted from investment to commercial banks. The expectations of investors, employees, clients and regulators all need to shift, and each company will need to influence how these perceptions change. Doing so involves repositioning the entire firm.

This is especially true of small and medium-sized firms, many of which often lack strong brands for individual product lines. In a prolonged recession, business approaches that were effective during healthy economies often become ineffective and it becomes necessary to change a firm's positioning. Upscale restaurants, for example, which previously flourished on expense account dinners and corporate events, may for the first time need to stress value as a sale tool. Repositioning a company involves more than a marketing challenge. It involves making hard decisions about how a market is shifting and how a firm's competitors will react. Often these decisions must be made without the benefit of sufficient information, simply because the definition of "volatility" is that change becomes difficult or impossible to predict.

Product Life Cycle Management

Product life cycle management is the succession of strategies used by management as a product goes through its product life cycle. The conditions in which a product is sold changes over time and must be managed as it moves through its succession of stages.

Product Life Cycle

The product life cycle goes through many phases, involves many professional disciplines, and requires many skills, tools and processes. Product life cycle (PLC) has to do with the life of a product in the market with respect to business/commercial costs and sales measures; whereas product life cycle management (PLM) has more to do with managing descriptions and properties of a product through its development and useful life, mainly from a business/engineering point of view. To say that a product has a life cycle is to assert four things:

- that products have a limited life.
- product sales pass through distinct stages, each posing different challenges, opportunities, and problems to the seller.
- profits rise and fall at different stages of product life cycle, and.
- products require different marketing, financial, manufacturing, purchasing, and human resource strategies in each life cycle stage.

Request for Deviation

In the process of building a product following defined procedure, an RFD is a request for authorization, granted prior to the manufacture of an item, to depart from a particular performance or design requirement of a specification, drawing or other document, for a specific number of units or a specific period of time.....

Market Identification

A "micro-market" can be used to describe a Walkman, more portable, as well as individually and privately recordable; and then Compact Discs ("CDS") brought increased capacity and CD-R offered individual private recording...and so the process goes. The below section on the "technology lifecycle" is a most appropriate concept in this context. Most of the context is not in English so you may need a translator.

In short, termination is not always the end of the cycle; it can be the end of a micro-entrant within the grander scope of a macro-environment. The auto industry, fast-food industry, petro-chemical industry, are just a few that demonstrate a macro-environment that overall has not terminated even while micro-entrants over time have come and gone.

Lessons of the Product Life Cycle (PLC)

It is claimed that every product has a life period, It is launched, it grows, and at some point, may die. A fair comment is that-at least in the short term-not all products or services die. Jeans may die, but clothes probably will not. Legal services or medical services may die, but depending on the social and political climate, probably will not.

Even though its validity is questionable, it can offer a useful 'model' for managers to keep at the back of their mind. Indeed, if their products are in the introductory or growth phases, or in that of decline, it perhaps should be at the front of their mind; for the predominant features of these phases may be those revolving around such life and death. Between these two extremes, it is salutary for them to have that vision of mortality in front of them.

However, the most important aspect of product life-cycles is that, even under normal conditions, to all practical intents and purposes they often do not exist (hence, there needs to be more emphasis on model/reality mappings). In most markets the majority of the major brands have held their position for at least two decades. The dominant product life-cycle, that of the brand leaders which almost monopolize many markets, is therefore one of continuity.

In the Criticism of the Product Life Cycle, Dhalla & Yuspeh State

The PLC is a dependent variable which is determined by market actions; it is not an independent variable to which companies should adapt their marketing programs. Marketing management itself can alter the shape and duration of a brand's life cycle. Thus, the life cycle may be useful as a description, but not as a predictor; and usually should be firmly under the control of the marketer. The important point is that in many markets the product or brand life cycle is significantly longer than the planning cycle of the organisations involved. Thus, it offers little practical value for most marketers. Even if the PLC (and the related PLM support) exists for them, their plans will be based just upon that piece of the curve where they currently reside (most probably in the 'mature' stage); and their view of that part of it will almost certainly be 'linear' (and limited), and will not encompass the whole range from growth to decline.

Limitations

The PLC model is of some degree of usefulness to marketing managers, in that it is based on factual assumptions. Nevertheless, it is difficult for marketing management to gauge accurately where a product is on its PLC graph. A rise in sales *per se* is not necessarily evidence of growth. A fall in sales *per se* does not typify decline. Furthermore, some products do not (and to date, at the least, have not) experienced a decline. Coca Cola and Pepsi are examples of two products that have existed for many decades, but are still popular products all over the world. Both modes of cola have been in maturity for some years. Another factor is that differing products would possess different PLC "shapes".

A fad product would hold a steep sloped growth stage, a short maturity stage, and a steep sloped decline stage. A product such as Coca Cola and Pepsi would experience growth, but also a constant level of sales over a number of decades.

It can probably be said that a given product (or products collectively within an industry) may hold a unique PLC shape, and the typical PLC model can only be used as a rough guide for marketing management.

The Product Life Cycle (PLC) is based upon the biological life cycle. For example, a seed is planted (introduction); it begins to sprout (growth); it shoots out leaves and puts down roots as it becomes an adult (maturity); after a long period as an adult the plant begins to shrink and die out (decline). In theory it's the same for a product.

After a period of development it is introduced or launched into the market; it gains more and more customers as it grows; eventually the market stabilises and the product becomes mature; then after a period of time the product is overtaken by development and the introduction of superior competitors, it goes into decline and is eventually withdrawn.

Strategies for the Differing Stages of the Product Life Cycle

The need for immediate profit is not a pressure. The product is promoted to create awareness. If the product has no or few competitors, a skimming price strategy is employed. Limited numbers of product are available in few channels of distribution.

Growth

Competitors are attracted into the market with very similar offerings. Products become more profitable and companies form alliances, joint ventures and take each other over. Advertising spend is high and focuses upon building brand. Market share tends to stabilise.

Maturity

Those products that survive the earlier stages tend to spend longest in this phase. Sales grow at a decreasing rate and then stabilise. Producers attempt to differentiate products and brands are key to this.

Price wars and intense competition occur. At this point the market reaches saturation. Producers begin to leave the market due to poor margins. Promotion becomes more widespread and use a greater variety of media.

Decline

At this point there is a downturn in the market. For example more innovative products are introduced or consumer tastes have changed. There is intense price-cutting and many more products are withdrawn from the market. Profits can be improved by reducing marketing spend and cost cutting.

Problems with Product Life Cycle

In reality very few products follow such a prescriptive cycle. The length of each stage varies enormously. The decisions of marketers can change the stage, for example from maturity to decline by price-cutting. Not all products go through each stage. Some go from introduction to decline.

It is not easy to tell which stage the product is in. Remember that PLC is like all other tools. Use it to inform your gut feeling. Another marketing tool for evaluating PRODUCT is the Three Levels of a Product.

Research and Development

The phrase research and development (also R and D or, more often, R&D), according to the Organization for Economic Co-operation and Development, refers to "creative work undertaken on a systematic basis in order to increase the stock of knowledge, including knowledge of man, culture and society, and the use of this stock of knowledge to devise new applications".

R&D

New product design and development is more often than not a crucial factor in the survival of a company. In an industry that is fast changing, firms must continually revise their design and range of products. This is necessary due to continuous technology change and development as well as other competitors and the changing preference of customers. A system driven by marketing is one that puts the customer needs first, and only produces goods that are known to sell. Market research is carried out, which establishes what is needed. If the development is technology driven then it is a matter of selling what it is possible to make. The product range is developed so that production processes are as efficient as possible and the products are technically superior, hence possessing a natural advantage in the market place.

R&D has a special economic significance apart from its conventional association with scientific and technological development. R&D investment generally reflects a government's or organization's willingness to forgo current operations or profit to improve future performance or returns, and its abilities to conduct research and development. In 2006, the world's four largest spenders of R&D were the United States (US$343 billion), the EU (US$231 billion), China (US$136 billion), and Japan (US$130 billion). In terms of percentage of GDP, the order of these spenders for 2006 was China (US$115 billion of US$2,668 billion GDP), Japan, United States, EU with approximate percentages of 4.3, 3.2, 2.6, and 1.8 respectively. The top 10 spenders in terms of percentage of GDP were Israel (4.53%), Sweden (3.73%), Finland (3.45%), Japan (3.39%), South Korea (3.23%), Switzerland (2.9%), Iceland (2.78%), United States (2.62%), Germany (2.53%) and Austria (2.45%).

In general, R&D activities are conducted by specialized units or centres belonging to companies, universities and state agencies. In the context of commerce, "research and development" normally refers to future-oriented, longer-term activities in science or technology, using similar techniques to scientific research without predetermined outcomes and with broad forecasts of commercial yield. Statistics on organizations devoted to "R&D" may express the state of an industry, the degree of competition or the lure of progress. Some common measures include: budgets, numbers of patents or on rates of peer-reviewed publications. Bank ratios are one of the best measures, because they are continuously maintained, public and reflect risk.

In the U.S., a typical ratio of research and development for an industrial company is about 3.5% of revenues. A high technology company such as a computer manufacturer might spend 7%. Although Allergan (a biotech company) tops the spending table 43.4% investment, anything over 15% is remarkable and usually gains a reputation for being a high technology company. Companies in this category include pharmaceutical companies such as Merck & Co. (14.1%) or Novartis (15.1%), and engineering companies like Ericsson (24.9%). Such companies are often seen as poor credit risks because their spending ratios are so unusual.

Generally such firms prosper only in markets whose customers have extreme needs, such as medicine, scientific instruments, safety-critical mechanisms (aircraft) or high technology military armaments. The extreme needs justify the high risk of failure and consequently high gross margins from 60% to 90% of revenues. That is, gross profits will be as much as 90% of the sales cost, with manufacturing costing only 10% of the product price, because so many individual projects yield no exploitable product.

Most industrial companies get only 40% revenues. On a technical level, high tech organisations explore ways to re-purpose and repackage advanced technologies as a way of amortizing the high overhead. They often reuse advanced manufacturing processes, expensive safety certifications, specialized embedded software, computer-aided design software, electronic designs and mechanical subsystems. Research has shown that firms with a persistent R&D strategy outperform those with an irregular or no R&D investment programme.

Pharmaceuticals

Research often refers to basic experimental research; development refers to the exploitation of discoveries. Research involves the identification of possible chemical compounds or theoretical mechanisms. In the United States, universities are the main provider of research level products. In the United States, corporations buy licences from universities or hire scientists directly when economically solid research level products emerge and the development phase of drug delivery is almost entirely managed by private enterprise.

Development is concerned with proof of concept, safety testing, and determining ideal levels and delivery mechanisms. Development often occurs in phases that are defined by drug safety regulators in the country of interest. In the United States, the development phase can cost between \$10 to \$200 million and approximately one in ten compounds identified by basic research pass all development phases and reach market.

Business

Research and development is nowadays of great importance in business as the level of competition, production processes and methods are rapidly increasing. It is of special importance in the field of marketing where companies keep an eagle eye on competitors and customers in order to keep pace with modern trends and analyse the needs, demands and desires of their customers. Unfortunately, research and development are very difficult to manage, since the defining feature of research is that the researchers do not know in advance exactly how to accomplish the desired result. As a result, higher R&D spending does not guarantee "more creativity, higher profit or a greater market share."

R&D Alliance

An R&D alliance is a mutually beneficial formal relationship formed between two or more parties to pursue a set of agreed upon goals while remaining independent organisations, where acquiring new knowledge is a goal by itself. The different parties agree to combine their knowledge to create new innovative products. Thanks to funding from government organizations, like the European Union's Seventh Framework Programme (FP7), and modern advances in technology, such as Eures Tools, R&D alliances have now become more efficient. Research and development is nowadays of great importance in business as the level of competition, production processes and methods are rapidly increasing. It is of special importance in the field of marketing where companies keep an eagle eye on competitors and customers in order to keep pace with modern trends and analyse the needs, demands and desires of their customers.

Unfortunately, research and development are very difficult to manage, since the defining feature of research is that the researchers do not know in advance exactly how to accomplish the desired result. As a result, higher R&D spending and does not guarantee "more creativity, higher profit or a greater market share."

Chapter 3

Development of Product and the Emergence of E-commerce

The innovation of e-commerce has affected not only the marketplace through the facilitation of the exchange of goods and services, but also human behaviour in response to the mechanisms of online services. Researchers have identified and hypothesized on relevant subject matters ranging from Web usability, marketing channels and other factors influencing online buying behaviour. Though researchers have focused on what appear different aspects of online buying behaviour, their studies may be shown to be interrelated and interdependent, even to the extent of revealing constructs upon which e-commerce, in terms of future design and research, could be built upon.

Constructs

A construct is defined as an abstract or general idea inferred or derived from specific instances (Hyperdictionary). This paper researched a number of studies on e-commerce with each providing examples in order to substantiate their respective hypotheses. Even with the varying number and nature of these studies, some constructs emerge which seem interdependent in contributing to the holistic view of e-commerce and associated consumer interactions. For example, Li, Kuo and Russel (2002) extrapolated from an online survey of 999 U.S. Internet users, that marketing channel knowledge is the strongest predictor of online buying behaviour. They draw this construct in the due course of presenting ten hypotheses. Three of their finding demonstrates that there is no difference in price, recreation orientation or age differences between those who make online purchases and those who don't. They did find that online buyers are better educated and male, with a higher income than those who don't purchase online. As would be expected, they further determined that online consumers are lower in experiential orientation than non-Web buyers and more convenience oriented. The remaining two hypotheses propose that online consumers view the Web as having higher utilities in communication, distribution as well as hold the self-perception that they are more knowledgeable about the Web as a marketing channel, than non-Web consumers. Ultimately however, these authors identify a weakness in their study in that their methodologies for measuring channel utilities may need to be modified to accommodate attributes such as information customization and degree of interactivity.

Web Usability Construct

Becker (2002) in a separate and unrelated study, which in contrast to the focus on individual users studied seventeen U.S. based e-businesses, theorizes on the construct of Web Usability. The weakness" with regard to information customization identified by Li et al above, appears addressable via Becker's mechanism of Web Usability. Becker represents Web Usability as the sum of eleven factors, which are navigation, design standards, personalization, design layout, performance, customer satisfaction, design consistency, reliability, security, information content and accessibility. The design standard speaks to the generalized "look and feel", which can be achieved by employing, for example, HTML style sheets. We could also include emerging World Wide Web Consortium technologies such as XHTML and CSS, used for data formatting. Personalization is the meeting, through customization (i.e., display of personal data, buying preferences etc.,) of individual needs.

Design layout is the presentation of the visual content as achieved through the positioning of Web-objects along with colours, fonts, styles etc. Navigation is the travellers mechanisms as well as the breadth and depth of search paths. Design consistency is the uniform placement of Web objects in all of the Web site's pages. Customer service is those added functionalities that enhance the online experience, such as, chat and e-mail. Reliability is the consistent availability of the customer's access to the Website as realized through the mitigation/elimination of any downtime. Security is the access limitation and privacy of personal information. Yeung, Shim and Lai for instance, state that, "Clearly, online payment security and data privacy are the major barriers for any business deploying e-commerce". Performance is the network related metrics of consumer wait and system response times. For example, Liu, Dixon and Murphy (2002) note that in China, "an underdeveloped infrastructure, expensive access, slow access speed...hamper Internet adoption". Information content is described as the accurate and complete translation of text into a native language. Finally, accessibility is how well its comprehension requirements are aligned with the visual, physical and cognitive limitations of the Web user.

Marketing Channel Construct

What seems to emerge here is that Web Usability is a construct upon which marketing's communication channel construct rests. In other words, when the Web site's intent transitions from conveying information to a true commercial venture, what appear super-imposable on the Web-usability infrastructure are the marketing channels; namely, communication channel, transaction channel and distribution channel. Li et al, argue that these three channels may or may not overlap through a commerce-oriented Website. The function of these marketing channels includes information, promotion, negotiation, ordering, financing, risk taking, physical possession, payment and the actual transfer of product ownership.

The purpose of the communication channel is to provide the customers' information needs for decision-making. Li et al argue that the communications channel can be judged on its characteristics of quality, quantity, and recency of information. It could be further argued that the communication channel, by holistically addressing the attributes of information, evolves the eleven Web Usability factors into the marketing activities of information and promotion. In short, this communication channel facilitates and perhaps even enhances, the flow of various types of information between sellers and buyers. If this line of reasoning is pursued, then the transaction channel seems responsible for the marketing functions of negotiations, ordering, financing, risk taking and payment. In essence, the transaction channel holds the range of activities between ordering and payment between buyers and sellers. The distribution channel could then be said to hold the remaining marketing functions of physical possession and the actual transfer of product ownership.

Design Construct

Nah and Davis (2002) take a different approach to Web Usability by simply distilling it to the ease of two distinct activities; namely, search and navigation. They present search, as an information seeking behaviour directed by goals. They give the example of a user seeking specific population growth data in her hometown over the last five years. In contrast, they make navigation synonymous with the common behaviour of browsing, defining it as an activity where the information space is explored without an explicit goal in mind. They also offer that, "searching tasks are best supported by a hierarchical information structure, such as those used by many online stores" in opposition to exploratory tasks, which are best supported by a network structure and a graphical browser. They suggest three design strategies or constructs, which are related in a top-down fashion: "(1) the task to be performed, (2) how information is structured within the system, and (3) navigational support".

Katz and Byrne (2003) use the same terms of searching and browsing to actually mean a subset of a goal-directed, information seeking behaviour. They define search as the "use of a site-specific search function accessed by typing a search query into a text field" and browsing as the "alternative methods of navigating a particular Web site, particularly the traversal of the site's menu of hierarchy". Furthermore, they hypothesize on information scent: "In the context of shopping online, information scent could refer to the amount of information a user could attain regarding the location of a product in a site based solely on the design of the site's home page...Presumably, information scent can play a large role in a user's decision to traverse the menus or use the site search function". Since all e-commerce transactions begin with either navigation/browsing or searching (as defined by Nah and Davis), these constructs along with the subset offered by Katz and Byrne, could act as strategic predecessors in building Becker's Web Usability segments.

Purchasing Decision Support Construct

Similarly, the decision support system presented by Nah and Davis could be said to precede Li et al's marketing channels. Nah and Davis (2002) define the decision support construct as one that supports the stages of the purchasing decision. The stages include product search, criteria management and comparison support. Product search contains the metaphor type of the site (search engine or browsable Web structure) and information structure (network or hierarchical). Criteria management is concerned with the product presentation type (graphics, colors, size, etc.,) and how the information on the product is provided (reviews from professionals, customers, etc.,). Of interest is Becker' note that, " many localized Web sites use national colors (e.g., yellow appears on many Germany Web sites) for navigation bars, images, and other Web objects to promote customer loyalty and national pride, as well as for 'branding' the customer experience". Lastly, comparison support involves the comparison scope (inter-site or intra-site) and comparison tools. In a Web site's transition from conveying information to a true commercial venture with marketing channels, Nah and Davis's three, decision support criteria could serve as the intermediary framework on which the e-commerce portion could be based.

Qualitative HCI Construct

The degree of interactivity, left opened by Li et al, is investigated in yet another separate study by Sun Lim of fourteen interviewees. Lim argues that systematic analysis of human-computer interaction (HCI) must be predicated on the understanding of how and why users perform their activities (Lim 2002). He bypasses quantitative methods like the study of the progression of movement within Web pages, temporal differences in online actions, etc., in favor of a qualitative framework of study construct, which seeks to comprehend the cognitive processes fueling online behaviour. The tool that Lim uses is the Self-Confrontational Interview. In this technique, the subjects are asked to perform the behaviour being analysed, i.e., online activity, which is then recorded. Subsequently, the subjects view their recorded actions and are asked to recount both thoughts and emotions as best they can recall. The interviews are then transcribed to correlate the actor's actions with their thoughts and emotions.

Lim (2002) surmises that such qualitative understanding of human interaction will in turn contribute to improve Web usability. For example, he finds that online consumers favor sequential progression from larger activity units to smaller component units. This is illustrated in the narrowing process where online buyers begin with a search engine to identify pertinent stores and then funnel further to a range of stores within which to select a range of products until they get to the item they wish to purchase. Similarly, consumers expect hyperlinks to elaborate on parent hyperlink. This appears to further support the direction that Becker's Web usability factor of navigation should be divided to produce Nah and Davis's hierarchical model of search activity.

Lim also introduces the concept that Websites should mimic real life scripts. In other words, any online purchasing interface, should imitate a brick-and-mortar process. For example, if when one needs to purchase an airline ticket, all one has to do is state different destinations to the travel agent, then an online ticket system should mirror requiring the same, and not more information, in order to provide the service.

A study of an interviewee is given in this exact same scenario where the online interface requires more data input/additional traversal paths and the ensuing tension and confusion experienced by the consumer. This correlates with what Nah and Davis (2002) identify as cognitive overhead, "the challenge of maintaining several tasks or hyperlink trails simultaneously". They term the user's "experiences in planning, managing and executing digressions from a course of action", as the digression problem. In drawing a comparison between Becker's Web usability factor of accessibility and designing Web sites for real life scripts/cognitive overhead, it initially appears unrelated.

For in fact, Becker discusses accessibility in terms of mitigating consumer's physical impairments and from an international perspective, the users' reading and language comprehension limitations. However, it could be argued that comprehension limitations exist not only due to physical or foreign language translations and understanding, but also as a byproduct of the consumer's specious expectation to use their real life shopping scripts to function in an Internet store and/or the consumer's inability to cope with the increasing cognitive demands. If this perception is considered, then Becker's view of accessibility is given an entirely new dimension.

Visual indicators as presented by Lim (2002), involve those clues which consumers have become accustomed to in a brick-and-mortar store. For example, one may look for box cover or a product design and logo rather than simply a product name when shopping. Becker's Web usability factor of information content might need to be deliberately stratified to accommodate emerging categories of information content such as these visual indicators. Nah and Davis (2002), take this further by calling for future studies in effective visual representations. For example, they query whether or not products should be presented on the Web using 3D imaging with interior and exterior views, for items such as automobiles. Li et al claim that such experience-oriented functionalities (e.g., 3D, virtual reality and surround video) will be dominant characteristics of the next generation of e-commerce stores. They state that simulating the real-life shopping experience, with which the consumer is familiar, will drive future, online consumer marketing.

Lim (2002) is careful to point out though, that functionality has to be dominant over aesthetics. He gives an example where a technically savvy user continued on a Website despite lack of functional clarity. A less technically competent user, he states, would simply have given up. There may be some correlation between this hypothesis and that of Li et al, which describes some online consumers belief that the Web has higher utilities in communication. It could be argued that the belief, the higher expectation of communication utility of the Web and the self-view of competency of experienced online consumers, allows them to persist in Web sites, which fail to meet the design layout, consistency and navigation as defined by Becker.

However, Lim (2002) makes the last point of guarding against Web site designs that encourage conditioning of automatic actions, as opposed to the thorough processing of information. For instance, a design layout that calls for pop-windows as a means of a communication channel, would fail in its intent if the shopper instinctively responds to remove these perceived obstructions to their line of vision, by summarily closing all pop-ups. Here again, Becker and Li's (2002) definition of design layout and communication channel respectively, achieve a greater level of granularity through the filter of Lim's hypothesis.

Trust Construct

Going beyond effective technical infrastructure, design and communication, a critical element influencing all e-commerce behaviour is the construct of trust. Wang and Vassileva distinguish between trust and reputation as; trust is "an agent's belief in an another agent's capabilities, honesty and reliability based on its own direct experiences", while reputation is the same belief, but based on other agents' recommendations.

Smith and Brynjolfsson (2000) also offer that an Internet market, in response to lower search costs, yields a Perfect Bayesian Equilibrium in which buyers and sellers select actions based on their beliefs about each other. Nah and Davis (2002) define trust as " the willingness of the consumer (trustor) to be vulnerable to the actions of an online party (trustee) by engaging in online relationship exchanges with the party". They outline thirteen principles of trust under three major categories of Content, Design and External Certifications and References.

Under Content as it pertains to trust, Nah and Davis (2002) state that it is necessary for e-commerce Web sites to provide the identity of the company (address, contact information, mission statement, etc.,) disclose performance history of the company and have a clear privacy and security policy. Becker notes that the "same security issues facing US users regarding the misuse and unauthorized distribution of credit card numbers, addresses, phone number, income and other personal data extend to all users in the international, online market".

Nah and Davis elaborate that these policies should have information outlining, "how and what types of consumers' personal and transaction information will be collected, how they will be used" and "how they will be protected from unauthorized access". They also indicate that the Web site must provide accurate and comprehensive product and pricing information along with a candid disclosure of all customer relationships aspects.

The latter includes specifications of each participant's obligations and responsibilities, guarantees and pertinent compensation along with support for mediation services and dispute resolution.

Under Design, Nah and Davis suggest that the following traits will promote trust; timely and professional we site design, reliable and secure technology, informed consent and personalization. Nielsen states that, "a professional appearance brings confidence to consumers, clear navigation conveys respect for the customer and an implied promise of good service, and typos or difficult navigation communicate disregard for the users".

Nah and Davis suggest that informed consent can be achieved by providing consumers the technical functionality to opt-in/opt-out of those online interactions that can either potentially benefit or harm the users. They go on to say that with the customers' privacy protected, personalization (such as selective recommendations to customers) can provide the experience that will increase the levels of trust and loyalty. Becker defines personalization as meeting the needs of a user and Nah and Davis complements this by suggesting that customer's needs must be understood via mechanisms such as data mining and collaborative filtering. Xu and Yadov, indicate "three sources of trust between trading parties in business relationship: familiarity, calculativeness, and values" with "the most practical trust source is calculativeness: trading parties estimate the trustworthiness of each other through calculation based on the other party's past performance, which is reflected by reputation".

Under External Certifications and References, Nah and Davis propose four guidelines for fostering trust indirectly. Credibility of online services can be cultivated by obtaining certifications either in the form of approvals from professional associations or from third party assurance services, which certify security and privacy practices. Online traders can be afforded protection from Internet fraud through escrow services. Reputation systems, which gather, disseminate and compile participant feedback, are also effective in aiding consumers' assessment of an online service's trustworthiness.

Finally, credibility can be enhanced by association, via hyperlinks to and from, with other credible third parties. It could be argued that trust, (in the accuracy of information, competency of the vendor to deliver expected service, privacy of client information, reliability of performance and security of all data transfers and transactions), permeates the entire cycle of e-commerce constructs.

Conclusion

Consumer shopping behaviour is being fundamentally changed by electronic commerce. Recent, independent and seemingly unrelated studies, show general patterns of dependencies or constructs, in how the virtual marketplace, as presented by e-commerce Web sites, need to be approached in terms of construction in order to accommodate consumers' needs. Nah and Davis's design paradigm of the task to be performed, structure of the information within the system (with Katz and Byrnes subsets of information seeking) and navigational support, all appear to be a unifying design construct in building Becker's eleven segments of Web Usability.

In turn, Web Usability itself seems to be a construct upon which Li et al's marketing-communication channel rests. Another of Nah and Davis's constructs, the three, purchasing decision support criteria of product search, criteria management and comparison support, could then serve as the intermediary framework on which the e-commerce portion, including Li et al's remaining marketing channels of transaction and distribution, could rest. The maturing marketing channels are then likely to complete the construct circle as constructs themselves in evolving and effectively leveraging not only the current quantitative mechanisms of data mining, collaborative filtering, real-life scripts (mimicking shopping and support), but also in contributing to the genesis and use of new constructs of qualitative techniques, such as Lim's Self-Confrontational Interview, cognitive overhead research and social constructs of trust.

Understanding the Quality and Customer Service

Customer Service

Customer service is the provision of service to customers before, during and after a purchase. According to Jamier L. Scott. (2002), "Customer service is a series of activities designed to enhance the level of customer satisfaction – that is, the feeling that a product or service has met the customer expectation."

Its importance varies by product, industry and customer; defective or broken merchandise can be exchanged, often only with a receipt and within a specified time frame. Retail stores will often have a desk or counter devoted to dealing with returns, exchanges and complaints, or will perform related functions at the point of sale.

Customer service may be provided by a person (e.g., sales and service representative), or by automated means called self-service. Examples of self service are Internet sites.

However, In the Internet era, a challenge has been to maintain and/or enhance the personal experience while making use of the efficiencies of online commerce. Writing in Fast Company, entrepreneur and customer systems innovator Micah Solomon has made the point that "Online customers are literally invisible to you (and you to them), so it's easy to short-change them emotionally. But this lack of visual and tactile presence makes it even more crucial to create a sense of personal, human-to-human connection in the online arena."

Customer service is normally an integral part of a company's customer value proposition. In their book *Rules to Break and Laws to Follow*, Don Peppers and Martha Rogers, Ph.D. write that "customers have memories.

They will remember you, whether you remember them or not." Further, "customer trust can be destroyed at once by a major service problem, or it can be undermined one day at a time, with a thousand small demonstrations of incompetence." From the point of view of an overall sales process engineering effort, customer service plays an important role in an organization's ability to generate income and revenue. From that perspective, customer service should be included as part of an overall approach to systematic improvement.

Some have argued that the quality and level of customer service has decreased in recent years, and that this can be attributed to a lack of support or understanding at the executive and middle management levels of a corporation and/or a customer service policy.

Instant Feedback

Recently, many organizations have implemented feedback loops that allow them to capture feedback at the point of experience. For example, National Express, one of the UK's leading travel companies invites passengers to send text messages whilst riding the bus. This has been shown to be useful as it allows companies to improve their customer service before the customer defects, thus making it far more likely that the customer will return next time.

Setting the Right KPIs

A challenge working with Customer Service is to ensure that you have focused your attention on the right key areas, measured by the right Key Performance Indicator. There is no challenge to come up with a lot of meaningful KPIs, but the challenge is to select a few which reflects your overall strategy. In addition to reflecting your strategy it should also enable staff to limit their focus to the areas that really matter.

The focus must be of those KPIs, which will deliver the most value to the overall objective, e.g. cost saving, service improving etc. It must also be done in such a way that staff sincerly believe that they can make a difference with the effort.

One of the most important aspects of a customer service KPI is that of what is often referred to as the "Feel Good Factor". Basically the goal is to not only help the customer have a good experience, but to offer them an experience that exceeds their expectations. Several key points are listed as follows:

1. Know your product-Know what products/service you are offering back to front. In other words be an information expert. It is okay to say "I don't know", but it should always be followed up by... "but let me find out" or possibly " but my friend knows!" Whatever the situation may be, make sure that you don't leave your customer with an unanswered question.
2. Body Language/Communication-Most of the communication that we relay to others is done through body language. If we have a negative body language when we interact with others it can show our lack of care. Two of the most important parts of positive body language are smiling, and eye contact. Make sure to look your customers in the eye. It shows that we are listening to them, not at them. And then of course smiling is just more inviting than someone who has a blank look on their face.
3. Anticipate Guest Needs-Nothing surprises your customer more than an employee going the extra mile to help them. Always look for ways to serve your customer more than they expect. In doing so it helps them to know that you care and it will leave them with the "Feel Good Factor" that we are searching for.

Standardization

There are few standards on this topic. ISO and The International Customer Service Institute (TICSI) have published the following ones:

- ISO 9004:2000, on performance improvement
- ISO 10001:2007, on customer service conduct
- ISO 10002:2004, on quality management in handling customer complaints
- ISO 10003:2007, on dispute resolution
- The International Customer Service Standard (TICSS).

There is also an Information Technology service management standard: ISO/IEC 20000:2005. Its first part concerns specifications and its second part the code of practice.

Understanding and Managing Customer Perception

In today's globalising economy competition is getting more and more fierce. That means it becomes more difficult for products and services to differentiate themselves from other offerings than ever before. Not only is the number of competitive offerings rising due to globalisation of production, sourcing, logistics and access to information. Many products and services face new competition from substitutes and from completely new offerings or bundles from industry outsiders. Since product differences are closed at an increasing speed and many companies try to win the battle for customers by price reductions, products and services tend to become commodities.

On the other hand, customer behaviour becomes more hybrid. On one hand, customers are increasingly price sensitive – searching for bargains at marketplaces like ebay or buying their groceries at discount markets. On the other hand they enjoy branded and luxury goods. One and the same person may plan a weekend trip with a no-frills airline and a stay at a five-star-hotel.

In the result, customers have a wider choice of often less distinguishable products and they are much better informed. For many offerings the balance of power shifts towards the customer. Customers are widely aware of their greater power, which raises their expectations on how companies should care for them. Bringing it all together, it becomes ever more difficult to differentiate a product or service by traditional categories like price, quality, functionality etc.

In this situation the development of a strong relationship between customers and a company could likely prove to be a significant opportunity for competitive advantage. This relationship is not longer based on features like price and quality alone. Today it is more the perceived experience a customer makes in his various interactions with a company (e.g. how fast, easy, efficient and reliable the process is) that can make or break the relationship. Problems during a single transaction can damage a so far favourable customer attitude. The consequence for companies is that they have to adapt their ways of competing for customers. Traditionally, companies have focused their efforts of customer relationship management on issues like customer satisfaction and targeted marketing activities like event marketing, direct marketing or advertising. Although doubtless necessary and beneficial, these activities are not longer enough. They narrow the relationship between company and customer down to a particular set of contacts in which the company invests its efforts. Most likely this will produce not more than a satisfied customer who is well aware of the companies offerings and has a positive attitude towards them. However, a satisfied customer is not necessarily a loyal one.

If a customer is satisfied that means that a product of service has met his expectations and that he was not dissatisfied by it. Customer satisfaction is doubtlessly very important. It is the precondition for repeat purchases and it prevents the customer from telling others about his disappointing experiences. A loyal customer, however, is more than a customer who frequently purchases from a company.

The difference is the emotional bond which links the customer so closely to the company that he develops a clear preference for these products or brands and is even willing to recommend them to others. Loyal customers truly prefer a product, brand or company over competitive offerings. Thus loyalty goes beyond a rational decision for known quality or superior price-performance-ratio. It is about the customers' feelings and perceptions about the brand or product.

When the customer makes his buying decision, he evaluates the benefits he perceives from a particular product and compares them with the costs. The value a customer perceives when buying and using a product or service go beyond usability. There is a set of emotional values as well, such as social status, exclusivity, friendliness and responsiveness or the degree to which personal expectations and preferences are met. Similarly, the costs perceived by the customer, normally comprise more than the actual price. They also include costs of usage, the lost opportunity to use an other offering, potential switching costs etc. Hence, the customer establishes an equation between perceived benefits and perceived costs of one product and compares this to similar equations of other products.

Based on this, customer loyalty can be understood as to how customers feel about a product, service or brand and whether their perceived total investments with a it live up to their expectations. The important point here is the involvement of feelings, emotions and perceptions. In today's competitive marketplace, these perceptions are becoming much more important for gaining sustainable competitive advantage.

Customer perceptions are influenced by a variety of factors. Besides the actual outcome – i.e. did the product or service deliver the expected function and did it fulfil the customers need – the whole process of consumption and all interactions involved are of crucial importance. In today's globalised information driven economy this can also comprise issues like

- How other customers or influencing groups perceive the product or brand.
- The degree to which the customer feels the actual marketing campaign addresses the most important issues.
- Responsiveness and service quality of any affiliates, e.g. distribution partners.

Customer perceptions are dynamic. First of all, with the developing relationship between customer and company, his perceptions of the company and its products or services will change. The more experience the customer accumulates, the more his perceptions will shift from fact-based judgements to a more general meaning the whole relationship gains for him. Over time, he puts a stronger focus on the consequence of the product or service consumption.

Moreover, if the customers' circumstances change, their needs and preferences often change too. In the external environment, the offerings of competitors, with which a customer compares a product or service will change, thus altering his perception of the best offer around. Another point is that the public opinion towards certain issues can change. This effect can reach from fashion trends to the public expectation of good corporate citizenship.

Shells intention to dump its Brent Spar platform into the ocean significantly altered many customers perception of which company was worth buying fuel from. Research has been don on the impact of market share on the perceived quality of a product. Depending on the nature of the product and the customers' preferences, increasing market share can have positive or negative effects on how the customer perceives the product.

Positive Effects of Increasing Market share on Customer Perception

Increasing market share can send out positive signals by acting as an indicator of superior quality that is recognised by more and more other customers. This effect is particularly strong for premium priced products. Customers normally assume that a product must be of exceptional quality if it can gain such an unexpected market success despite its high price.

Many brands offer positive emotional benefits of using a product that is popular in the markets. The value of a product or service can rise through increasing number of users of the same product, e.g. number of members of an online community, better availability of software for popular computer systems.

Negative Effects of Increasing Market share on Customer Perception

For premium and luxury products, customers may translate an increasing market share into a loss of exclusivity and thus perceive it as less valuable.

The quality of services may suffer if they are consumed by increasing numbers of users. Dis-economies of scales and congestions can be observed with busy airports and many other services so that customers may look out for other providers that promise more timely service and convenience.

The concept of customer perception does not only relate to individual customers in consumer markets. It is also valid in business to business situations. For example, a competitor Benchmarking survey of a large industrial supplier revealed that the market leader, although recognised for excellent quality and service and known to be highly innovative, was perceived as arrogant in some regions. If we take into consideration that there are about four other large players with a similar level of quality and innovative ideas, this perceived arrogance could develop into a serious problem. Customers here are well aware the main characteristics of all the offerings available at the market are largely comparable. So they might use the development of a new product generation of their own to switch to a supplier that can serve them not better or worse, but with more responsiveness and understanding.

Companies have done a lot to improve customer satisfaction and customer relationships in the past. As discussed above, this will not be enough any more.

Any serious effort to manage customer perceptions starts with a good measurement system. Companies must be truly willing to look at the whole process of interaction through the customers eyes. For many companies, this requires a more or less extensive shift in mindset, since most departments from development to sales will be involved.

Example: France Telecom has set up a 'Quality of Perceived Value Lab' at its R&D department. Aiming at a better understanding of customer perception, this unit's main objective is in fact to give a better definition of the correlation that exists between technical problems in products an those perceived by users. By anticipation customers' feelings on product qualities, the laboratory provides perceived quality expertise on new solutions. Thus, France Telecom implements the issue of how customers perceive their products as early as in the product development process.

The backbone of any customer perception management and measurement system, however, is thorough market research and surveys. There are several aspects of measuring customer perceptions.

- First of all the company has to find out how itself and its offerings are perceived by the customers. It is essential to identify what the customer is actually buying and which features are most important to him. Only this way it is possible to align the internal focus and resources to the customers expectation. This information is of greater value if it can be compared to the customers' perception of competitive offerings. Not only will this reveal relative strengths and weaknesses, it is also a valuable source of ideas for improvement.
- Besides that, surveys should also identify the relative importance of several influencing variables in the eyes of the customer. To know what matters most to the customer helps to set priorities for projects.
- Of course, as with any market research activities, it should be based on a careful customer segmentation. Customer groups that differ by frequency of use, social status, geographical region or other criteria, are likely to have different expectations and preferences. Hence, they will probably perceive an offering in different ways.
- Zeithaml et al suggest to incorporate several behavioural-intentions questions to identify signals that are potentially favourable or unfavourable for the company. Questions for behaviour intentions are potentially of higher validity and richer

diagnostic value than the "overall service quality" or "customer satisfaction" variables. Since these questions are directed at potential future actions they can not only indicate of changes in demand and market trends. They also provide early warning signs and help to take to take timely corrective action.

Only if a company knows which features of its products and services or which other points of contact with the customer are considered most important by the customers, it can develop appropriate strategies. Such a strategy will not only help the company to strengthen the emotional bond with the customer through targeted improvements and activities. It may also have the positive side effect that the customers' whole experience leads him to the conclusion that this company really understands his distinctive needs and really takes him seriously. Hence, the customers perception of the whole company may improve beyond a positive attitude towards a particular product.

Based on thorough research, companies can develop strategies and initiate targeted activities to manage and improve customer perceptions. This article finishes with some examples of how this can be done. It has to be taken into consideration, however, that there is no one right strategy. Since these measures shall provide a distinctive competitive advantage, they should be based on the particular competencies and resources of a company and they should aim at setting the company apart from the other market participants.

- The service experience is closely linked to his perception of the total company and its offerings – be it products or service. A common idea of many authors is that it is not always necessary to deliver the absolutely perfect customer experience. Instead it is important to solve the customers need or problem in a matter that is perceived appropriate. For many retail products, for example, it will be sufficient in most cases to offer an appropriate group of substitute products, but not all particular products. In service situations, customers will-depending on the actual nature of the service-not expect an immediate service delivery. They will however expect a delivery within a time frame that is either market standard or meets the service promise of the actual service provider. As long as the company keeps this promise, the customer will perceive this as satisfying. Byrnes even suggests that you earn more customer loyalty when you do a good job fixing a service problem, than if there had been no problem at all. The point is to meet or excel the customers' expectations, not to achieve some ideal level of product or service delivery.

- Companies should try to make sure that their customers are fully aware of all the ways their offering can provide value to them. They have to explain the customer how this particular product can deliver more value than those from competitors. This approach means to widen the customer perception and to extend their awareness and appreciation to more features or aspects of the offering. However, this point has to be considered very carefully in order not to produce an diametrical effect.

Example

A customer who uses a large part of the functionality of his mobile phone might be delighted to learn about additional features and functions of the next generation product. Here the perceived value of the new product could be increased by highlighting the utility of the new functions. Another type of customer only uses his mobile phone to make and receive phone calls. He would probably not appreciate this type of communication. His equation of product value and cost will shift to the perception that he should pay an higher price for even more features he does not need and will not use.

This point again highlights the critical importance of market research. In this example, market research would help the company to develop different communication strategies that focus on those product features that are of high priority for particular market segments.

- A commonplace strategy to circumvent the loss of exclusivity associated with high market share is to leverage the brand by introducing new related brands. This is very efficient with fragrances or fashion brands.
- In situations in which customers perceive high market shares lead as a sign of quality, it is advisable to advertise a favourable high share, e.g. "Americas most popular SUV", "Three out of five people already use ...".
- It is advisable to contact customers who indicate low results for loyalty or perception of the company in the surveys. Direct contact allows to identify the roots of the problem and – if possible – to solve the issue. Besides solving some customer-specific problems and thus improving the perception of some individuals, such follow-ups may reveal some causes for problems that are common to wider parts of the customer base.

These are the starting points for some improvements with potentially significant effects.

The 9 Principles of Quality Customer Service

The quality of customer service is the key differentiator between good, bad and indifferent companies. Good quality customer service keeps customers coming back; bad customer service drives customers away, taking their friends, family and workmates with them.

All else being equal, good quality customer service gives the edge over competitors. Regardless of industry, here are the 9 key principals of good customer service that always make business sense.

Attracting new customers costs more than retaining existing customers: A satisfied customer stays with a company longer, spends more and may deepen the relationship. For example a happy credit card customer may enlist the company's financial services and later take travel insurance. This is an easy "sell", compared with direct marketing campaigns, television advertisements and other sophisticated and expensive approaches to attract new customers.

Customer service costs real money: Real costs are associated with providing customer service and companies spend in line with a customer's value. If you are a high value customer or have the potential of being high value, you will be serviced more carefully.

Companies reduce the cost of customer service by using telephone voice response systems, out sourcing call centres to cheaper locations, and self-servicing on the internet. However, companies risk alienating customers through providing an impersonal service.

Some internet banking companies are bucking the trend by charging customers to contact them. In exchange, customers receive better interest rates due to reduced overheads and are satisfied with that.

Understand your customers' needs and meet them: How can you meet your customers' needs, if you don't know them? To understand your customer's needs, just listen to the "voice of the customer" and take action accordingly.

Customer listening can be done in many ways, for example feedback forms, mystery shopping, and satisfaction surveys. Some companies involve senior employees in customer listening to ensure decisions benefit the customer as much as the company.

Good process and product design is important: Good quality customer service is only one factor in meeting customer needs. Well designed products and processes will meet customers' needs more often. Quality movements, such as Six Sigma, consider the "cost of quality" resulting from broken processes or products. Is it better to service the customer well than to eradicate the reason for them to contact you in the first instance?

Customer service must be consistent: Customers expect consistent quality of customer service; with a similar, familiar look and feel whenever and however they contact the company.

Say you visit an expensive hairdressing salon and receive a friendly welcome, a drink and a great haircut. You are out of town and visit the same hairdressing chain and get no friendly welcome, no drink and a great hair-cut. Are you a satisfied customer who will use that chain again? Probably not, as you did not receive the same customer service – which is more than a good hair-cut.

Employees are customers too: The quality management movement brought the concept of internal and external customers. Traditionally the focus was on external customers with little thought given to how internal departments interacted. Improving relationships with internal customers and suppliers assists delivery of better customer service to external customers, through reduced lead-times, increased quality and better communication.

The "Service-Profit Chain" model developed by Harvard University emphasizes the circular relationship between employees, customers and shareholders. Under-staffed, under-trained employees will not deliver good quality customer service, driving customers away. Equal effort must be made in attracting, motivating and retaining employees as is made for customers, ultimately delivering improved shareholder returns. Better shareholder returns mean more money is available to invest in employees and so the circle continues.

Open all communications channels: The customer wants to contact you in many ways – face to face, by mail, phone, fax, and email- and will expect all of these communication channels to be open and easily inter-mingled. This presents a technical challenge, as it requires an integrated, streamlined solution providing the employee with the information they need to effectively service the customer.

Every customer contact is a chance to shine: If a customer contact concerns a broken process, then empowered employees will be able to resolve the complaint swiftly, possibly enhancing the customer's perception of the company. Feeding back this information allows corrective action to be made, stopping further occurrences of the error.

If you inform customers about new products or services when they contact you, you may make a valuable sale, turning your cost centre into a profit centre. This is only possible when you have a good relationship with your customer, where you understand their specific needs. A targeted sales pitch will have a good chance of success, as the customer is pre-sold on the company's reputation.

People expect good customer service everywhere: Think about an average day – you travel on a train, you buy coffee, you work. You expect your train to be on time, clean and be a reasonable cost. You expect your coffee to be hot and delivered quickly. You expect your work mates to work with you, enabling you to get the job done. People become frustrated when their expectations are not met, and increasingly demand higher service quality in more areas of their lives. Providing outstanding customer service at the right price is the holy grail of most companies. It is worth remembering that we all experience customer service every day. We can learn from these and apply them in our own line of work, whatever it may be. The quality of customer service will make you stand out from your competitors – make sure it's for the right reasons!

Understanding the Pricing Policies and Strategies

Pricing Policy and Strategy

Managers should start setting prices during the development stage as part of strategic pricing to avoid launching products or services that cannot sustain profitable prices in the market. This approach to pricing enables companies to either fit costs to prices or scrap products or services that cannot be generated cost-effectively. Through systematic pricing policies and strategies, companies can reap greater profits and increase or defend their market shares. Setting prices is one of the principal tasks of marketing and finance managers in that the price of a product or service often plays a significant role in that product's or service's success, not to mention in a company's profitability. Generally, pricing policy refers how a company sets the prices of its products and services based on costs, value, demand, and competition. Pricing strategy, on the other hand, refers to how a company uses pricing to achieve its strategic goals, such as offering lower prices to increase sales volume or higher prices to decrease backlog. Despite some degree of difference, pricing policy and strategy tend to overlap, and the different policies and strategies are not necessarily mutually exclusive.

After establishing the bases for their prices, managers can begin developing pricing strategies by determining company pricing goals, such as increasing short-term and long-term profits, stabilizing prices, increasing cash flow, and warding off competition. Managers also must take into account current market conditions when developing pricing strategies to ensure that the prices they choose fit market conditions. In addition, effective pricing strategy involves considering customers, costs, competition, and different market segments.

Pricing strategy entails more than reacting to market conditions, such as reducing pricing because competitors have reduced their prices. Instead, it encompasses more thorough planning and consideration of customers, competitors, and company goals. Furthermore, pricing strategies tend to vary depending on whether a company is a new entrant into a market or an established firm. New entrants sometimes offer products at low cost to attract market share, while incumbents' reactions vary. Incumbents that fear the new entrant will challenge the incumbents' customer base may match prices or go even lower than the new entrant to protect its market share. If incumbents do not view the new entrant as a serious threat, incumbents may simply resort to increased advertising aimed at enhancing customer loyalty, but have no change in price in efforts to keep the new entrant from stealing away customers.

The following sections explain various ways companies develop pricing policy and strategy. First, cost-based pricing is considered. This is followed by the second topic of value-based pricing. Third, demand-based pricing is addressed followed by competition-based pricing. After this, several strategies for new and established pricing strategies are explained.

Cost-based Pricing

The traditional pricing policy can be summarized by the formula:

Cost + Fixed profit percentage = Selling price.

Cost-based pricing involves the determination of all fixed and variable costs associated with a product or service. After the total costs attributable to the product or service have been determined, managers add a desired profit margin to each unit such as a 5 or 10 percent markup. The goal of the cost-oriented approach is to cover all costs incurred in producing or delivering products or services and to achieve a targeted level of profit.

By itself, this method is simple and straightforward, requiring only that managers study financial and accounting records to determine prices. This pricing approach does not involve examining the market or considering the competition and other factors that might have an impact on pricing. Cost-oriented pricing also is popular because it is an age-old practice that uses internal information that managers can obtain easily. In addition, a company can defend its prices based on costs, and demonstrate that its prices cover costs plus a markup for profit.

However, critics contend that the cost-oriented strategy fails to provide a company with an effective pricing policy. One problem with the cost-plus strategy is that determining a unit's cost before its price is difficult in many industries because unit costs may vary depending on volume. As a result, many business analysts have criticized this method, arguing that it is no longer appropriate for modern market conditions. Cost-based pricing generally leads to high prices in weak markets and low prices in strong markets, thereby impeding profitability because these prices are the exact opposites of what strategic prices would be if market conditions were taken into consideration.

While managers must consider costs when developing a pricing policy and strategy, costs alone should not determine prices. Many managers of industrial goods and service companies sell their products and services at incremental cost, and make their substantial profits from their best customers and from short-notice deliveries. When considering costs, managers should ask what costs they can afford to pay, taking into account the prices the market allows, and still allow for a profit on the sale. In addition, managers must consider production costs in order to determine what goods to produce and in what amounts. Nevertheless, pricing generally involves determining what prices customers can afford before determining what amount of products to produce. By bearing in mind the prices they can charge and the costs they can afford to pay, managers can determine whether their costs enable them to compete in the low-cost market, where customers are concerned primarily with price, or whether they must compete in the premium-price market, in which customers are primarily concerned with quality and features.

Value-based Pricing

Value pricers adhere to the thinking that the optimal selling price is a reflection of a product or service's perceived value by customers, not just the company's costs to produce or provide a product or service. The value of a product or service is derived from customer needs, preferences, expectations, and financial resources as well as from competitors' offerings. Consequently, this approach calls for managers to query customers and research the market to determine how much they value a product or service. In addition, managers must compare their products or services with those of their competitors to identify their value advantages and disadvantages.

Yet, value-based pricing is not just creating customer satisfaction or making sales because customer satisfaction may be achieved through discounting alone, a pricing strategy that could also lead to greater sales. However, discounting may not necessarily lead to profitability. Value pricing involves setting prices to increase profitability by tapping into more of a product or service's value attributes. This approach to pricing also depends heavily on strong advertising, especially for new products or services, in order to communicate the value of products or services to customers and to motivate customers to pay more if necessary for the value provided by these products or services.

Demand-based Pricing

Managers adopting demand-based pricing policies are, like value pricers, not fully concerned with costs. Instead, they concentrate on the behavior and characteristics of customers and the quality and characteristics of their products or services. Demand-oriented pricing focuses on the level of demand for a product or service, not on the cost of materials, labour, and so forth.According to this pricing policy, managers try to determine the amount of products or services they can sell at different prices. Managers need demand schedules in order to determine prices based on demand. Using demand schedules, managers can figure out which production and sales levels would be the most profitable. To determine the most profitable production and sales levels, managers examine production and marketing costs estimates at different sales levels. The prices are determined by considering the cost estimates at different sales levels and expected revenues from sales volumes associated with projected prices.

The success of this strategy depends on the reliability of demand estimates. Hence, the crucial obstacle managers face with this approach is accurately gauging demand, which requires extensive knowledge of the manifold market factors that may have an impact on the number of products sold. Two common options managers have for obtaining accurate estimates are enlisting the help from either sales representatives or market experts. Managers frequently ask sales representatives to estimate increases or decreases in demand stemming from specific increases or decreases in a product or service's price, since sales representatives generally are attuned to market trends and customer demands. Alternatively, managers can seek the assistance of experts such as market researchers or consultants to provide estimates of sales levels at various unit prices.

Competition-based Pricing

With a competition-based pricing policy, a company sets its prices by determining what other companies competing in the market charge. A company begins developing competition-based prices by identifying its present competitors. Next, a company assesses its own product or service. After this step, a company sets it prices higher than, lower than, or on par with the competitors based on the advantages and disadvantages of a company's product or service as well as on the expected response by competitors to the set price. This last consideration-the response of competitors-is an important part of competition-based pricing, especially in markets with only a few competitors. In such a market, if one competitor lowers its price, the others will most likely lower theirs as well.

This pricing policy allows companies to set prices quickly with relatively little effort, since it does not require as accurate market data as the demand pricing. Competitive pricing also makes distributors more receptive to a company's products because they are priced within the range the distributor already handles. Furthermore, this pricing policy enables companies to select from a variety of different pricing strategies to achieve their strategic goals. In other words, companies can choose to mark their prices above, below, or on par with their competitors' prices and thereby influence customer perceptions of their products. For example, if a Company A sets its prices above those of its competitors, the higher price could suggest that Company A's products or services are superior in quality. Harley Davidson used this with great success. Although Harley-Davidson uses many of the same parts suppliers as Honda, Kawasaki, Yamaha, and Honda, they price well above the competitive price of these competitors. Harley's high prices combined with its customer loyalty and mystique help overcome buyer resistance to higher prices. Production efficiencies over the last two decades, however, have made quality among motorcycle producers about equal, but pricing above the market signals quality to buyers, whether or not they get the quality premium they pay for.

Strategies for New and Established Products

Product pricing strategies frequently depend on the stage a product or service is in its life cycle; that is, new products often require different pricing strategies than established products or mature products.

New Product Pricing Strategy

Entrants often rely on pricing strategies that allow them to capture market share quickly. When there are several competitors in a market, entrants usually use lower pricing to change consumer spending habits and acquire market share.

To appeal to customers effectively, entrants generally implement a simple or transparent pricing structure, which enables customers to compare prices easily and understand that the entrants have lower prices than established incumbent companies.

Complex pricing arrangements, however, prevent lower pricing from being a successful strategy in that customers cannot readily compare prices with hidden and contingent costs. The long-distance telephone market illustrates this point; large corporations have lengthy telephone bills that include numerous contingent costs, which depend on location, use, and service features. Consequently, competitors in the corporate long-distance telephone service market do not use lower pricing as the primary pricing strategy, as they do in the consumer and small-business markets, where telephone billing is much simpler.

Another example is the computer industry. Dell, Fujitsu, HP, and many others personal computer makers offer bundles of products that make it more difficult for consumers to sort out the true differences among these competitors.

For example, consumers purchasing an HP computer from the retailer, Best Buy, will have not only the computer itself, but also six months of "free" Internet access bundled into the price. Comparing the absolute value of each personal computer become more difficult as an increasing number of other products such as Quicken, Adobe's Photoshop Elements, and other software are sold together with the purchase.

For Macintosh users or for those who might consider switching from a personal computer to a Macintosh, Apple announced in 2005 that it would begin selling the Mac Mini, a Macintosh that, as with PC makers, bundles its iLife® software into the mix. By extending its brand to non-premium price tiers, Apple will compete head-to-head with established firms. And although the Mac Mini is at a low price point, starting at $499, it will be difficult for consumers to directly compare the bundled products of PCs directly with the bundled products of Apple's Mac Mini. The complexity of these comparisons is what can make such new product pricing successful.

Established Product Pricing Strategy

Sometimes established companies need not adjust their prices at all in response to entrants and their lower prices, because customers frequently are willing to pay more for the products or services of an established company to avoid perceived risks associated with switching products or services.

However, when established companies do not have this advantage, they must implement other pricing strategies to preserve their market share and profits. When entrants are involved, established companies sometimes attempt to hide their actual prices by embedding them in complex prices. This tactic makes it difficult for customers to compare prices, which is advantageous to established companies competing with entrants that have lower prices. In addition, established companies also may use a more complex pricing plan, such as a two-part pricing tactic. This tactic especially benefits companies with significant market power. Local telephone companies, for example, use this strategy, charging both fixed and per-minute charges.

Market Segmentation

Because all customers do not have the same needs, expectations, and financial resources, managers can improve their pricing strategies by segmenting markets. Successful segmentation comes about when managers determine what motivates particular markets and what differences exist in the market when taken as a whole. For example, some customers may be motivated largely by price, while others are motivated by functionality and utility. The idea behind segmentation is to divide a large group into a set of smaller groups that share significant characteristics such as age, income, geographic location, lifestyle, and so on. By dividing a market into two or more segments, a company can devise a pricing scheme that will appeal to the motivations of each of the different market segments or it can decide to target only particular segments of the market that best correspond to its products or services and their prices.

Managers can use market segmentation strategically to price products or services in order to attain company objectives. Companies can set prices differently for different segments based on factors such as location, time of sale, quantity of sale, product design, and a number of others, depending on the way companies divide up the market. By doing so, companies can increase their profits, market share, cash flow, and so forth.

Pricing Strategies

There are many ways to price a product. Let's have a look at some of them and try to understand the best policy/strategy in various situations.

Premium Pricing

Use a high price where there is a uniqueness about the product or service. This approach is used where a substantial competitive advantage exists. Such high prices are charge for luxuries such as Cunard Cruises, Savoy Hotel rooms, and Concorde flights.

Penetration Pricing

The price charged for products and services is set artificially low in order to gain market share. Once this is achieved, the price is increased. This approach was used by France Telecom and Sky TV.

Economy Pricing

This is a no frills low price. The cost of marketing and manufacture are kept at a minimum. Supermarkets often have economy brands for soups, spaghetti, etc.

Price Skimming

Charge a high price because you have a substantial competitive advantage. However, the advantage is not sustainable. The high price tends to attract new competitors into the market, and the price inevitably falls due to increased supply. Manufacturers of digital watches used a skimming approach in the 1970s. Once other manufacturers were tempted into the market and the watches were produced at a lower unit cost, other marketing strategies and pricing approaches are implemented. Premium pricing, penetration pricing, economy pricing, and price skimming are the four main pricing policies/ strategies. They form the bases for the exercise. However there are other important approaches to pricing.

Psychological Pricing

This approach is used when the marketer wants the consumer to respond on an emotional, rather than rational basis. For example 'price point perspective' 99 cents not one dollar.

Product Line Pricing

Where there is a range of product or services the pricing reflect the benefits of parts of the range. For example car washes. Basic wash could be $2, wash and wax $4, and the whole package $6.

Captive Product Pricing

Where products have complements, companies will charge a premium price where the consumer is captured. For example a razor manufacturer will charge a low price and recoup its margin from the sale of the only design of blades which fit the razor.

Product Bundle Pricing

Here sellers combine several products in the same package. This also serves to move old stock. Videos and CDs are often sold using the bundle approach.

Promotional Pricing

Pricing to promote a product is a very common application. There are many examples of promotional pricing including approaches such as BOGOF (Buy One Get One Free).

Geographical Pricing

Geographical pricing is evident where there are variations in price in different parts of the world. For example rarity value, or where shipping costs increase price.

Value Pricing

This approach is used where external factors such as recession or increased competition force companies to provide 'value' products and services to retain sales e.g. value meals at McDonalds.

Chapter 4

The Marketing Mix and Management Process of Brand

Marketing mix modelling is a term of art for the use of statistical analysis such as multivariate regressions on sales and marketing time series data to estimate the impact of various promotional tactics on sales and then forecast the impact of future sets of promotional tactics. It is often used to optimize promotional tactics with respect to sales revenue or profit. The techniques were developed by econometricians and were first applied to consumer packaged goods, since manufacturers of those goods had access to good data on sales and marketing support. In the recent times MMM has found acceptance as a trustworthy marketing tool among the major consumer marketing companies.

History

The term Market Mix Modelling was developed by Neil Borden who first started using the phrase in 1949. "An executive is a mixer of ingredients, who sometimes follows a recipe as he goes along, sometimes adapts a recipe to the ingredients immediately available, and sometimes experiments with or invents ingredients no one else has tried." (Culliton, J. 1948)

According to Borden,"When building a marketing program to fit the needs of his firm, the marketing manager has to weigh the behavioural forces and then juggle marketing elements in his mix with a keen eye on the resources with which he has to work." Jerome McCarthy (McCarthy, J. 1960), was the first person to suggest the four P's viz price, promotion, product and distribution which constitute the most common variables used in constructing a marketing mix.

According to McCarthy the marketers essentially have these four variables which they can use while crafting a marketing strategy and writing a marketing plan. In the long term, all four of the mix variables can be changed, but in the short term it is difficult to modify the product or the distribution channel.

Another set of marketing mix variables were developed by Albert Frey (Frey, A. 1961) who classified the marketing variables into two categories: the offering, and process variables. The "offering" consists of the product, service, packaging, brand, and price. The "process" or "method" variables included advertising, promotion, sales promotion, personal selling, publicity, distribution channels, marketing research, strategy formation, and new product development.

Recently, Bernard Booms and Mary Bitner built a model consisting of seven P's. They added "People" to the list of existing variables, in order to recognize the importance of the human element in all aspects of marketing. They added "process" to reflect the fact that services, unlike physical products, are experienced as a process at the time that they are purchased.

Marketing Mix Model

Marketing mix modelling is an analytical approach that use historic information, such as syndicated point-of-sale data and companies' internal data, to quantify the sales impact of various marketing activities. Mathematically, this is done by establishing a simultaneous relation of various marketing activities with the sales, in the form of a linear or a non-linear equation, through the statistical technique of regression. MMM defines the effectiveness of each of the marketing elements in terms of its contribution to sales-volume, effectiveness (volume generated by each unit of effort), efficiency (sales volume generated divided by cost) and ROI. These learnings are then adopted to adjust marketing tactics and strategies, optimize the marketing plan and also to forecast sales while simulating various scenarios.

This is accomplished by setting up a model with the sales volume/ value as the dependent variable and independent variables created out of the various marketing efforts. The creation of variables for Marketing Mix Modelling is a complicated affair and is as much an art as it is a science. Once the variables are created, multiple iterations are carried out to create a model which explains the volume/value trends perfectly. Further validations are carried out, either by using a validation data, or by the consistency of the business results.

The output can be used to analyse the impact of the marketing elements on various dimensions. The contribution of each element as a percentage of the total plotted year on year is a good indicator of how the effectiveness of various elements changes over the years.

The yearly change in contribution is also measure by a due-to analysis which shows what percentage of the change in total sales is attributable to each of the elements. For activities like television advertising and trade promotions, more sophisticated analysis like effectiveness can be carried out.

This analysis tells the marketing manager the incremental gain in sales that can be obtained by increasing the respective marketing element by one unit. If detailed spend information per activity is available then it is possible to calculate the Return on Investment of the marketing activity.

Not only is this useful for reporting the historical effectiveness of the activity, it also helps in optimizing the marketing budget by identifying the most and least efficient marketing activities.

Once the final model is ready, the results from it can be used to simulate marketing scenarios for a 'What-if' analysis. The marketing manager can reallocate this marketing budget in different proportions and see the direct impact on sales/value. He can optimize the budget by allocating spends to those activities which give the highest return on investment.

Components

Marketing-mix models decompose total sales into two components:

Base Sales: This is the natural demand for the product driven by economic factors like pricing, long-term trends, seasonality, and also qualitative factors like brand awareness and brand loyalty.

Incremental Sales: Incremental sales are the component of sales driven by marketing and promotional activities.

This component can be further decomposed into sales due to each marketing component like Television advertising or Radio advertising, Print Advertising (magazines, newspapers etc.), Coupons, Direct Mail, Internet, Feature or Display Promotions and Temporary Price Reductions. Some of these activities have short-term returns (Coupons, Promotions), while others have longer term returns (TV, Radio, Magazine/Print). Marketing-Mix analyses are typically carried out using Linear Regression Modelling.

Nonlinear and lagged effects are included using techniques like Advertising Adstock transformations. Typical output of such analyses include a decomposition of total annual sales into contributions from each marketing component, a.k.a Contribution pie-chart.

Elements Measured in MMM

Base and Incremental Volume

The very break-up of sales volume into base (volume that would be generated in absence of any marketing activity) and incremental (volume generated by marketing activities in the short run) across time gain gives wonderful insights. The base grows or declines across longer periods of time while the activities generating the incremental volume in the short run also impact the base volume in the long run. The variation in the base volume is a good indicator of the strength of the brand and the loyalty it commands from its users.

Television Advertising

For the TV advertising activity, it is possible to examine how each ad execution has performed in the market in terms of its impact on sales volume. MMM can also provide information on TV effectiveness at different media weight levels, as measured by Gross Rating Points in relation to sales volume response within a time frame, be it a week or a month. Information can also be gained on the minimum level of GRPs (threshold limit) in a week that need to be aired in order to make an impact, and conversely, the level of GRPs at which the impact on volume maximizes (saturation limit) and that the further activity does not have any payback. While not all MMM's will be able to produce definitive answers to all questions, some additional areas in which insights can sometimes be gained include:

1) the effectiveness of 15-second vis-a-vis 30-second executions;
2) comparisons in ad performance when run during prime-time vis-a-vis off-prime-time dayparts;
3) comparisons into the direct and the halo effect of TV activity across various products or sub-brands.

The role of new product based TV activity and the equity based TV activity in growing the brand can also be compared

Trade Promotions

Trade promotion is a key activity in every marketing plan. It is aimed at increasing sales in the short term by employing promotion schemes which effectively increases the customer awareness of the business and its products. The response of consumers to trade promotions is not straight forward and is the subject of much debate. Non-linear models exist to simulate the response. Using MMM we can understand the impact of trade promotion at generating incremental volumes. It is possible to obtain an estimate of the volume generated per promotion event in each of the different retail outlets by region.

This way we can identify the most and least effective trade channels. If detailed spend information is available we can compare the Return on Investment of various trade activities like Every Day Low Price, Off-Shelf Display etc. We can use this information to optimize the trade plan by choosing the most effective trade channels and targeting the most effective promotion activity.

Pricing

Price changes of the brand impacts the sales negatively. This effect can be captured through modelling the price in MMM. The model provides the price elasticity of the brand which tells us the percentage change in the sales for each percentage change in price. Using this, the marketing manager can evaluate the impact of a price change decision.

Distribution

For the element of distribution, we can know how the volume will move by changing distribution efforts or, in other words, by each percentage shift in the width or the depth of distribution. This can be identified specifically for each channel and even for each kind of outlet for off-take sales. In view of these insights, the distribution efforts can be prioritized for each channel or store-type to get the maximum out of the same. A recent study of a laundry brand showed that the incremental volume through 1% more presence in a neighbourhoods Kirana store is 180% greater than that through 1% more presence in a supermarket. Based upon the cost of such efforts, managers identified the right channel to invest more for distribution.

Launches

When a new product is launched, the associated publicity and promotions typically results in higher volume generation than expected. This extra volume cannot be completely captured in the model using the existing variables. Often special variables to capture this incremental effect of launches are used. The combined contribution of these variables and that of the marketing effort associated with the launch will give the total launch contribution. Different launches can be compared by calculating their effectiveness and ROI.

Competition

The impact of competition on the brand sales is captured by creating the competition variables accordingly. The variables are created from the marketing activities of the competition like television advertising, trade promotions, product launches etc. The results from the model can be used to identify the biggest threat to own brand sales from competition. The cross-price elasticity and the cross-promotional elasticity can be used to devise appropriate response to competition tactics. A successful competitive campaign can be analysed to learn valuable lesson for the own brand.

Studies in MMM

Typical MMM studies provide the following insights:

- Contribution by marketing activity
- ROI by marketing activity
- Effectiveness of marketing activity
- Optimal distribution of spends
- Learnings on how to execute each activity better e.g. optimal GRPs per week, optimal distribution between 15s and 30s, which promos to run, what SKUS to put on promotion etc.

Adoption of MMM by the Industry

MMM is a relatively new area of application. In the last 10 years though many CPG companies have adopted MMM. Many Fortune 500 companies such as P&G, Kraft, Coca-Cola and Pepsi have made MMM an integral part of their marketing planning. This has also been made possible due to the availability of specialist firms that are now providing MMM services. Marketing-mix models were more popular initially the CPG industry and quickly spread to Retail and Pharma industries because of the availability of Syndicated Data in these industries (primarily from Nielsen Company and IRI and to a lesser extent from NPD Group). Availability of Time-series data is crucial to robust modelling of marketing-mix effects and with the systematic management of customer data through CRM systems in other industries like Financial Services, Automotive and Hospitality industries helped its spread to these industries.

In addition competitive and industry data availability through third-party sources like Forrester Research's Ultimate Consumer Panel (Financial Services), Polk Insights (Automotive) and Smith Travel Research (Hospitality), further enhanced the application of marketing-mix modelling to these industries. Application of marketing-mix modelling to these industries is still in a nascent stage and a lot of standardization needs to be brought about especially in these areas:

- Interpretation of promotional activities across industries for e.g. promotions in CPG do not have lagged effects as they happen in-store, but automotive and hospitality promotions are usually deployed through the internet or through dealer marketing and can have longer lags in their impact. CPG promotions are usually absolute price discounts, whereas Automotive promotions can be cash-books or loan incentives, and Financial Services promotions are usually interest rate discounts.
- Hospitality industry marketing has a very heavy seasonal pattern and most marketing-mix models will tend to confound marketing effectiveness with seasonality, thus over or under estimating marketing ROI. Time-series Cross-Sectional models like 'Pooled Regression' need to be utilized, which increase sample size and variation and thus make a robust separation of pure marketing-effects from seasonality.
- Automotive Manufacturers spend a substantial amount of their marketing budgets on dealer advertising, which may not be accurately measurable if not modelled at the right level of aggregation. If modelled at the national level or even the market or DMA level, these effects may be lost in aggregation bias. On the other hand going all the way down to dealer-level may over-estimate marketing effectiveness as it would ignore consumer switching between dealers in the same area.

  The correct albeit rigorous approach would be to determine what dealers to combine into 'addable' common groups based on overlapping 'trade-areas' determined by consumer zip codes and cross-shopping information. At the very least 'Common Dealer Areas' can be determined by clustering dealers based on geographical distance between dealers and share of county sales. Marketing-mix models built by 'pooling' monthly sales for these dealer clusters will be effectively used to measure the impact of dealer advertising effectively.

The proliferation of marketing-mix modelling was also accelerated due to the focus from Sarbanes-Oxley Section 404 that required internal controls for financial reporting on significant expenses and outlays. Marketing for consumer goods can be in excess of a 10th of total revenues and until the advent of marketing-mix models, relied on qualitative or 'soft' approaches to evaluate this spend.

Marketing-mix modelling presented a rigorous and consistent approach to evaluate marketing-mix investments as the CPG industry had already demonstrated. A study by American Marketing Association pointed out that top management was more likely to stress the importance of marketing accountability than middle management, suggesting a top-down push towards greater accountability.

Limitations

While marketing mix models provide much useful information, there are two key areas in which these models have limitations that should be taken into account by all of those that use these models for decision making purposes. These limitations, discussed more fully below, include:

1) the focus on short-term sales can significantly under-value the importance of longer-term equity building activities; and
2) when used for media mix optimization, these models have a clear bias in favour of time-specific media (such as TV commercials) versus less time-specific media (such as ads appearing in monthly magazines); biases can also occur when comparing broad-based media versus regionally or demographically targeted media.

In relation to the bias against equity building activities, marketing budgets optimized using marketing-mix models may tend too much towards efficiency because marketing-mix models measure only the short-term effects of marketing. Longer term effects of marketing are reflected in its brand equity. The impact of marketing spend on [brand equity] is usually not captured by marketing-mix models. One reason is that the longer duration that marketing takes to impact brand perception extends beyond the simultaneous or, at best, weeks-ahead impact of marketing on sales that these models measure. The other reason is that temporary fluctuation in sales due to economic and social conditions do not necessarily mean that marketing has been ineffective in building brand equity. On the contrary, it is very possible that in the short term sales and market-share could deteriorate, but brand equity could actually be higher. This higher equity should in the long run help the brand recover sales and market-share.

Because marketing-mix models suggest a marketing tactic has a positive impact on sales doesn't necessarily mean it has a positive impact on long-term brand equity. Different marketing measures impact short-term and long-term brand sales differently and adjusting the marketing portfolio to maximize either the short-term or the long-term alone will be sub-optimal. For example the short-term positive effect of promotions on consumers' utility induces consumers to switch to the promoted brand, but the adverse impact of promotions on brand equity carries over from period to period. Therefore the net effect of promotions on a brand's market share and profitability can be negative due to their adverse impact on brand. Determining marketing ROI on the basis of marketing-mix models alone can lead to misleading results. This is because marketing-mix attempts to optimize marketing-mix to increase incremental contribution, but marketing-mix also drives brand-equity, which is not part of the incremental part measured by marketing-mix model-it is part of the baseline.

True 'Return on Marketing Investment' is a sum of short-term and long-term ROI. The fact that most firms use marketing-mix models only to measure the short-term ROI can be inferred from an article by Booz Allen Hamilton, which suggests that there is a significant shift away from traditional media to 'below-the-line' spending, driven by the fact that promotional spending is easier to measure. But academic studies have shown that promotional activities are in fact detrimental to long-term marketing ROI (Ataman et al., 2006). Short-term marketing-mix models can be combined with brand-equity models using brand-tracking data to measure 'brand ROI', in both the short-and long-term. The second limitation of marketing mix models comes into play when advertisers attempt to use these models to determine the best media allocation across different media types. The traditional use of MMM's to compare money spent on TV versus money spent on couponing was relatively valid in that both TV commercials and the appearance of coupons (for example, in a FSI run in a newspaper) were both quite time specific. However, as the use of these models has been expanded into comparisons across a wider range of media types, extreme caution should be used.

Even with traditional media such as magazine advertising, the use of MMM's to compare results across media can be problematic; while the modellers overlay models of the 'typical' viewing curves of monthly magazines, these lack in precision, and thus introduce additional variability into the equation. Thus, comparisons of the effectiveness of running a TV commercial versus the effectiveness of running a magazine ad would be biased in favour of TV, with its greater precision of measurement. As new new forms of media proliferate, these limitations become even more important to consider if MMM's are to be used in attempts to quantify their effectiveness. For example, Sponsorship Marketing, Sports Affinity Marketing, Viral Marketing, Blog Marketing and Mobile Marketing all vary in terms of the time-specificity of exposure.

Further, most approaches to marketing-mix models try to include all marketing activities in aggregate at the national or regional level, but to the extent that various tactics are targeted to different demographic consumer groups, their impact may be lost. For example, Mountain Dew sponsorhip of NASCAR may be targeted to NASCAR fans, which may include multiple age groups, but Mountain Dew advertising on gaming blogs may be targeted to the Gen Y population. Both of these tactics may be highly effective within the corresponding demographic groups but, when included in aggregate in a national or regional marketing-mix model, may come up as ineffective.

Aggregation bias, along with issues relating to variations in the time-specific natures of different media, pose serious problems when these models are used in ways beyond those for which they were originally designed. As media become even more fragmented, it is critical that these issues are taken into account if marketing-mix models are used to judge the relative effectiveness of different media and tactics.

Marketing-mix models use historical performance to evaulate marketing performance and so are not an effective tool to manage marketing investments for new products. This is because the relatively short history of new products make marketing-mix results unstable. Also relationship between marketing and sales may be radically different in the launch and stable periods. For example the initial performance of Coke Zero was really poor and showed low advertising elasticity. In spite of this Coke increased its media spend, with an improved strategy and radically improved its performance resulting in advertising effectiveness that is probably several times the effectiveness during the launch period. A typical marketing-mix model would have recommended cutting media spend and instead resorting to heavy price discounting.

Direct Marketing

Direct marketing is a form of advertising that reaches its audience without using traditional formal channels of advertising, such as TV, newspapers or radio. Businesses communicate straight to the consumer with advertising techniques such as fliers, catalogue distribution, promotional letters, and street advertising.

Direct Advertising is a sub-discipline and type of marketing. There are two main definitional characteristics which distinguish it from other types of marketing. The first is that it sends its message directly to consumers, without the use of intervening commercial communication media. The second characteristic is the core principle of successful Advertising driving a specific "call-to-action." This aspect of direct marketing involves an emphasis on trackable, measurable, positive responses from consumers (known simply as "response" in the industry) regardless of medium.

If the advertisement asks the prospect to take a specific action, for instance call a free phone number or visit a website, then the effort is considered to be direct response advertising.

Direct Marketing is predominantly used by Small to Medium Enterprises with limited Advertising Budgets which do not have a well recognized Brand Message. A well executed Direct Advertising campaign offers positive Return on Investment, as the message is not hidden with over complicated branding, "Vorsprung Durch Technik" does not directly sell more cars, instead Direct Advertising is straight to the point, it offers a Product, Service or Event "Buy a New Car" and explains how to get the offered Product, Service or Event "At Daves Autos".

History

The term *direct marketing* is believed to have been first used in 1967 in a speech by Lester Wunderman, who pioneered direct marketing techniques with brands such as American Express and Columbia Records. The term *junk mail*, referring to unsolicited commercial ads delivered via post office or directly deposited in consumers' mail boxes, can be traced back to 1954. The term spam, meaning "unsolicited commercial email", can be traced back to March 31, 1993, although in its first few months it merely referred to inadvertently posting a message so many times on Use Net that the repetitions effectively drowned out the normal flow of conversation.

Although Wunderman may have been the first to use the term *direct marketing*, the practice of mail order selling (direct marketing via mail) essentially began in the U.S. upon invention of the typewriter in 1867. The first modern mail-order catalog was produced by Aaron Montgomery Ward in 1872. The Direct Mail Advertising Association, predecessor of the present-day Direct Marketing Association, was first established in 1917. Third class bulk mail postage rates were established in 1928.

Direct marketing's history in Europe can be traced to the 15th century. Upon Gutenberg's invention of movable type, the first trade catalogs from printer-publishers appeared sometime around 1450.

Benefits and Drawbacks

Direct marketing is attractive to many marketers, because in many cases its positive effect (but not negative results) can be measured directly. For example, if a marketer sends out one thousand solicitations by mail, and one hundred respond to the promotion, the marketer can say with some confidence that the campaign led directly to 10% direct responses. The number of recipients who are offended by the junk mail/ spam, however, is not easily measured. By contrast, measurement of other media must often be indirect, since there is no direct response from a consumer. Measurement of results, a fundamental element in successful direct marketing, is explored in greater detail elsewhere in this article.

The Internet has made it easier for Marketing Managers to measure the results of a campaign. This is often achieved by using a specific website landing page directly relating to the promotional material, a call to action will ask the consumer to visit the landing page and the effectiveness of the campaign can be measured by taking the number of promotional messages distributed (e.g. 1000) and divide it by the number of responses (people visiting the unique website page). Another way to measure the results is to compare the projected sales for a given term with the actual sales after a Direct Advertising Campaign.

While many marketers recognize the financial benefits of increasing targeted awareness, some direct marketing efforts using particular media have been criticized for generating unwanted solicitations, not due to the method of communication but because of poorly complied demographic databases, advertisers do not wish to waste money on communicating with consumers not interested in their products. For example, direct mail that is irrelevant to the recipient is considered *junk mail*, and unwanted email messages are considered *spam*. Some consumers are demanding an end to direct marketing for privacy and environmental reasons, which direct marketers are able to provide by using "opt out" lists, variable printing and more targeted mailing lists. In response to consumer demand and increasing business pressure to increase the effectiveness of reaching the right consumer with Direct Marketing, companies such as Ireland Advertising specialize in targeted Direct Advertising to great effect, reducing advertising budget waste and increasing the effectiveness of delivering a marketing message with better geo-demography information, delivering the advertising message to only the consumers interested in the product, service or event on offer.

Channels

Direct Mail

The most common form of direct marketing is direct mail, sometimes called junk mail, used by advertisers who send paper mail to all postal customers in an area or to all customers on a list.

Any low-budget medium that can be used to deliver a communication to a customer can be employed in direct marketing. Probably the most commonly used medium for direct marketing is mail, in which marketing communications are sent to customers using the postal service. The term direct mail is used in the direct marketing industry to refer to communication deliveries by the Post Office, which may also be referred to as "junk mail" or "admail" or "crap mail" and may involve bulk mail. Junk mail includes advertising circulars, catalogs, free trial CDs, pre-approved credit card applications, and other unsolicited merchandising invitations delivered by mail or to homes and businesses, or delivered to consumers' mailboxes by delivery services other than the Post Office. Bulk mailings are a particularly popular method of promotion for businesses operating in the financial services, home computer, and travel and tourism industries.

In many developed countries, direct mail represents such a significant amount of the total volume of mail that special rate classes have been established. In the United States and United Kingdom, for example, there are bulk mail rates that enable marketers to send mail at rates that are substantially lower than regular first-class rates. In order to qualify for these rates, marketers must format and sort the mail in particular ways – which reduces the handling (and therefore costs) required by the postal service.

Advertisers often refine direct mail practices into *targeted mailing*, in which mail is sent out following database analysis to select recipients considered most likely to respond positively. For example a person who has demonstrated an interest in golf may receive direct mail for golf related products or perhaps for goods and services that are appropriate for golfers. This use of database analysis is a type of database marketing. The United States Postal Service calls this form of mail "advertising mail".

Tele-marketing

The second most common form of direct marketing is Tele-marketing, in which marketers contact consumers by phone. The unpopularity of cold call Tele-marketing (in which the consumer does not expect or invite the sales call) has led some US states and the US federal government to create "no-call lists" and legislation including heavy fines. This process may be out sourced to specialist call centres.

In the US, a national do-not-call list went into effect on October 1, 2003. Under the law, it is illegal for tele-marketers to call anyone who has registered themselves on the list.

After the list had operated for one year, over 62 million people had signed up. The Tele-marketing industry opposed the creation of the list, but most tele-marketers have complied with the law and refrained from calling people who are on the list.

Canada has passed legislation to create a similar Do Not Call List. In other countries it is voluntary, such as the New Zealand Name Removal Service.

Email Marketing

Email Marketing may have passed Tele-marketing in frequency at this point, and is a third type of direct marketing. A major concern is spam, which actually predates legitimate email marketing.

As a result of the proliferation of mass spamming, ISPs and email service providers have developed increasingly effective E-Mail Filtering programs. These filters can interfere with the delivery of email marketing campaigns, even if the person has subscribed to receive them, as legitimate email marketing can possess the same hallmarks as spam.

Door-to-Door Leaflet Marketing

Leaflet Distribution services are used extensively by the fast food industries, and many other business focussing on a local catchment Business to consumer business model, similar to direct mail marketing, this method is targeted purely by area, and costs a fraction of the amount of a mailshot due to not having to purchase stamps, envelopes or having to buy address lists and the names of home occupants.

Broadcast Faxing

A fourth type of direct marketing, broadcast faxing, is now less common than the other forms. This is partly due to laws in the United States and elsewhere which make it illegal.

Voicemail Marketing

A fifth type of direct marketing has emerged out of the market prevalence of personal voice mailboxes, and business voicemail systems. Due to the ubiquity of email marketing, and the expense of direct mail and Tele-marketing, voicemail marketing presented a cost effective means by which to reach people directly, by voice. Abuse of consumer marketing applications of voicemail marketing resulted in an abundance of "voice-spam", and prompted many jurisdictions to pass laws regulating consumer voicemail marketing.

More recently, businesses have utilized guided voicemail (an application where pre-recorded voicemails are guided by live callers) to accomplish personalized business-to-business marketing formerly reserved for Tele-marketing. Because guided voicemail is used to contact only businesses, it is exempt from Do Not Call regulations in place for other forms of voicemail marketing.

Couponing

Couponing is used in print media to elicit a response from the reader. An example is a coupon which the reader cuts out and presents to a super-store check-out counter to avail of a discount. Coupons in newspapers and magazines cannot be considered direct marketing, since the marketer incurs the cost of supporting a third-party medium (the newspaper or magazine); direct marketing aims to circumvent that balance, paring the costs down to solely delivering their unsolicited sales message to the consumer, without supporting the newspaper that the consumer seeks and welcomes.

Direct Response Television Marketing

Direct marketing on TV (commonly referred to as DRTV) has two basic forms: long form (usually half-hour or hour-long segments that explain a product in detail and are commonly referred to as infomercials) and short form which refers to typical 0:30 second or 0:60 second commercials that ask viewers for an immediate response (typically to call a phone number on screen or go to a website).

TV-response marketing—i.e. infomercials—can be considered a form of direct marketing, since responses are in the form of calls to telephone numbers given on-air.

This both allows marketers to reasonably conclude that the calls are due to a particular campaign, and allows the marketers to obtain customers' phone numbers as targets for Tele-marketing. Under the Federal Do-Not-Call List rules in the US, if the caller buys anything, the marketer would be exempt from Do-Not-Call List restrictions for a period of time due to having a prior business relationship with the caller. Major players are firms like QVC, Thane Direct, and Interwood Marketing Group then cross-sell, and up-sell to these respondents.

One of the most famous DRTV commercials was for Ginsu Knives by Ginsu Products, Inc. of RI. Several aspects of ad, such as it's use of adding items to the offer and the guarantee of satisfaction were much copied and came to be considered part of the formula for success with short form direct response TV ads (DRTV).

Direct Selling

Direct selling is the sale of products by face-to-face contact with the customer, either by having sales people approach potential customers in person, or through indirect means such as Tupperware parties.

Popularity of Direct Advertising

In a report conducted by the Direct Marketing Association, it was found that 57% of the campaigns studied were employing integrated strategies. Of those, almost half (47%) launched with a direct mail campaign, typically followed by e-mail and then Tele-marketing.

Multi-Level Marketing

Multi-level marketing (MLM), (also called network marketing, direct selling, referral marketing, and pyramid selling) is a term that describes a marketing structure used by some companies as part of their overall marketing strategy. The structure is designed to create a marketing and sales force by compensating promoters of company products not only for sales they personally generate, but also for the sales of other promoters they introduce to the company, creating a downline of distributors and a hierarchy of multiple levels of compensation in the form of a pyramid.The products and company are usually marketed directly to consumers and potential business partners by means of relationship referrals and word of mouth marketing.

MLM companies have been a frequent subject of controversy as well as the target of lawsuits. Criticisms have focused on their similarity to illegal pyramid schemes, price-fixing of products, high initial start-up costs, emphasis on recruitment of lower-tiered sales people over actual sales, encouraging if not requiring sales people to purchase and use the company's products, potential exploitation of personal relationships which are used as new sales and recruiting targets, complex and sometimes exaggerated compensation schemes, and cult-like techniques which some groups use to enhance their members enthusiasm and devotion. Not all MLM companies operate the same way, and MLM groups have persistently denied that their techniques are anything but legitimate business practices.

Setup

Independent, unsalaried sales people of multi-level marketing, referred to as distributors (or associates, independent business owners, dealers, franchise owners, sales consultants, consultants, independent agents, etc.), represent the company that produces the products or provides the services they sell. They are awarded a commission based upon the volume of product sold through their own sales efforts as well as that of their downline organization.

Independent distributors develop their organizations by either building an active customer base, who buy direct from the company, or by recruiting a *downline* of independent distributors who also build a customer base, thereby expanding the overall organization. Additionally, distributors can also earn a profit by retailing products they purchased from the company at wholesale price.

This arrangement of distributors earning a commission based on the sales of their independent efforts as well as the leveraged sales efforts of their downline is similar to franchise arrangements where royalties are paid from the sales of individual franchise operations to the franchiser as well as to an area or regional manager. Commissions are paid to multi-level marketing distributors according to the company's compensation plan. There can be individuals at multiple levels of the structure receiving royalties from a single person's sales.

Legality and Legitimacy

MLM businesses operate in the United States in all 50 states and in more than 100 other countries, and new businesses may use terms like "affiliate marketing" or "home-based business franchising". However, many pyramid schemes try to present themselves as legitimate MLM businesses.

The FTC states "Steer clear of multilevel marketing plans that pay commissions for recruiting new distributors. They're actually illegal pyramid schemes. Why is *pyramiding* dangerous? Because plans that pay commissions for recruiting new distributors inevitably collapse when no new distributors can be recruited. And when a plan collapses, most people-except perhaps those at the very top of the pyramid-end up empty-handed."

In a 2004 United States Federal Trade Commission (FTC) Staff Advisory letter to the Direct Selling Association states:

Much has been made of the personal, or internal, consumption issue in recent years. In fact, the amount of internal consumption in any multi-level compensation business does not determine whether or not the FTC will consider the plan a pyramid scheme. The critical question for the FTC is whether the revenues that primarily support the commissions paid to all participants are generated from purchases of goods and services that are not simply incidental to the purchase of the right to participate in a money-making venture.

The FTC warns "Not all multilevel marketing plans are legitimate. Some are pyramid schemes. It's best not to get involved in plans where the money you make is based primarily on the number of distributors you recruit and your sales to them, rather than on your sales to people outside the plan who intend to use the products." and states that research is your best tool and gives eight steps to follow:

- Find — and study — the company's track record.
- Learn about the product
- Ask questions
- Understand any restrictions
- Talk to other distributors (beware shills)
- Consider using a friend or adviser as a neutral sounding board or for a gut check.
- Take your time.
- Think about whether this plan suits your talents and goals.

However there are people who hold that all MLMs are nothing more than pyramid schemes even if they are legal rendering the whole issue of a particular MLM being legal moot.

Compensation Plans

Companies have devised a variety of MLM compensation plans over the decades.

- Unilevel plans This type of plan is often considered the simplest of compensation plans. As the name suggests, the plan allows a person to sponsor one line of distributors, called a "frontline." Every distributor the person sponsors is considered to be on that sponsor's frontline and there are no width limitations, meaning there is no limit to the amount of people one can sponsor in the frontline. The common goal of this plan is to recruit a large number of frontline distributors and then encourage them to do the same. This is due to the fact that commissions are normally paid out on a limited depth, which typically means sponsor can earn commissions on sales between 5 and 7 levels deep.

- Stairstep Breakaway plans This type of plan is characterized as having representatives who are responsible for both personal and group sales volumes. Volume is created by recruiting and by retailing product. Various discounts or rebates may be paid to group leaders and a group leader can be any representative with one or more downline recruits. Once predefined personal and/or group volumes are achieved, a representative moves up a commission level.

  This continues until the representative's sales volume reaches the top commission level and "breaks away" from their upline. From that point on, the new group is no longer considered part of his upline's group and the multi-level compensation aspect ceases. The original upline usually continues to be compensated through override commissions and other incentives.

- Matrix plans This type of plan is similar to a Uni-Level plan, except there is also a limited number of representatives who can be placed on the first level. Recruits beyond the maximum number of first level positions allowed are automatically placed in other downline (lower level) positions. Matrix plans often have a maximum width and depth.

  When all positions in a representative's downline matrix are filled (maximum width and depth is reached for all participants in a matrix), a new matrix may be started. Like Uni-Level plans, representatives in a matrix earn unlimited commissions on limited levels of volume with minimal sales quotas.

- Binary plans: A binary plan is a multilevel marketing compensation plan which allows distributors to have only two front-line distributors. If a distributor sponsors more than two distributors, the excess are placed at levels below the sponsoring distributor's front-line. This "spillover" is one of the most attractive features to new distributors since they need only sponsor two distributors to participate in the compensation plan. The primary limitation is that distributors must "balance" their two downline legs to receive commissions. Balancing legs typically requires that the number of sales from one downline leg constitute no more than a specified percentage of the distributor's total sales.

- Hybrid plans are compensation plans that are constructed using elements of more than one type of compensation plan.

Income Levels

Several sources have commented on the income level of specific MLMs or MLMs in general:

- The Times: "The Government investigation claims to have revealed that just 10 per cent of Amway's agents in Britain make any profit, with less than one in ten selling a single item of the group's products."
- Scheibeler, a high level "Emerald" Amway member: "UK Justice Norris found in 2008 that out of an IBO [Independent Business Owners] population of 33,000, 'only about 90 made sufficient incomes to cover the costs of actively building their business.' That's a 99.7 percent loss rate for investors."
- Newsweek: based on Mona Vie's own 2007 income disclosure statement "fewer than 1 percent qualified for commissions and of those, only 10 percent made more than $100 a week."
- Business Students Focus on Ethics: "In the USA, the average annual income from MLM for 90% MLM members is no more than US $5,000, which is far from being a sufficient means of making a living (San Lian Life Weekly 1998)"
- USAToday: "While earning potential varies by company and sales ability, DSA says the median annual income for those in direct sales is $2,400."

Criticism of MLM

The Federal Trade Commission (FTC) issued a decision, *In re Amway Corp.*, in 1979 in which it indicated that multi-level marketing was not illegal *per se* in the United States. However, Amway was found guilty of price fixing (by requiring "independent" distributors to sell at the low price) and making exaggerated income claims.

The FTC advises that multi-level marketing organizations with greater incentives for recruitment than product sales are to be viewed skeptically. The FTC also warns that the practice of getting commissions from recruiting new members is outlawed in most states as "pyramiding".

In April 2006, it proposed a Business Opportunity Rule intended to require all sellers of business opportunities—including MLMs—to provide enough information to enable prospective buyers to make an informed decision about their probability of earning money. In March 2008, the FTC removed Network Marketing (MLM) companies from the proposed Business Opportunity Rule:

The revised proposal, however, would not reach multi-level marketing companies or certain companies that may have been swept inadvertently into scope of the April 2006 proposal.

Walter J. Carl stated in a 2004 *Western Journal of Communication* article that "MLM organizations have been described by some as cults (Butterfield, 1985), pyramid schemes, or organizations rife with misleading, deceptive, and unethical behavior (Carter, 1999), such as the questionable use of evangelical discourse to promote the business, and the exploitation of personal relationships for financial gain.

Because of encouraging recruits to further recruit their competitors, some people have even gone so far as to say at best MLMs are nothing more than legalized pyramid schemes with one stating "Multi-level marketing companies have become an accepted and legally sanctioned form of pyramid scheme in the United States" while another states "Multi-Level Marketing, a form of Pyramid Scheme, is not necessarily fraudulent.

Chapter 5

Developing and Managing Products

The noun product is defined as a "thing produced by labour or effort" or the "result of an act or a process", and stems from the verb produce, from the Latin *producers* '(to) lead or bring forth'. Since 1575, the word "product" has referred to anything produced. Since 1695, the word has referred to "thing or things produced". The economic or commercial meaning of product was first used by political economist Adam Smith

In marketing, a product is anything that can be offered to a market that might satisfy a want or need. In retailing, products are called merchandise. In manufacturing, products are purchased as raw materials and sold as finished goods. Commodities are usually raw materials such as metals and agricultural products, but a commodity can also be anything widely available in the open market. In project management, products are the formal definition of the project deliverable that make up or contribute to delivering the objectives of the project. In general usage, product may refer to a single item or unit, a group of equivalent products, a grouping of goods or services, or an industrial classification for the goods or services. A related concept is sub-product, a secondary but useful result of a production process.

Product Groups

Tangible and Intangible Products

Products can be classified as tangible or intangible. A tangible product is any physical product that can be touched like a computer, automobile, etc. An intangible product is a non-physical product like an insurance policy.

In its online product catalog, retailer Sears, Roebuck and Company divides its products into departments, then presents products to shoppers according to (1) function or (2) brand. Each product has a Sears item number and a manufacturer's model number. The departments and product groupings that Sears uses are intended to help customers browse products by function or brand within a traditional department store structure.

Sizes and Colours

A catalog number, especially for clothing, may group sizes and colours. When ordering the product, the customer specifies size, colour and other variables. example: you walk into a store and see a group of shoes and in that group are sections of different colours of that type of shoe and sizes for that shoe to satisfy your need.

Product Line

A product line is "a group of products that are closely related, either because they function in a similar manner, are sold to the same customer groups, are marketed through the same types of outlets, or fall within given price ranges."

Many businesses offer a range of product lines which may be unique to a single organization or may be common across the business's industry. In 2002 the US Census compiled revenue figures for the finance and insurance industry by various product lines such as "accident, health and medical insurance premiums" and "income from secured consumer loans". Within the insurance industry, product lines are indicated by the type of risk coverage, such as auto insurance, commercial insurance and life insurance.

National and International Product Classifications

Various classification systems for products have been developed for economic statistical purposes. The North American Industry Classification System (NAICS) classifies companies by their primary product [this is not even close to true, NAICS is a production-oriented classification system, not a product-oriented classification system — the NAFTA signatories are working on a system that classifies products called NAPCS as a companion to NAICS. The European Union uses a "Classification of Products by Activity" among other product classifications. The United Nations also classifies products for international economic activity reporting.

The Aspinwall Classification System

(Leo Aspinwall, 1958) classifies and rates products based on five variables:

1. Replacement rate (How frequently is the product repurchased?)
2. Gross margin (How much profit is obtained from each product?)
3. Buyer goal adjustment (How flexible are the buyers' purchasing habits with regard to this product?)
4. Duration of product satisfaction (How long will the product produce benefits for the user?)
5. Duration of buyer search behavior (How long will consumers shop for the product?).

The National Institute of Governmental Purchasing (NIGP) developed a commodity and services classification system for use by state and local governments, the NIGP Code. The NIGP Code is used by 33 states within the United States as well as thousands of cities, counties and political subdivisions. The NIGP Code is a hierarchical schema consisting of a 3 digit class, 5 digit class-item, 7 digit class-item-group and an 11 digit class-item-group-detail. Applications of the NIGP Code include vendor registration, inventory item identification, contract item management, spend analysis and strategic sourcing.

Levels of Product Management:

- Product Item Level – At this level responsibilities are associated with marketing a single product or brand. By "single" we are limiting the marketer's responsibility to one item. For instance, a startup software development company may initially market just one product. In some organizations the person in charge has the title Product Manager, though in smaller companies this person may simply be the Marketing Manager.
- Brand Product Line Level – At this level responsibilities are associated with managing two or more similar product items. By "similar" we are referring to products carrying the same brand name that fit within the same product category and offer similar solutions to customers' needs. Procter & Gamble, one of the largest consumer products companies in the world, markets Tide laundry detergent in several different packaging sizes (e.g., 50oz., 100oz., 200oz.), in different forms (e.g., powder, liquid) and with different added features (e.g., softener, bleach). Tide's product line consists of over 100 different versions of the product. Differences in the product offerings indicate these are

targeted to different segments within the larger market (e.g., those preferring liquid vs. those preferring powder), however, it may also represent a choice for the same target market who may seek variety. A product line is often measured by its depth, relative to competitors, with deep product lines offering extensive product items. Brand product lines are often managed by a Brand or Product Line Manager.

- Category Product Line Level – At this level responsibilities are associated with managing two or more brand product lines within the same product category. In this situation the marketer may manage products that offer similar basic benefits (e.g., clean clothes) but target their offerings to slightly different needs (e.g., product for tough to clean clothing vs. product to clean delicate clothing). Multiple brand product lines allow the marketer to cover the needs of more segments and, consequently, increase their chance to generate sales. Often in larger companies category product lines are the responsibility of the Product Category or Divisional Marketing Manager who may have Brand Product Managers reporting to him/her.
- Product Mix Level – At this level responsibilities include two or more category product lines that are directed to different product categories. In some cases the category product lines may yield similar general solutions (e.g., cleaning) but are aimed at entirely different target markets (e.g., cleaning dishes vs. cleaning automobiles). In large companies, the product lines are very diverse and offer different solutions. For example, BIC sells writing instruments, shaving products, and lighters. This diversification strategy cushions against an "all-eggs-in-one-basket" risk that may come if a company directs all resources to one product category. A product mix can be classified based on its width (how many different category product lines) and its depth (how many different brand product lines within a category product line). Generally responsibility for this level belongs to a company's Vice President for Marketing.

Branding Strategy

Branding is an important decision designed to enhance the identity of the product through the use of unique brand names, symbols and other distinctive measures. With competition growing more intense in almost all industries, establishing a strong brand allows an organization's products to stand out and avoid potential pitfalls, such as price wars, that have befallen many products. Therefore, a clear understanding of branding strategy is essential in order to build solid products and product lines. In particular, marketers should be aware of various branding approaches that can be pursued.By branding approach we are referring to different product identification strategies that can be deployed to establish a product within the market. As we will see, the purpose of these approaches is to build a brand that will exist for the long term. Making smart decisions up front is crucial since a company may have to live with the decision for a long time.

Approaches to Branding

Branding approaches include the following:

- Individual Product Branding – Under this branding approach new products are assigned new names with no obvious connection to existing brands offered by the company. Under individual product branding the marketing organization must work hard to establish the brand in the market since it cannot ride the coattails of previously introduced brands. The chief advantage of this approach is it allows brands to stand on their own thus lessening threats that may occur to other brands marketed by the company. For instance, if another company brand receives negative publicity this news is less likely to rub off on the company's other brands that carry their own unique names. Additionally, as mentioned in the Product Decisions tutorial, brands can create financial gains through the concept known as brand equity. Under an individual branding approach, each brand builds its own separate equity which allows the company, if they choose, to sell off individual brands without impacting other brands owned by the company. The most famous marketing organization to follow this strategy is Procter and Gamble, which has historically introduced new brands without any link to other brands or even to the company name.
- Family Branding – Under this branding approach new products are placed under the umbrella of an existing brand. The principle advantage of this approach is that it enables the organization to rapidly build market awareness and acceptance since the brand is already established and known to the market. But the potential disadvantage is that the market has already established certain perceptions of the brand. For instance, a company that sells low-end, lower priced products may have a brand that is viewed as an economy brand. This brand image may create customer confusion and hinder the company if they attempt to introduce higher-end,

higher priced products using the same brand name. Additionally, with family branding any negative publicity that may occur for one product within a brand could spread to all other products that share the same name.

- Co-Branding – This approach takes the idea of individual and family branding a step further. With co-branding a marketer seeks to partner with another firm, which has an established brand, in hopes synergy of two brands on a product is even more powerful than a single brand. The partnership often has both firms sharing costs but also sharing the gains. For instance, major credit card companies, such as Visa and Master Card, offer co-branding options to companies and organizations. The cards carry the name of a co-branded organization (e.g., University name) along with the name of the issuing bank (e.g., Citibank) and the name of the credit card company. Besides tapping into awareness for multiple brands, the co-branding strategy is also designed to appeal to a larger target market, especially if each brand, when viewed separately, does not have extensive overlapping target markets with the other brand. Thus, co-branding allows both firms to tap into market segments where they did not previously have a strong position.
- Private or Store Branding – Some suppliers are in the business of producing products for other companies including placing another company's brand name on the product. This is most often seen in the retail industry where stores or online sellers contract with suppliers to manufacture the retailer's own branded products. In some cases the supplier not only produces product for the retailer's brand but also markets their own brand so that store shelves will contain both brands.
- No-Name or Generic Branding – Certain suppliers supply products that are intentionally "brandless." These products are mostly basic commodity-type products that consumer or business customers purchase as low price alternatives to branded products. Basic household products such as paper products, over-the-counter medicines such as buprofen, and even dog food are available in a generic form.
- Brand Licensing – Under brand licensing a contractual arrangement is created in which a company owning a brand name allows others to produce and supply products carrying the brand name. This is often seen when a brand is not directly connected with a product category. For instance, several famous

children's characters, such as Sesame Street's Elmo, have been licensed to toy and food manufacturers who market products using the branded character's name and image.

Developing New Products

By its nature marketing requires new ideas. Unlike some organizational functions, where basic processes follow a fairly consistent routine (e.g., accounting), successful marketers are constantly making adjustments to their marketing efforts.

New ideas are essential for responding to changing demand by the target market and by pressure exerted by competitors. These changes are manifested in decisions in all marketing areas including the development of new products.

In addition to being responsive to changing customer tastes and competitive forces, there are many other reasons why new product development is vital. These include:

- Many new products earn higher profits than older products. This is often the case for products considered innovative or unique which, for a period of time, may enjoy success and initially face little or no competition.
- New products can help reposition the company in customer's minds. For instance, a company that traditionally sold low priced products with few features may shift customers' perceptions about the company by introducing products with more features and slightly higher pricing.
- Fierce global competition and technological developments make it much easier for competitors to learn about products and replicate them. To stay ahead of competitors marketers must innovate and often create and introduce new products on a consistent schedule.
- Companies with limited depth in a product line may miss out on more sales unless they can add new products to fill out the line.
- Some firms market seasonal products that garner their highest sales during a certain time of the year or sell cyclical products whose sales fluctuate depending on economic or market factors. Expanding the firm's product mix into new areas may help offset these fluctuations. For manufacturing firms an additional benefit is realized as new products utilize existing production capacity that is under-used when seasonal or cyclical products are not being produced.

Categories of New Products

New products can fall into one of several categories. These categories are defined by the type of market the product is entering (i.e., newly created, existing but not previously targeted, existing and targeted) and the level of product innovation (i.e., radically new, upgrade).

- Creates New Market with Radically New Product or Product Line – This category is represented by new breakthrough products that are so revolutionary they create an entirely new market. Recent examples include digital music players, such as Apple's iPod, that have spawned new delivery methods (downloadable music) and new media (podcasting). Highly innovative products are rare so very few new products fall into this category.
- Enters Existing But Not Previously Targeted Market with New-Product or Product Line – In this category a marketer introduces a new product item or product line to an existing market which they did not previously target. Often these products are similar to competitors' products already available in the market but with some level of difference (e.g., different features, lower price, etc.). Microsoft's entry into the video gaming system market with their Xbox is an example.
- Stays in Existing and Previously Targeted Market by Enhancing Existing Product or Product Line – Under this development category the marketer attempts to improve its current position in the market by either improving or upgrading existing products or by extending a product line by adding new products. This type of new product is seen in our earlier example of Procter and Gamble's Tide product line which contains many product variations of the basic Tide product.

How New Products are Obtained

Marketers have several options for obtaining new products. First, products can be developed within an organization's own research operations. For some companies, such as service firms, this may simply mean the marketer designs new service options to sell to target markets. For instance, a marketer for a mortgage company may design new mortgage packages that offer borrowers different rates or payment options. At the other extreme companies may support an extensive research and development effort where engineers, scientists or others are engaged in new product discovery. A second way to obtain products is to acquire them from external sources.

This can occur in several ways including:

- Purchase the Product-With this option a marketer purchases the product outright from another firm that currently owns the product. The advantage is that the product is already developed, which reduces the purchasing company's time and cost of trying to develop it themselves. On the negative side the purchase cost may be high.
- License the Product – Under this option the marketer negotiates with the owner of the product for the rights to market the product. This may be a particularly attractive option for companies who have to fill a product need quickly (e.g., give a product line more depth) or it may be used as a temporary source of products while the marketer's company is developing its own product. On the negative side the arrangement may have a limited time frame at which point the licensor may decide to end the relationship leaving the marketer without a source for the product.
- Purchase Another Firm-Instead of purchasing another company's products marketers may find it easier to just purchase the whole company selling the products. One key advantage to this is that the acquisition often includes the people and resources that developed the product which may be a key consideration if the acquiring company wants to continue to develop the acquired products.

New Product Development Process

Because introducing new products on a consistent basis is important to the future success of many organizations, marketers in charge of product decisions often follow set procedures for bringing products to market. In the scientific area that may mean the establishment of ongoing laboratory research programs for discovering new products (e.g., medicines) while less scientific companies may pull together resources for product development on a less structured timetable.

In this section we present a 7-step process comprising the key elements of new product development. While some companies may not follow a deliberate step-by-step approach, the steps are useful in showing the information input and decision making that must be done in order to successfully develop new products. The process also shows the importance market research plays in developing products. We should note that while the 7-step process works for most industries, it is less effective in developing radically new products. The main reason lies in the inability of the target market to provide sufficient feedback on advanced product concepts since they often find it difficult to understand radically different ideas. So while many of these steps are used to research breakthrough ideas, the marketer should exercise caution when interpreting the results.

Product Development Steps 1-3

Step 1. Idea Generation

The first step of new product development requires gathering ideas to be evaluated as potential product options. For many companies idea generation is an ongoing process with contributions from inside and outside the organization. Many market research techniques are used to encourage ideas including: running focus groups with consumers, channel members, and the company's sales force; encouraging customer comments and suggestions via toll-free telephone numbers and website forms; and gaining insight on competitive product developments through secondary data sources.

One important research technique used to generate ideas is brainstorming where open-minded, creative thinkers from inside and outside the company gather and share ideas. The dynamic nature of group members floating ideas, where one idea often sparks another idea, can yield a wide range of possible products that can be further pursued.

Step 2. Screening

In Step 2 the ideas generated in Step 1 are critically evaluated by company personnel to isolate the most attractive options. Depending on the number of ideas, screening may be done in rounds with the first round involving company executives judging the feasibility of ideas while successive rounds may utilize more advanced research techniques. As the ideas are whittled down to a few attractive options, rough estimates are made of an idea's potential in terms of sales, production costs, profit potential, and competitors' response if the product is introduced. Acceptable ideas move on to the next step.

Step 3. Concept Development and Testing

With a few ideas in hand the marketer now attempts to obtain initial feedback from customers, distributors and its own employees.

Generally, focus groups are convened where the ideas are presented to a group, often in the form of concept board presentations (i.e., story boards) and not in actual working form. For instance, customers may be shown a concept board displaying drawings of a product idea or even an advertisement featuring the product. In some cases focus groups are exposed to a mock-up of the ideas, which is a physical but generally non-functional version of product idea. During focus groups with customers the marketer seeks information that may include: likes and dislike of the concept; level of interest in purchasing the product; frequency of purchase (used to help forecast demand); and price points to determine how much customers are willing to spend to acquire the product.

Step 4. Business Analysis

At this point in the new product development process the marketer has reduced a potentially large number of ideas down to one or two options. Now in Step 4 the process becomes very dependent on market research as efforts are made to analyse the viability of the product ideas. (Note, in many cases the product has not been produced and still remains only an idea.) The key objective at this stage is to obtain useful forecasts of market size (e.g., overall demand), operational costs (e.g., production costs) and financial projections (e.g., sales and profits). Additionally, the organization must determine if the product will fit within the company's overall mission and strategy. Much effort is directed at both internal research, such as discussions with production and purchasing personnel, and external marketing research, such as customer and distributor surveys, secondary research, and competitor analysis.

Step 5. Product and Marketing Mix Development

Ideas passing through business analysis are given serious consideration for development. Companies direct their research and development teams to construct an initial design or prototype of the idea. Marketers also begin to construct a marketing plan for the product. Once the prototype is ready the marketer seeks customer input. However, unlike the concept testing stage where customers were only exposed to the idea, in this step the customer gets to experience the real product as well as other aspects of the marketing mix, such as advertising, pricing, and distribution options (e.g., retail store, direct from company, etc.). Favourable customer reaction helps solidify the marketer's decision to introduce the product and also provides other valuable information such as estimated purchase rates and understanding how the product will be used by the customer. Reaction that is less favourable may suggest the need for adjustments to elements of the marketing mix. Once these are made the marketer may again have the customer test the product. In addition to gaining customer feedback, this step is used to gauge the feasibility of large-scale, cost effective production for manufactured products.

Step 6. Market Testing

Products surviving to Step 6 are ready to be tested as real products. In some cases the marketer accepts what was learned from concept testing and skips over market testing to launch the idea as a fully marketed product. But other companies may seek more input from a larger group before moving to commercialization. The most common type of market testing makes the product available to a selective small segment of the target market (e.g., one city), which is exposed to the full marketing effort as they would be to any product they could purchase. In some cases, especially with consumer products sold at retail stores, the marketer must work hard to get the product into the test market by convincing distributors to agree to purchase and place the product on their store shelves.

In more controlled test markets distributors may be paid a fee if they agree to place the product on their shelves to allow for testing. Another form of market testing found with consumer products is even more controlled with customers recruited to a "laboratory" store where they are given shopping instructions. Product interest can then be measured based on customer's shopping response.

Finally, there are several high-tech approaches to market testing including virtual reality and computer simulations. With virtual reality testing customers are exposed to a computer-projected environment, such as a store, and are asked to locate and select products. With computer simulations customers may not be directly involved at all. Instead certain variables are entered into a sophisticated computer program and estimates of a target market's response are calculated.

Step 7. Commercialization

If market testing displays promising results the product is ready to be introduced to a wider market. Some firms introduce or roll-out the product in waves with parts of the market receiving the product on different schedules. This allows the company to ramp up production in a more controlled way and to fine tune the marketing mix as the product is distributed to new areas.

Managing Existing Products

Marketing strategies developed for initial product introduction almost certainly need to be revised as the product settles into the market. While commercialization may be the last step in the new product development process it is just the beginning of managing the product.

Adjusting the product's marketing strategy is required for many reasons including:

- Changing customer tastes
- Domestic and foreign competitors
- Economic conditions
- Technological advances.

To stay on top of all possible threats the marketer must monitor all aspects of the marketing mix and make changes as needed. Such efforts require the marketer to develop and refine the product's marketing plan on a regular basis.

Physical Distribution Management (PDM)

Physical distribution management (PDM) is concerned with *ensuring the* product is in the right place at the right time. 'Place' has always been thought of as being the least dynamic of the 'Four Ps'. Marketing practitioners and academics have tended to concentrate on the more conspicuous aspects of marketing. It is now recognised that PDM is a critical area of overall marketing management, and much of its expertise is 'borrowed' from military practice. During the Second World War and the Korean and Vietnam Wars, supplies officers had to perform extraordinary feats of PDM, in terms of food, clothing, ammunition, weapons and a whole range of support equipment having to be transported across the world. The military skill that marketing has adopted and applied to PDM is that of logistics. Marketing management realised that distribution could be organised in a scientific way and so the concept of business logistics developed, focusing attention on and increasing the importance of PDM.

As marketing analysis became increasingly sophisticated, managers became more aware of the costs of physical distribution. Whilst the military must win battles, the primary aim of business is to provide customer satisfaction in a manner that results in profit for the company. Business logistical techniques can be applied to PDM so that costs and customer satisfaction are optimised. There is little point in making large savings in the cost of distribution if, in the long run, sales are lost because of customer dissatisfaction. Similarly, it does not make economic sense to provide a level of service that is not really required by the customer and leads to erosion of profits. This cost/service balance is a basic dilemma that faces physical distribution managers.

Definition

Physical distribution management (PDM) is concerned with ensuring the product is in the right place at the right time.

A final reason for the growing importance of PDM as a marketing function is the increasingly demanding nature of the business environment. In the past, it was not uncommon for companies to hold large inventories of raw materials and components. Although industries and individual firms differ widely in their stockholding policies, nowadays stock levels are kept to a minimum wherever possible. Holding stock is wasting working capital, for it is not earning money for the company. A more financially analytical approach by management has combined to move the responsibility for carrying stock onto the supplier and away from the customer. Gilbert and Strebel (1989) pointed out that this has a 'domino' effect throughout the marketing channel, with each member putting pressure on the next to provide higher levels of service.

A logistical issue facing physical distribution managers today is the increasing application by customers of just-in-time management techniques or lean manufacturing. Hutchins (1988) stresses that companies who demand 'JIT' service from their suppliers carry only a few hours' stock of material and components, and rely totally on supplier service to keep their production running. This demanding distribution system is supported by company expediters whose task it is to 'chase' the progress of orders and deliveries, not only with immediate suppliers, but right along the chain of supply (called 'supply chain integration'). Lean manufacturing has been widely adopted throughout the automotive industry, where companies possess the necessary purchasing power to impose such delivery conditions on their suppliers.

Their large purchasing power also necessitates stringent financial controls, and huge financial savings can be made in the reduction or even elimination of stockholding costs where this method of manufacturing is employed. To think of the logistical process merely in terms of transportation is much too narrow a view. Physical distribution management (PDM) is concerned with the flow of goods from the receipt of an order until the goods are delivered to the customer. In addition to transportation, PDM involves close liaison with production planning, purchasing, order processing, material control and warehousing. All these areas must be managed so that they interact efficiently with each other to provide the level of service that the customer demands and at a cost that the company can afford.

Supply Chain Management

Supply chain management (SCM) is the management of a network of interconnected businesses involved in the ultimate provision of product and service packages required by end customers (Harland, 1996). Supply Chain Management spans all movement and storage of raw materials, work-in-process inventory, and finished goods from point of origin to point of consumption (supply chain).

Another definition is provided by the APICS Dictionary when it defines SCM as the "design, planning, execution, control, and monitoring of supply chain activities with the objective of creating net value, building a competitive infrastructure, leveraging worldwide logistics, synchronizing supply with demand, and measuring performance globally."

Idea

More common and accepted definitions of Supply Chain Management are:

- Supply Chain Management is the systemic, strategic coordination of the traditional business functions and the tactics across these business functions within a particular company and across businesses within the supply chain, for the purposes of improving the long-term performance of the individual companies and the supply chain as a whole (Mentzer et al, 2001).
- Global Supply Chain Forum-Supply Chain Management is the integration of key business processes across the supply chain for the purpose of adding value for customers and stockholders (Lambert, 2008)
- According to the Council of Supply Chain Management Professionals (CSCMP), Supply chain management encompasses the planning and management of all activities involved in sourcing, procurement, conversion, and logistics management. It also includes the crucial components of coordination and collaboration with channel partners, which can be suppliers, intermediaries, third-party service providers, and customers. In essence, supply chain management integrates supply and demand management within and across companies. More recently, the loosely coupled, self-organizing network of

businesses that cooperate to provide product and service offerings has been called the *Extended Enterprise*.

A supply chain, as opposed to supply chain management, is a set of organizations directly linked by one or more of the upstream and downstream flows of products, services, finances, and information from a source to a customer. Managing a supply chain is 'supply chain management' (Mentzer et al., 2001).

Supply chain management software includes tools or modules used to execute supply chain transactions, manage supplier relationships and control associated business processes.

Supply chain event management (abbreviated as SCEM) is a consideration of all possible events and factors that can disrupt a supply chain. With SCEM possible scenarios can be created and solutions devised.

Supply Chain Management Problems

Supply chain management must address the following problems:

- Distribution Network Configuration: number, location and network missions of suppliers, production facilities, distribution centres, warehouses, cross-docks and customers.
- Distribution Strategy: questions of operating control (centralized, decentralized or shared); delivery scheme, e.g., direct shipment, pool point shipping, cross docking, DSD (direct store delivery), closed loop shipping; mode of transportation, e.g., motor carrier, including truckload, LTL, parcel; railroad; intermodal transport, including TOFC (trailer on flatcar) and COFC (container on flatcar); ocean freight; airfreight; replenishment strategy (e.g., pull, push or hybrid); and transportation control (e.g., owner-operated, private carrier, common carrier, contract carrier, or 3PL).
- Trade-Offs in Logistical Activities: The above activities must be well coordinated in order to achieve the lowest total logistics cost. Trade-offs may increase the total cost if only one of the activities is optimized. For example, full truckload (FTL) rates are more economical on a cost per pallet basis than less than truckload (LTL) shipments. If, however, a full truckload of a product is ordered to reduce transportation costs, there will be an increase in inventory holding costs which may increase total logistics costs. It is therefore imperative to take a systems approach when planning logistical activities. These trade-offs

and SCM strategy. are key to developing the most efficient and effective Logistics

- Information: Integration of processes through the supply chain to share valuable information, including demand signals, forecasts, inventory, transportation, potential collaboration, etc.
- Inventory Management: Quantity and location of inventory, including raw materials, work-in-progress (WIP) and finished goods.
- Cash-Flow: Arranging the payment terms and methodologies for exchanging funds across entities within the supply chain.

Supply chain execution means managing and coordinating the movement of materials, information and funds across the supply chain. The flow is bi-directional.

Activities/Functions

Supply chain management is a cross-function approach including managing the movement of raw materials into an organization, certain aspects of the internal processing of materials into finished goods, and the movement of finished goods out of the organization and toward the end-consumer. As organizations strive to focus on core competencies and becoming more flexible, they reduce their ownership of raw materials sources and distribution channels. These functions are increasingly being out sourced to other entities that can perform the activities better or more cost effectively. The effect is to increase the number of organizations involved in satisfying customer demand, while reducing management control of daily logistics operations. Less control and more supply chain partners led to the creation of supply chain management concepts. The purpose of supply chain management is to improve trust and collaboration among supply chain partners, thus improving inventory visibility and the velocity of inventory movement.

Several models have been proposed for understanding the activities required to manage material movements across organizational and functional boundaries. SCOR is a supply chain management model promoted by the Supply Chain Council. Another model is the SCM Model proposed by the Global Supply Chain Forum (GSCF). Supply chain activities can be grouped into strategic, tactical, and operational levels. The CSCMP has adopted The American Productivity & Quality Centre (APQC) Process Classification Framework a high-level, industry-neutral enterprise process model that allows organizations to see their business processes from a cross-industry viewpoint·

Strategic:

- Strategic network optimization, including the number, location, and size of warehousing, distribution centres, and facilities.
- Strategic partnerships with suppliers, distributors, and customers, creating communication channels for critical information and operational improvements such as cross docking, direct shipping, and third-party logistics.
- Product life cycle management, so that new and existing products can be optimally integrated into the supply chain and capacity management activities.
- Information technology chain operations.
- Where-to-make and what-to-make-or-buy decisions.
- Aligning overall organizational strategy with supply strategy.
- It is for long term and needs resource comittement.

Tactical:

- Sourcing contracts and other purchasing decisions.
- Production decisions, including contracting, scheduling, and planning process definition.
- Inventory decisions, including quantity, location, and quality of inventory.
- Transportation strategy, including frequency, routes, and contracting.
- Benchmarking of all operations against competitors and implementation of best practices throughout the enterprise.
- Milestone payments.
- Focus on customer demand.

Operational:

- Daily production and distribution planning, including all nodes in the supply chain.
- Production scheduling for each manufacturing facility in the supply chain (minute by minute).
- Demand planning and forecasting, coordinating the demand forecast of all customers and sharing the forecast with all suppliers.
- Sourcing planning, including current inventory and forecast demand, in collaboration with all suppliers.

- Inbound operations, including transportation from suppliers and receiving inventory.
- Production operations, including the consumption of materials and flow of finished goods.
- Outbound operations, including all fulfillment activities, warehousing and transportation to customers.
- Order promising, accounting for all constraints in the supply chain, including all suppliers, manufacturing facilities, distribution centres, and other customers.

Supply Chain Management

Organizations increasingly find that they must rely on effective supply chains, or networks, to compete in the global market and networked economy. In Peter Drucker's (1998) new management paradigms, this concept of business relationships extends beyond traditional enterprise boundaries and seeks to organize entire business processes throughout a value chain of multiple companies.

During the past decades, globalization, out sourcing and information technology have enabled many organizations, such as Dell and Hewlett Packard, to successfully operate solid collaborative supply networks in which each specialized business partner focuses on only a few key strategic activities (Scott, 1993).

This inter-organizational supply network can be acknowledged as a new form of organization. However, with the complicated interactions among the players, the network structure fits neither "market" nor "hierarchy" categories (Powell, 1990). It is not clear what kind of performance impacts different supply network structures could have on firms, and little is known about the coordination conditions and trade-offs that may exist among the players. From a systems perspective, a complex network structure can be decomposed into individual component firms (Zhang and Dilts, 2004). Traditionally, companies in a supply network concentrate on the inputs and outputs of the processes, with little concern for the internal management working of other individual players. Therefore, the choice of an internal management control structure is known to impact local firm performance (Mintzberg, 1979).

In the 21st century, changes in the business environment have contributed to the development of supply chain networks. First, as an outcome of globalization and the proliferation of multinational companies, joint ventures, strategic alliances and business partnerships, significant success factors were identified, complementing the earlier "Just-In-Time", "Lean Manufacturing" and "Agile Manufacturing" practices. Second, technological changes, particularly the dramatic fall in information communication costs, which are a significant component of transaction costs, have led to changes in coordination among the members of the supply chain network (Coase, 1998).

Many researchers have recognized these kinds of supply network structures as a new organization form, using terms such as "Keiretsu", "Extended Enterprise", "Virtual Corporation", "Global Production Network", and "Next Generation Manufacturing System". In general, such a structure can be defined as "a group of semi-independent organizations, each with their capabilities, which collaborate in ever-changing constellations to serve one or more markets in order to achieve some business goal specific to that collaboration" (Akkermans, 2001). The security management system for supply chains is described in ISO/IEC 28000 and ISO/IEC 28001 and related standards published jointly by ISO and IEC.

Developments in Supply Chain Management

Six major movements can be observed in the evolution of supply chain management studies: Creation, Integration, and Globalization, Specialization Phases One and Two, and SCM 2.0.

Creation Era

The term supply chain management was first coined by a U.S. industry consultant in the early 1980s. However, the concept of a supply chain in management was of great importance long before, in the early 20th century, especially with the creation of the assembly line. The characteristics of this era of supply chain management include the need for large-scale changes, re-engineering, downsizing driven by cost reduction programs, and widespread attention to the Japanese practice of management.

Integration Era

This era of supply chain management studies was highlighted with the development of Electronic Data Interchange (EDI) systems in the 1960s and developed through the 1990s by the introduction of Enterprise Resource Planning (ERP) systems. This era has continued to develop into the 21st century with the expansion of internet-based collaborative systems. This era of supply chain evolution is characterized by both increasing value-adding and cost reductions through integration.

Globalization Era

The third movement of supply chain management development, the globalization era, can be characterized by the attention given to global systems of supplier relationships and the expansion of supply chains over national boundaries and into other continents. Although the use of global sources in the supply chain of organizations can be traced back several decades (e.g., in the oil industry), it was not until the late 1980s that a considerable number of organizations started to integrate global sources into their core business. This era is characterized by the globalization of supply chain management in organizations with the goal of increasing their competitive advantage, value-adding, and reducing costs through global sourcing.

Specialization Era—Phase One: Out sourced Manufacturing and Distribution

In the 1990s industries began to focus on "core competencies" and adopted a specialization model. Companies abandoned vertical integration, sold off non-core operations, and out sourced those functions to other companies. This changed management requirements by extending the supply chain well beyond company walls and distributing management across specialized supply chain partnerships.

This transition also re-focused the fundamental perspectives of each respective organization. OEMs became brand owners that needed deep visibility into their supply base. They had to control the entire supply chain from above instead of from within. Contract manufacturers had to manage bills of material with different part numbering schemes from multiple OEMs and support customer requests for work-in-process visibility and vendor-managed inventory (VMI).

The specialization model creates manufacturing and distribution networks composed of multiple, individual supply chains specific to products, suppliers, and customers who work together to design, manufacture, distribute, market, sell, and service a product. The set of partners may change according to a given market, region, or channel, resulting in a proliferation of trading partner environments, each with its own unique characteristics and demands.

Specialization Era—Phase Two: Supply Chain Management as a Service

Specialization within the supply chain began in the 1980s with the inception of transportation brokerages, warehouse management, and non-asset-based carriers and has matured beyond transportation and logistics into aspects of supply planning, collaboration, execution and performance management.

At any given moment, market forces could demand changes from suppliers, logistics providers, locations and customers, and from any number of these specialized participants as components of supply chain networks. This variability has significant effects on the supply chain infrastructure, from the foundation layers of establishing and managing the electronic communication between the trading partners to more complex requirements including the configuration of the processes and work flows that are essential to the management of the network itself.

Supply chain specialization enables companies to improve their overall competencies in the same way that out sourced manufacturing and distribution has done; it allows them to focus on their core competencies and assemble networks of specific, best-in-class partners to contribute to the overall value chain itself, thereby increasing overall performance and efficiency. The ability to quickly obtain and deploy this domain-specific supply chain expertise without developing and maintaining an entirely unique and complex competency in house is the leading reason why supply chain specialization is gaining popularity.

Out sourced technology hosting for supply chain solutions debuted in the late 1990s and has taken root primarily in transportation and collaboration categories. This has progressed from the Application Service Provider (ASP) model from approximately 1998 through 2003 to the On-Demand model from approximately 2003-2006 to the Software as a Service (SaaS) model currently in focus today.

Supply Chain Management 2.0 (SCM 2.0)

Building on globalization and specialization, the term SCM 2.0 has been coined to describe both the changes within the supply chain itself as well as the evolution of the processes, methods and tools that manage it in this new "era". o-touch via business process out sourcing, mid-touch via managed services and software as a service (SaaS), or high touch in the traditional software deployment model.

Supply Chain Business Process Integration

Successful SCM requires a change from managing individual functions to integrating activities into key supply chain processes. An example scenario: the purchasing department places orders as requirements become known. The marketing department, responding to customer demand, communicates with several distributors and retailers as it attempts to determine ways to satisfy this demand. Information shared between supply chain partners can only be fully leveraged through process integration. Supply chain business process integration involves collaborative work between buyers and suppliers, joint product development, common systems and shared information. According to Lambert and Cooper (2000), operating an integrated supply chain requires a continuous information flow. However, in many companies, management has reached the conclusion that optimizing the product flows cannot be accomplished without implementing a process approach to the business. The key supply chain processes stated by Lambert (2004) are:

- Customer relationship management
- Customer service management
- Demand management
- Order fulfillment
- Manufacturing flow management
- Supplier relationship management
- Product development and commercialization
- Returns management.

Much has been written about demand management. Best-in-Class companies have similar characteristics, which include the following: a) Internal and external collaboration b) Lead time reduction initiatives c) Tighter feedback from customer and market demand d) Customer level forecasting

One could suggest other key critical supply business processes which combine these processes stated by Lambert such as:

a. Customer service management
b. Procurement
c. Product development and commercialization
d. Manufacturing flow management/support
e. Physical distribution
f. Out sourcing/partnerships
g. Performance measurement.

Customer Service Management Process

Customer Relationship Management concerns the relationship between the organization and its customers. Customer service is the source of customer information. It also provides the customer with real-time information on scheduling and product availability through interfaces with the company's production and distribution operations. Successful organizations use the following steps to build customer relationships:

- Determine mutually satisfying goals for organization and customers
- Establish and maintain customer rapport
- produce positive feelings in the organization and the customers.

Procurement Process

Strategic plans are drawn up with suppliers to support the manufacturing flow management process and the development of new products. In firms where operations extend globally, sourcing should be managed on a global basis.

The desired outcome is a win-win relationship where both parties benefit, and a reduction in time required for the design cycle and product development. Also, the purchasing function develops rapid communication systems, such as electronic data interchange (EDI) and Internet linkage to convey possible requirements more rapidly. Activities related to obtaining products and materials from outside suppliers involve resource planning, supply sourcing, negotiation, order placement, inbound transportation, storage, handling and quality assurance, many of which include the responsibility to coordinate with suppliers on matters of scheduling, supply continuity, hedging, and research into new sources or programs.

Product Development and Commercialization

Here, customers and suppliers must be integrated into the product development process in order to reduce time to market. As product life cycles shorten, the appropriate products must be developed and successfully launched with ever shorter time-schedules to remain competitive. According to Lambert and Cooper (2000), managers of the product development and commercialization process must:

1. coordinate with customer relationship management to identify customer-articulated needs;
2. select materials and suppliers in conjunction with procurement, and
3. develop production technology in manufacturing flow to manufacture and integrate into the best supply chain flow for the product/market combination.

Manufacturing Flow Management Process

The manufacturing process produces and supplies products to the distribution channels based on past forecasts. Manufacturing processes must be flexible to respond to market changes and must accommodate mass customization. Orders are processes operating on a just-in-time (JIT) basis in minimum lot sizes. Also, changes in the manufacturing flow process lead to shorter cycle times, meaning improved responsiveness and efficiency in meeting customer demand. Activities related to planning, scheduling and supporting manufacturing operations, such as work-in-process storage, handling, transportation, and time phasing of components, inventory at manufacturing sites and maximum flexibility in the coordination of geographic and final assemblies postponement of physical distribution operations.

Physical Distribution

This concerns movement of a finished product/service to customers. In physical distribution, the customer is the final destination of a marketing channel, and the availability of the product/service is a vital part of each channel participant's marketing effort. It is also through the physical distribution process that the time and space of customer service become an integral part of marketing, thus it links a marketing channel with its customers (e.g., links manufacturers, wholesalers, retailers).

Out sourcing/Partnerships

This is not just out sourcing the procurement of materials and components, but also out sourcing of services that traditionally have been provided in-house. The logic of this trend is that the company will increasingly focus on those activities in the value chain where it has a distinctive advantage, and outsource everything else. This movement has been particularly evident in logistics where the provision of transport, warehousing and inventory control is increasingly subcontracted to specialists or logistics partners. Also, managing and controlling this network of partners and suppliers requires a blend of both central and local involvement. Hence, strategic decisions need to be taken centrally, with the monitoring and control of supplier performance and day-to-day liaison with logistics partners being best managed at a local level.

Performance Measurement

Experts found a strong relationship from the largest arcs of supplier and customer integration to market share and profitability. Taking advantage of supplier capabilities and emphasizing a long-term supply chain perspective in customer relationships can both be correlated with firm performance. As logistics competency becomes a more critical factor in creating and maintaining competitive advantage, logistics measurement becomes increasingly important because the difference between profitable and unprofitable operations becomes more narrow. A.T. Kearney Consultants (1985) noted that firms engaging in comprehensive performance measurement realized improvements in overall productivity. According to experts, internal measures are generally collected and analysed by the firm including

1. Cost
2. Customer Service
3. Productivity measures
4. Asset measurement, and
5. Quality.

External performance measurement is examined through customer perception measures and "best practice" Benchmarking, and includes:

1) customer perception measurement, and
2) best practice Benchmarking.

Components of Supply Chain Management are:

1. Standardization
2. Postponement
3. Customization.

Theories of Supply Chain Management

Currently there is a gap in the literature available on supply chain management studies: there is no theoretical support for explaining the existence and the boundaries of supply chain management. A few authors such as Halldorsson, et al. (2003), Ketchen and Hult (2006) and Lavassani, et al. (2008[b]) have tried to provide theoretical foundations for different areas related to supply chain by employing organizational theories. These theories include:

- Resource-Based View (RBV)
- Transaction Cost Analysis (TCA)
- Knowledge-Based View (KBV)
- Strategic Choice Theory (SCT)
- Agency Theory (AT)
- Institutional theory (InT)

- Systems Theory (ST)
- Network Perspective (NP).

Supply Chain Sustainability

Supply chain sustainability is a business issue affecting an organisation's supply chain or logistics network and is frequently quantified by comparison with SECH ratings. SECH ratings are defined as *social, ethical, cultural and health* footprints. Consumers have become more aware of the environmental impact of their purchases and companies' SECH ratings and, along with non-governmental organisations ([NGO]s), are setting the agenda for transitions to organically-grown foods, anti-sweatshop labour codes and locally-produced goods that support independent and small businesses. Because supply chains frequently account for over 75% of a company's carbon footprint many organisations are exploring how they can reduce this and thus improve their SECH rating.

Components of Supply Chain Management Integration

The Management Components of SCM

The SCM components are the third element of the four-square circulation framework. The level of integration and management of a business process link is a function of the number and level, ranging from low to high, of components added to the link.

Consequently, adding more management components or increasing the level of each component can increase the level of integration of the business process link. The literature on business process re-engineering, buyer-supplier relationships, and SCM suggests various possible components that must receive managerial attention when managing supply relationships. Lambert and Cooper (2000) identified the following components:

- Planning and control
- Work structure
- Organization structure
- Product flow facility structure
- Information flow facility structure
- Management methods
- Power and leadership structure
- Risk and reward structure
- Culture and attitude.

However, a more careful examination of the existing literature leads to a more comprehensive understanding of what should be the key critical supply chain components, the "branches" of the previous identified supply chain business processes, that is, what kind of relationship the components may have that are related to suppliers and customers. Bowersox and Closs states that the emphasis on cooperation represents the synergism leading to the highest level of joint achievement. A primary level channel participant is a business that is willing to participate in the inventory ownership responsibility or assume other aspects of financial risk, thus including primary level components. A secondary level participant (specialized) is a business that participates in channel relationships by performing essential services for primary participants, including secondary level components, which support primary participants. Third level channel participants and components that support the primary level channel participants and are the fundamental branches of the secondary level components may also be included.

Consequently, Lambert and Cooper's framework of supply chain components does not lead to any conclusion about what are the primary or secondary (specialized) level supply chain components. That is, what supply chain components should be viewed as primary or secondary, how should these components be structured in order to have a more comprehensive supply chain structure, and how to examine the supply chain as an integrative one.

Reverse Supply Chain Reverse logistics is the process of managing the return of goods. Reverse logistics is also referred to as "Aftermarket Customer Services". In other words, any time money is taken from a company's warranty reserve or service logistics budget one can speak of a reverse logistics operation.

Global Supply Chain Management

Global supply chains pose challenges regarding both quantity and value:

Supply and Value Chain Trends

- Globalization
- Increased cross border sourcing
- Collaboration for parts of value chain with low-cost providers
- Shared service centres for logistical and administrative functions
- Increasingly global operations, which require increasingly global coordination and planning to achieve global optimums

- Complex problems involve also midsized companies to an increasing degree.

These trends have many benefits for manufacturers because they make possible larger lot sizes, lower taxes, and better environments (culture, infrastructure, special tax zones, sophisticated OEM) for their products. Meanwhile, on top of the problems recognized in supply chain management, there will be many more challenges when the scope of supply chains is global. This is because with a supply chain of a larger scope, the lead time is much longer. Furthermore, there are more issues involved such as multi-currencies, different policies and different laws. The consequent problems include:

1. different currencies and valuations in different countries;
2. different tax laws (Tax Efficient Supply Chain Management);
3. different trading protocols; 4. lack of transparency of cost and profit.

Chapter 6

Customer Relationship Management

Customer Relationship Management (CRM) is fundamental to building a customer-centric organisation. CRM system links together the customer data into single and logical customer repository. CRM in banking is a key element of differentiation that allows a bank to develop its customer base and sales capacity.

The goal of CRM is to manage all aspects of customer interactions in a manner that enables banks to maximise profitability from every customer. Increasing competition, deregulation, and the internet have all contributed to the increase in customer power. Technology has reduced barriers to entry and exit for the customers, making it easier to switch banks or brokers without feeling the pinch in the wallet. Retaining customers is a major concern for banking institutions which underscores the importance of customer relationship management (CRM).

Customers, faced with an increasing array of banking products and services, are expecting more from banks in terms of customised offerings, attractive returns, ease of access and transparency in dealings. By using *knowledge of the customer*, banks can turn customer relationship into a key competitive advantage.

Banks can develop customer relationships across a broad spectrum of touch points ?branches, kiosks, ATMs, internet, electronic banking, smart cards, call centres and phone banking. The full integration of these systems, their associated business processes, and the methods for which information is extracted and used, forms the basis for CRM.

Technology and Customer Relationships Management in Banking Industry

Changing customer expectations, advances in technology and globalization of the economy are the new dimensions that have brought growing pressures on banks in terms of CRM. It is imperative that to a detailed study is undertaken to find out the existing ways of doing business by banks, their present marketing tech and to formulate enhanced CRM for the better performance of banking industry. The study results will be helpful in improving the effectiveness of internal marketing and to find out whether customization or standardization will be suitable for the present scenario in banking sector.

There is evidence of this trend in every industry. In the financial industry, banks have embraced customer relationship marketing. They offer packaged checking, loan, mortgage and investment account solutions based on usage patterns. Customers that bank on the Internet, via telephone, debit card and ATM might pay more for excess check usage and less or nothing at all in monthly fees. People who commonly use traditional teller services for their banking needs and rarely or never bank via telephone or online are offered solutions that provide low-priced or unlimited check writing with a more substantial monthly fee or a high per-transaction cost.

Organizations must nurture their client relationships to ensure customer satisfaction and subsequent loyalty. While this might sound like considerably more work, it is much more costly long term to focus solely on winning customers than it is to concentrate on keeping them. In the end, the cost of doing business is less because your customers are reached more successfully. Companies are able to target the right customer with the most appropriate solution, ensuring the most profitable promotions and highest propensity to buy.

Review of Literature

Parasuraman A.,(2000) made a study on "superior customer service and marketing Excellence: Two sides of the same success coin". The first half of the article studied the nature and determination of high quality customer service and the second half of the article made a study as to why superior customer service and marketing excellence are two faces of the same success coin.

The researches discussed the meaning and measurement of service quality and offers managerial guidelines for delivering superior service to customer. He argued for broadening the scope of marketing to include the delivery of customer service as an integral component and a judicious blend of conventional marketing and superior customer service is the best receipe for sustained market success.

Parimal Vyas(2000) made a study on "Measurement of customer satisfaction: A study of banking services". This paper attempted at studying empirically customer satisfaction with the services provided by different banks and also analysed the responses of customer towards the actual time taken by banks to complete the banking transaction. The finding of the study revealed that nationalised banks and co-operative banks need to improve on reducing the overall time taken to complete banking transaction, comparatively, the private and foreign banks took much less time for completing their transactions.

Nationalised and co-operative banks need to increase the use of information technology and CRM to deliver standardized customer specific banks service to its targeted customer.

Anjana Grewal (2000) in her article "winning strategies and processes for effective CRM in banking and financial services", presented a case study on relationship management practices developed in a leading foreign bank in India in the early nineties. It was a practical paper and provided insight into what made it happen, the developed model outlined ten stages for effective customer relationship practices in financial services. These span across defining customer relationship, understanding transaction behaviour and business volumes for different customer. Developing a customer profitability model, creating the organization structure to support relationship management practices, developing training programs, relationship pricing continuously evaluating the role of relationship managers with emerging technology are the new trends expected of the relationship role.

Sharlesh and Mohan(2000) carried out a study to gain an insight into one current status of CRM. In Indian services firms and their relationship management practices and programs being implemented by them. The research revealed that aspects such as business processes, information technology, employee empowerment, quality assurance and customer knowledge strategies should be made more customer-centric.

Aravind Brahme(2000) in his article "customer complaints" has stated that customer complaints are a universal phenomenon and a service industry like banking is no exception. Handling of complaints should be considered as a core activity and viewed as one of the key functions. He draws a clear distinction between verbal and written complaints and also the way to deal with both of them. The study elaborates on as to why organisations lose customer and states that 68% of the customers are lost due to short comings in customer service. A suggestion regarding the complaint handling cell or unit is made and characteristics of a complaint system have been enlisted by the author. He has proposed organizing of workshops on complaints handling for the bank staff to develop an awareness and positive approach.

Parimal Vyas(2004) made a study on a "Measurement of customer satisfaction on IT adoption in banking services". This study was an empirical study based on descriptive research design to measure customer satisfaction considering the prevalent state of IT adoption among selected branch of nationalized banks, private banks, co-operative bank and foreign banks located at baroda. The findings of the study revealed that there was an effective implementation of E-Banking services in the case of private banks and foreign bank whereas nationalised bank were found to have a lessor degree of computerization.

Customer Relationship Management: The Concept

Customer Relationship Management is the establishment, development, maintenance and optimization of long-term mutually valuable relationships between consumers and the organizations. Successful customer relationship management focuses on understanding the needs and desires of the customers and is achieved by placing these needs at the heart of the business by integrating them with the organization's strategy, people, technology and business processes.

At the heart of a perfect, CRM strategy is the creation of mutual value for all the parties involved in the business process. It is about creating a sustainable competitive advantage by being the best at understanding, communicating, and delivering, and developing existing customer relationships in addition to creating and keeping new customers. So the concept of product life cycle is giving way to the concept of customer life cycle focusing on the development of products and services that anticipate the future need of the existing customers and creating additional services that extend existing customer relationships beyond transactions.

Need of Crm in the Banking Industry

Over time, retail bank customers tend to increase their holding of the other products from across the range of financial products/services available.

* Long-term customers are more likely to become a referral source.
* The longer a relationship continues, the better a bank can understand the customer and his/her needs & preferences, and so greater the opportunity to tailor products and services and cross-sell the product/service range.
* Customers in long-term relationships are more comfortable with the service, the organization, methods and procedures. This helps reduce operating cost and costs arising out of customer error.

With increased number of banks, products and services and practically nil switching costs, customers are easily switching banks whenever they find better services and products. Banks are finding it tough to get new customers, and more importantly, retain existing customers. According to a research by Reichheld and Sasser in the Harvard Business Review, 5% increase in customer retention can increase profitability by 35% in banking business, 50% in insurance and brokerage, and 125% in the consumer credit card market. Therefore, banks are now stressing on retaining customers and increasing market share.

Technology and CRM in Banks

Customer Relationship Management (CRM) in the Indian banking system is fundamental to building a customer-centric organization. CRM systems link customer data into a single and logical customer repository. CRM in banking is a key element that allows a bank to develop its customer base and sales capacity. The goal of CRM is to manage all aspects of customer interactions in a manner that enables banks to maximize profitability from every customer. Increasing competition, deregulation, and the internet have all contributed to the increase in customer power. Customers, faced with an increasing array of banking products and services, are expecting more from banks in terms of customized offerings, attractive returns, ease of access, and transparency in dealings. Retaining customers is a major concern for banking institutions which underscores the importance of CRM. Banks can turn customer relationship into a key competitive advantage through strategic development across a broad spectrum.

The key to successfully making this switch in marketing focus is altering the way in which organizations analyse their customer data. Most of the data organizations need in order to yield integrated, accurate customer information comes directly from the customers themselves: their demographics, their purchasing patterns, their likes and dislikes, their means and methods of purchasing, their buying history.

The good news is most organizations are likely to have most of this data. The bad news is that most of this information is in bits and pieces and lives in disparate *data* sources across an organization. To compound the problem, those systems do not speak the same language; and many organizations have no means of efficiently consolidating and analysing the data into meaningful decision support information. This may cause organizations to think that from a marketing or customer relationship management perspective, they are back at square one. That is not the case. Knowing that the data is within reach is the first step to the solution. Next, it must be found, run through the data quality process and integrated based on business rules – then it can be analysed.

Undoubtedly, an organization that is not using information technology to understand and serve its customers better will be out-performed, out-sold, out-smarted and probably out of business before the end of the next decade. Competition within a global marketplace dictates that companies distinguish themselves from the competition through their customer relationships. It is impossible for employees to provide the level of service customers expect if information about them is scattered throughout an organization or is just plain unavailable. Good customer information architecture can effectively integrate data from many sources (e.g., financial, claims, customer and call Centre systems).

For example, In Banking systems – credit card, instalment loan, investments, trust account, mortgage, etc. – are isolated within each division, how can that institution leverage its customer information? The financial institution with fragmented customer information is bombarding customers with redundant, confusing propositions that often don't apply to their individual situations. Today's customers want to be able to glance at their entire financial portfolio and see how they can optimize their financial future. The financial industry has responded to this with consolidated monthly statements and e-commerce solutions that give clients real time access to their portfolios. Furthermore, financial institutions that enable customers' access to personal account information, loan payment and money managing services online will have a clear advantage over their competitors who do not offer sophisticated, e-commerce solutions.

Delivery channels provide sophisticated analysis tools and customer interfaces. When the dust settles, the clear market leaders will be the organizations taking advantage of the Internet age by implementing e-commerce solutions on top of robust analytical solutions that are supported by data warehousing technology.

Decision support systems are used for analysis of customer information. Decision support systems (supported by the data warehouse) are the tools that enable decision-makers to analyse their data. These systems are typically functionally specific (i.e., product performance analysis, risk analysis, call pattern analysis, etc.).

Developing and implementing an enterprise customer relationship management solution, facilitates business communication by collecting and combining customer-driven data into an easily accessible operational data store and data warehouse that makes information available to the enterprise and, potentially, to customers accessing organizations via the Internet. The financial services industry has been a leading adopter of leveraging the vast amounts of customer information locked in legacy systems.

Financial institutions have various goals and objectives. Some organizations want to maximize their cross-selling opportunities, understand customer buying patterns and demographics, and analyse loan performance. Others want to better increase the effectiveness of their customer service and conduct risk analysis.

Mergers and acquisitions often present the need to integrate financial, claims, customer and application data from companies that have merged. Some companies want to assess their credit risk, better understand market segmentation and more effectively detect fraud. Some organizations' main goal is to service their customers better. For example, they want to conduct credit line analysis so they can offer better consolidation rates and/or raise or lower credit lines. Other organizations want to streamline and maximize their marketing efforts. All of these business issues can be solved and objectives can be reached by using and analysing information appropriately. Although the initial investment in this technology is expensive, companies must focus on the long-term benefits.

CRM in Retail Banking: Current Trends and Dynamics

Today, more than ever before, the ability to maximize customer loyalty through close and durable relationships is critical to retail banks' ability to grow their businesses. As banks strive to create and manage customer relationships, several emerging trends affect the approach and tools banks employ to achieve sustainable growth. These trends reflect a fundamental change in the way banks interact with the customers they have " and those they want to acquire.

Trend: Focusing on Organic Growth

How can a retail bank drive growth? Traditionally, banks have grown through an aggressive strategy of acquiring direct competitors and taking over their branch networks. Today, that strategy is no longer sufficient, since it doesn't create organic growth for the financial institution.

To build stronger customer loyalty, banks need improved customer knowledge to develop products and deliver services targeted at specific market segments; resulting in more directed marketing, sales and service tactics.

This is not to say M&As will not continue to be an effective way to expand product offerings and service capabilities. However, retail banks will focus on acquiring businesses that have essential products or capabilities to complete the bank's portfolio of offerings. The goal? To gain greater wallet share of current customers and support their organic growth. A recent example of this is the acquisition of Providian by Washington Mutual that expanded its credit card offering for both banking and mortgage customers.

Trend: *Seeking out and better serving emerging customer segments.*

One of the ways banks can achieve improved organic growth is by focusing on new markets. Emerging demographic segments represent untapped revenue streams that can fuel a bank's growth. In the U.S., the Hispanic market represents a major opportunity. This fast-growing and under-served customer segment offers new potential revenue for retail banks.

Some of the recent 2000 U.S. Census demographics about this market are impressive: The United States is the fifth largest Spanish-speaking country in the world.

Between 1990 and 2000, the Hispanic population grew four times faster than the population as a whole (57.9 vs. 13.2 percent).

Hispanics now exceed 35 million people with 9.9 million households.

An estimated 40 percent of U.S. Hispanics have no relationship with any financial services institution.

As this demographic group continues to pass through different stages of cultural assimilation into the United States market, financial services companies need to address how to maximize their share of this emerging market segment.

While it would be ideal to have a 12-month timeframe and $50 million to establish Spanish-speaking capabilities like call Centres or financial product lines, these are luxuries virtually no bank can afford in today's market. The need every bank has is how to respond quickly and at low cost. And this need is increasing all the time.

Trend: *Creating deep business insight into customer preferences.*

Customer loyalty that drives organic growth can only be built through a consistent customer experience. This means under-standing each individual customer's needs and preferences. One of the largest challenges banks face is how to better understand their customers and provide personalized customer service.

A "one-size-fits-all" customer strategy no longer works. Banks need to serve the rapidly diverging needs of all markets: aging baby-boomers, time-stressed mid-lifers and younger technophiles (i.e., Gen-X and Gen-Y). Banks must move out of their "comfort zone" and develop services and products that address the specific needs of different market segments.

It is clear that financial service providers can no longer sustain growth and profitability targets through mass direct mail campaigns that deliver less than 1 percent response rates. Those that do will lose out to competitors implementing personalized communications that target the right customer, at the right time, with the right product or service.

To optimize customer relationships and loyalty, banks need to integrate processes and technologies that enable them to build " and then act upon " a detailed view of what each customer wants. This will require highly skilled customer service professionals, with the right combination of linguistic, culturally aligned and financial services skills, as well as the ability to deploy customer service strategies quickly, efficiently and cost-effectively.

Trend: *Responding to intensifying competition through revitalized offerings.*

The need to revitalize a company's portfolio of offerings happens in every industry. Examples in high-tech manufacturing, consumer industries and transportation show how important new offerings are in order to stay competitive as products and services become more "commoditized." The same is true in the financial services industry.

Today's retail banks face a relentless stream of new competitors, eager to take a share of the market's revenues. Three major competitors offering differentiated products, services or distribution models have emerged over the past decade:

Brokerage and insurance firms, expanding their offering portfolios into banking products beyond their traditional product sets.

Nontraditional players such as PayPal (expanding through technology-led channels of services) or telecommunications companies (expanding by bundling of payments for "like" services) are growing by becoming payment aggregators.

Nonbanking companies looking to (if not already) enter the market by offering banking products and services. The entry of nontraditional players will not only affect bank growth rates as they compete for consumers, but will also place downward pressure on operating margins and profitability created through their nonbanking business models.

An example of a nonbanking competitor is Wal-Mart, which is currently renewing its push into banking. If Wal-Mart does obtain this status and if they choose to provide expanded banking services in its 3,500 U.S. stores (Wal-Mart already offers money transfers, check cashing and credit services), Wal-Mart would immediately become one of the largest retail banks (by branch count) in the United States. Their international potential would be, subject to numerous political governance and cultural issues for expansion, an additional 1,500 stores throughout the world, including in China.

Renewing and reinvigorating product offerings and customer service strategies are essential ways to stay competitive in a changing marketplace. Proactive banks will respond to market opportunities and competitive threats by launching new products, entering new markets and acquiring new customer segments. A proactive CRM solution is the foundation that can help support this without disrupting current services that would put existing clients at risk.

Trend: *Improving distribution and channel management.*

How are retail banks responding to intensified market competition? To take themselves to the next level of improved sales and service, banks are focusing on developing, implementing and integrating their channels more rapidly and efficiently. Their goal is to meet three objectives:

- Improved and more consistent service based on a full customer view
- Increased revenue through adoption of new products
- Improved profitability through lower product development and service costs

- Forward-looking banks will simultaneously improve customer service quality and profitability by deploying an integrated CRM strategy. Deepening relationships with their customers means that banks must offer their products and services through appropriate delivery channels that appeal to their customers.

Deploying multiple channels and integrating them at the enterprise level give banks a consistent and full view of the customer. To be successful, this must include all service channels " both physical and virtual " including, call Centre, Web, branch, kiosk, ATM, phone and mobile devices.

To achieve this, banks need to develop technology, operational processes and customer strategies to make their channels more effective in reaching and serving their customers. By tailoring products or services to specific customers or market segments, banks will be able to increase their product adoption rate, revenues and return on investment (ROI) for new product development.

Trend: *Safeguarding customer information.*

Adding to this complexity, customer privacy and information security are under attack as never before. The threats come from many quarters " including increasingly sophisticated identity thieves, constant phishing expeditions by criminals seeking to trap unwary customers, and even "inside jobs" where staff sell customer data to criminals.

Expanding legislative and industry requirements for customer security are also increasing costs for financial services companies. Compliance with customer information regulations is becoming increasingly complex as regulations are growing at all operating levels:

At the global level – The Payment Card Industry (PCI) Act requires a single set of information security standards and requirements for all payment organizations.

At the national level –The Gramm-Leach-Bliley Act not only requires that financial institutions ensure the security and confidentiality of customer records and information but also requires companies to protect against anticipated threats and unauthorized access, which could result in substantial harm or inconvenience to a customer.

At the state level – The California Information Practice Act requires businesses in California to disclose any security breach that occurs to any California resident whose unencrypted personal information was, or is reasonably believed to have been, acquired by an unauthorized person.

Against this ever-expanding background, it is vital that banks ensure their customer data is secure from both internal and external threats. The following are three key reasons why this is so important:

If a bank loses a customer's information, it invariably loses the customer as well.

A security breach has an immense negative impact on the value of the bank's brand and reputation, hindering the bank's ability to acquire new customers.

Under Basel II, banks without required client data security as a part of their risk management program must maintain higher levels of capital reserves " reducing the amount of funds available to invest in the marketplace and generate revenue.

By preventing security breaches and avoiding losses, banks can actually realize a ROI from investing in security. This makes protecting customer data a prerequisite for competing effectively in the retail financial services market.

Banks must balance the cost of security against the need to share information and service the customer, while at the same time finding ways to secure vital customer and financial data for the purposes of risk management planning.

To achieve this, banks need to develop technology, operational processes and customer strategies to make their channels more effective in reaching and serving their customers.

By tailoring products or services to specific customers or market segments, banks will be able to increase their product adoption rate, revenues and return on investment (ROI) for new product development.

Reaping the Benefits of a CRM Solution

Faced with these numerous and varied trends, retail banks are reshaping the way they must interact with their customers. A fully integrated, enterprisewide CRM platform ensures banks have the core capabilities to take full advantage of their customer relationships and capitalize on these market dynamics, rather than losing out because of them.

Based on decades of experience in developing CRM solutions for our clients, EDS has developed best practice business requirements for CRM systems. These best practices reflect business results a financial services company must obtain by implementing its CRM solution.

Gaining Sales Momentum

In today's increasingly competitive environment, where maximizing organic growth is a bank's priority, sales momentum is essential. To build this momentum, banks need to focus simultaneously on:

Increasing acquisition rates of new and emerging customer segments, such as the Hispanic population in the U.S.

Improving retention of existing customers and saving "at risk" customers.

Increasing profitability of customer relationships, either at the top-line through increased sales, or at the bottom-line through more cost-effective service.

Improving integrated channel distribution strategies to get the right product, to the right client, at the moment the customer has the need.

Maximizing the value and return from CRM investments that have already been made Increasing acquisition of new customers.

A CRM solution should help a bank target customers based on the "value" they bring to the bank, now and throughout the life of the customer (and beyond through "next generation" marketing). Banks need to ensure that their value propositions have traction with the right market segments. This will enable the bank to identify, target and capture new customers. Clearly, customer insight and strategy are the core differentiators for the bank. CRM solutions (people, applications, systems and processes) must support these strategies to get the right products and services to the right customers.

Improving Retention of Existing Customers

Customer retention can be achieved by enhancing customer satisfaction and loyalty, improving problem resolution, and creating the ability to identify and save "at-risk" customers. In fact, an "at-risk" customer actually represents a major opportunity for additional revenue – if handled correctly. However, the greatest danger for banks is either not identifying "at risk" customers or not having the capabilities to do anything to recover them.

For example, a customer makes a large withdrawal from his or her account. This may signal that the customer is switching funds to another bank. Or the customer may be buying a house, a boat, or paying college tuition, in which case there are clear opportunities to sell additional products or investments. The identification and treatment of this customer should reflect his or her lifetime value. CRM-driven techniques will help retain customers and can migrate mere "account holders" into loyal, long-term, profitable customers.

Increasing the Profitability of Customer Relationships

Boosting revenues requires improving the product pipeline and close rates, while reducing sales and service costs. On the revenue side, the bank's CRM solution should use customer intelligence to target specific offers and manage marketing campaigns for a high likelihood of acceptance. Customer treatment strategies should be fully integrated with a CRM platform and the processes to support them. On the cost side, better channel management, CRM automation and integration will help increase the efficiency and effectiveness of sales and service.

Improving Distribution and Channel Management

To win profitable customers and build long-term relationships with them, banks need to have the right insight, products and services for the right customer at the lowest possible cost. From call Centres to Web sites, every one of a bank's multiple channels must be scalable, flexible, low-cost and fully integrated with all the other channels. This is the only way to consolidate customer information and provide consistent treatment across the enterprise. Each of the bank's channels must also be able to accommodate change and adapt to future trends in the marketplace.

Maximizing the Value of past CRM Investments

As new technologies and channels emerge, the need to control costs and maximize the ROI from existing CRM investments raises many questions:

How can a bank lower its operational cost structure while leveraging the newest technologies " such as interactive voice recognition-based routing " to improve service quality and customer experience?

Customer Relationship in Retail

Retail consists of the sale of goods or merchandise from a fixed location, such as a department store, boutique or kiosk, or by mail, in small or individual lots for direct consumption by the purchaser. Retailing may include subordinated services, such as delivery. Purchasers may be individuals or businesses. In commerce, a "retailer" buys goods or products in large quantities from manufacturers or importers, either directly or through a wholesaler, and then sells smaller quantities to the end-user. Retail establishments are often called shops or stores. Retailers are at the end of the supply chain. Manufacturing marketers see the process of retailing as a necessary part of their overall distribution strategy. The term "retailer" is also applied where a service provider services the needs of a large number of individuals, such as a public utility, like electric power.

Shops may be on residential streets, shopping streets with few or no houses or in a shopping mall. Shopping streets may be for pedestrians only. Sometimes a shopping street has a partial or full roof to protect customers from precipitation. Online retailing, a type of electronic commerce used for business-to-consumer (B2C) transactions and mail order, are forms of non-shop retailing. Shopping generally refers to the act of buying products. Sometimes this is done to obtain necessities such as food and clothing; sometimes it is done as a recreational activity. Recreational shopping often involves window shopping (just looking, not buying) and browsing and does not always result in a purchase.

Types of Retail Outlets

A marketplace is a location where goods and services are exchanged. The traditional market square is a city square where traders set up stalls and buyers browse the merchandise. This kind of market is very old, and countless such markets are still in operation around the whole world. In some parts of the world, the retail business is still dominated by small family-run stores, but this market is increasingly being taken over by large retail chains. Retail is usually classified by type of products as follows:

- Food products
- Hard goods ("hardline retailers")-appliances, electronics, furniture, sporting goods, etc.
- Soft goods-clothing, apparel, and other fabrics.

There are the following types of retailers by marketing strategy:

- Department stores-very large stores offering a huge assortment of "soft" and "hard goods; often bear a resemblance to a collection of specialty stores. A retailer of such store carries variety of categories and has broad assortment at average price. They offer considerable customer service.
- Discount stores-tend to offer a wide array of products and services, but they compete mainly on price offers extensive assortment of merchandise at affordable and cut-rate prices. Normally retailers sell less fashion-oriented brands.

- Supermarkets-sell mostly food products;
- Warehouse stores-warehouses that offer low-cost, often high-quantity goods piled on pallets or steel shelves; warehouse clubs charge a membership fee;
- Variety stores or "dollar stores"-these offer extremely low-cost goods, with limited selection;
- Demographic-retailers that aim at one particular segment (e.g., high-end retailers focusing on wealthy individuals).
- Mom-And-Pop : is a retail outlet that is owned and operated by individuals. The range of products are very selective and few in numbers. These stores are seen in local community often are family-run businesses. The square feet area of the store depends on the store holder.
- Specialty stores: A typical speciality store gives attention to a particular category and provides high level of service to the customers. A pet store that specializes in selling dog food would be regarded as a specialty store. However, branded stores also come under this format. For example if a customer visits a Reebok or Gap store then they find just Reebok and Gap products in the respective stores.
- General store-a rural store that supplies the main needs for the local community;
- Convenience stores: is essentially found in residential areas. They provide limited amount of merchandise at more than average prices with a speedy checkout. This store is ideal for emergency and immediate purchases.
- Hypermarkets: provides variety and huge volumes of exclusive merchandise at low margins. The operating cost is comparatively less than other retail formats. *Supermarkets: is a self service store consisting mainly of grocery and limited products on non food items. They may adopt a Hi-Lo or an EDLP strategy for pricing. The supermarkets can be anywhere between 20,000 and 40,000 square feet. Example: SPAR supermarket.
- Malls: has a range of retail shops at a single outlet. They endow with products, food and entertainment under a roof.
- Category killers or Category Specialist: By supplying wide assortment in a single category for lower prices a retailer can "kill" that category for other retailers. For few categories, such

as electronics, the products are displayed at the centre of the store and sales person will be available to address customer queries and give suggestions when required. Other retail format stores are forced to reduce the prices if a category specialist retail store is present in the vicinity.

- E-tailers: The customer can shop and order through internet and the merchandise are dropped at the customer's doorstep. Here the retailers use drop shipping technique. They accept the payment for the product but the customer receives the product directly from the manufacturer or a wholesaler. This format is ideal for customers who do not want to travel to retail stores and are interested in home shopping. However it is important for the customer to be wary about defective products and non secure credit card transaction. Example: Amazon, Pennyful and Ebay.
- Vending Machines: This is an automated piece of equipment wherein customers can drop in the money in machine and acquire the products.

Some stores take a no frills approach, while others are "mid-range" or "high end", depending on what income level they target.

Other types of retail store include:

- Automated Retail stores are self service, robotic kiosks located in airports, malls and grocery stores. The stores accept credit cards and are usually open 24/7. Examples include ZoomShops and Redbox.
- Big-box stores encompass larger department, discount, general merchandise, and warehouse stores.
- Convenience store-a small store often with extended hours, stocking everyday or roadside items;
- General store-a store which sells most goods needed, typically in a rural area;

Retailers can opt for a format as each provides different retail mix to its customers based on their customer demographics, lifestyle and purchase behaviour. A good format will lend a hand to display products well and entice the target customers to spawn sales.

Retail Pricing

The pricing technique used by most retailers is cost-plus pricing. This involves adding a markup amount (or percentage) to the retailer's cost. Another common technique is suggested retail pricing. This simply involves charging the amount suggested by the manufacturer and usually printed on the product by the manufacturer.

In Western countries, retail prices are often called psychological prices or odd prices. Often prices are fixed and displayed on signs or labels. Alternatively, when prices are not clearly displayed, there can be price discrimination, where the sale price is dependent upon who the customer is. For example, a customer may have to pay more if the seller determines that he or she is willing and/or able to. Another example would be the practice of discounting for youths, students, or senior citizens..

Transfer Mechanism

There are several ways in which consumers can receive goods from a retailer:

- Counter service, where goods are out of reach of buyers and must be obtained from the seller. This type of retail is common for small expensive items (e.g. jewellery) and controlled items like medicine and liquor. It was common before the 1900s in the United States and is more common in certain countries like India.
- Delivery, where goods are shipped directly to consumer's homes or workplaces. Mail order from a printed catalog was invented in 1744 and was common in the late 19th and early 20th centuries. Ordering by telephone is now common, either from a catalog, newspaper, television advertisement or a local restaurant menu, for immediate service (especially for pizza delivery). Direct marketing, including telemarketing and television shopping channels, are also used to generate telephone orders. started gaining significant market share in developed countries in the 2000s.
- Door-to-door sales, where the salesperson sometimes travels with the goods for sale.
- Self-service, where goods may be handled and examined prior to purchase.

Second Hand Retail

Some shops sell second-hand goods. In the case of a nonprofit shop, the public donates goods to the shop to be sold. In giveaway shops goods can be taken for free.

Another form is the pawnshop, in which goods are sold that were used as collateral for loans. There are also "consignment" shops, which are where a person can place an item in a store and if it sells, the person gives the shop owner a percentage of the sale price. The advantage of selling an item this way is that the established shop gives the item exposure to more potential buyers.

ChallengesTo become a truly flourishing industry, retailing needs to cross the following hurdles:

Automatic approval is not allowed for foreign investment in retail. Regulations restricting real estate purchases, and cumbersome local laws. Taxation, which favours small retail businesses. Absence of developed supply chain and integrated IT management. Lack of trained work force. Low skill level for retailing management. Lack of Retailing Courses and study options Intrinsic complexity of retailing – rapid price changes, constant threat of product obsolescence and low margins

Sales Techniques

Behind the scenes at retail, there is another factor at work. Corporations and independent store owners alike are always trying to get the edge on their competitors. One way to do this is to hire a merchandising solutions company to design custom store displays that will attract more customers in a certain demographic. The nation's largest retailers spend millions every year on in-store marketing programs that correspond to seasonal and promotional changes.

As products change, so will a retail landscape. Retailers can also use facing techniques to create the look of a perfectly stocked store, even when it is not.

A destination store is one that customers will initiate a trip specifically to visit, sometimes over a large area. These stores are often used to "anchor" a shopping mall or plaza, generating foot traffic, which is capitalized upon by smaller retailers.

Customer Service

Customer service is the "sum of acts and elements that allow consumers to receive what they need or desire from your retail establishment." It is important for a sales associate to greet the customer and make himself available to help the customer find whatever he needs. When a customer enters the store, it is important that the sales associate does everything in his power to make the customer feel welcomed, important, and make sure he leave the store satisfied. Giving the customer full, undivided attention and helping him find what he is looking for will contribute to the customer's satisfaction.

Retail Sales

The Retail Sales report is published every month. It is a measure of consumer spending, an important indicator of the US GDP. Retail firms provide data on the dollar value of their retail sales and inventories. A sample of 12,000 firms is included in the final survey and 5,000 in the advanced one. The advanced estimated data is based on a subsample from the US CB complete retail & food services sample.

It has been published by the US Census Bureau since 1951.

Consolidation

Among retailers and retails chains a lot of consolidation has appeared over the last couple of decades. Between 1988 and 2010, worldwide 40'788 mergers & acquisitions with a total known value of 2'255 bil. USD have been announced. The largest transactions with involvement of retailers in/from the United States have been: the acquisition of Albertson's Inc. for 17 bil. USD in 2006, the merger between Federated Department Stores Inc with May Department Stores valued at 16.5 bil. USD in 2005-now Macy's, and the merger between Kmart Holding Corp and Sears Roebuck & Co with a value of 10.9 bil. USD in 2004.

Develop customer-friendly policies, train your employees to provide excellent customer service skills, and learn how to personalize your shop's customer service. Browse our list of Mystery Shopper providers. We also have tips for creating customer loyalty, dealing with disgruntled customers and other customer relations advice.

Chapter 7

Delivering Customer—Focused Value

Marketing is the process by which companies determine what products or services may be of interest to customers, and the strategy to use in sales, communications and business development. It generates the strategy that underlies sales techniques, business communication, and business developments. It is an integrated process through which companies build strong customer relationships and create value for their customers and for themselves.

Marketing is used to identify the customer, satisfy the customer, and keep the customer. With the customer as the focus of its activities, it can be concluded that marketing management is one of the major components of business management. Marketing evolved to meet the stasis in developing new markets caused by mature markets and overcapacities in the last 2-3 centuries. The adoption of marketing strategies requires businesses to shift their focus from production to the perceived needs and wants of their customers as the means of staying profitable.

The term *marketing concept* holds that achieving organizational goals depends on knowing the needs and wants of target markets and delivering the desired satisfactions. It proposes that in order to satisfy its organizational objectives, an organization should anticipate the needs and wants of consumers and satisfy these more effectively than competitors.

Marketing is further defined by the AMA as an organizational function and a set of processes for creating, communicating, and delivering value to customers and for managing customer relationships in ways that benefit the organization and its stakeholders. The term developed from an original meaning which referred literally to going to a market to buy or sell goods or services. Seen from a systems point of view, sales process engineering marketing is *"a set of processes that are interconnected and interdependent with other functions, whose methods can be improved using a variety of relatively new approaches."*

The Chartered Institute of Marketing defines marketing as *"the management process responsible for identifying, anticipating and satisfying customer requirements profitably."* A different concept is the *value-based marketing* which states the role of marketing to contribute to increasing shareholder value. In this context, marketing is defined as *"the management process that seeks to maximize returns to shareholders by developing relationships with valued customers and creating a competitive advantage."*

Marketing practice tended to be seen as a creative industry in the past, which included advertising, distribution and selling. However, because the academic study of marketing makes extensive use of social sciences, psychology, sociology, mathematics, economics, anthropology and neuroscience, the profession is now widely recognized as a science, allowing numerous universities to offer Master-of-Science (MSc) programmes. The overall process starts with marketing research and goes through market segmentation, business planning and execution, ending with pre-and post-sales promotional activities. It is also related to many of the creative arts. The marketing literature is also adept at re-inventing itself and its vocabulary according to the times and the culture.

Browne (2010) reveals that supermarkets intensively research and study consumer behaviour, spending millions of dollars. Their aim is to make sure that shoppers leave spending much more that they originally planned. 'Choice' examined the theory of trolleyology finding that many shoppers instinctively look to the right when they're in the supermarket. Supermarkets prey on this biological trait by positioning many expensive impulse buying products to the right of the every checkout. These products consist of the latest DVDs, magazines, chocolates, expensive batteries and other tempting products that wouldn't be on your shopping list. Naturally shoppers pick up the items because of the marketing strategies, victimizing their sub-conscience natures.

Supermarket move products around to confuse shoppers, the entry point is another marketing tactic. Consumer psychologist Dr. Paul Harrison (cited in Browne, 2010) states that supermarkets are constantly using different methodologies of selling. One method is performing regular overhauls changing the locations of products all around to break habitual shopping, and break your budget. Harrison also contends that people who are shopping in a counter clockwise direction are likely to spend more money than people shopping in a clockwise direction. Consumer psychologists (cited in Browne, 2010) reported that most people write with their right hand, thus it is a biological trait that people have the tendency of veering to the right when shopping, it is understood that supermarkets capitalize on this fact. Found on the capturing right-hand side are usually appealing products that a shopper might impulsively e.g. an umbrella when the weather is dull.

Evolution of Marketing

An orientation, in the marketing context, related to a perception or attitude a firm holds towards its product or service, essentially concerning consumers and end-users. Throughout history, marketing has changed considerably in conjunction with consumer tastes.

Earlier Approaches

The marketing orientation evolved from earlier orientations, namely, the production orientation, the product orientation and the selling orientation.

Contemporary Approaches

Recent approaches in marketing include *relationship marketing* with focus on the customer, *business marketing* or *industrial marketing* with focus on an organization or institution and *social marketing* with focus on benefits to society. New forms of marketing also use the internet and are therefore called *internet marketing* or more generally *e-marketing, online marketing,* search engine marketing, *desktop advertising* or *affiliate marketing.* It attempts to perfect the segmentation strategy used in traditional marketing. It targets its audience more precisely, and is sometimes called personalized marketing or one-to-one marketing. Internet marketing is sometimes considered to be broad in scope, because it not only refers to marketing on the Internet, but also includes marketing done via e-mail and wireless media.

Customer Orientation

A firm in the market economy survives by producing goods that persons are willing and able to buy. Consequently, ascertaining consumer demand is vital for a firm's future viability and even existence as a going concern. Many companies today have a customer focus (or market orientation). This implies that the company focuses its activities and products on consumer demands. Generally, there are three ways of doing this: the customer-driven approach, the market change identification approach and the product innovation approach.

In the consumer-driven approach, consumer wants are the drivers of all strategic marketing decisions. No strategy is pursued until it passes the test of consumer research. Every aspect of a market offering, including the nature of the product itself, is driven by the needs of potential consumers. The starting point is always the consumer. The rationale for this approach is that there is no reason to spend R&D funds developing products that people will not buy. History attests to many products that were commercial failures in spite of being technological breakthroughs.

A formal approach to this customer-focused marketing is known as *SIVA* (Solution, Information, Value, Access). This system is basically the four Ps renamed and reworded to provide a customer focus. The SIVA Model provides a demand/customer-centric alternative to the well-known 4Ps supply side model (product, price, placement, promotion) of marketing management.

If any of the 4Ps were problematic or were not in the marketing factor of the business, the business could be in trouble and so other companies may appear in the surroundings of the company, so the consumer demand on its products will decrease.

Consumer Behaviour

Consumer behaviour is the study of when, why, how, and where people do or do not buy a product. It blends elements from psychology, sociology, social anthropology and economics. It attempts to understand the buyer decision making process, both individually and in groups. It studies characteristics of individual consumers such as demographics and behavioural variables in an attempt to understand people's wants. It also tries to assess influences on the consumer from groups such as family, friends, reference groups, and society in general.

Customer behaviour study is based on consumer buying behaviour, with the customer playing the three distinct roles of user, payer and buyer.

Relationship marketing is an influential asset for customer behaviour analysis as it has a keen interest in the re-discovery of the true meaning of marketing through the re-affirmation of the importance of the customer or buyer. A greater importance is also placed on consumer retention, customer relationship management, personalisation, customisation and one-to-one marketing. Social functions can be categorized into social choice and welfare functions.

Each method for vote counting is assumed as social function but if Arrow's possibility theorem is used for a social function, social welfare function is achieved. Some specifications of the social functions are decisiveness, neutrality, anonymity, monotonicity, unanimity, homogeneity and weak and strong Pareto optimality.

No social choice function meets these requirements in an ordinal scale simultaneously. The most important characteristic of a social function is identification of the interactive effect of alternatives and creating a logical relation with the ranks. Marketing provides services in order to satisfy customers.

With that in mind, the productive system is considered from its beginning at the production level, to the end of the cycle, the consumer (Kioumarsi et al., 2009).

Black Box Model

The black box model shows the interaction of stimuli, consumer characteristics, decision process and consumer responses. It can be distinguished between interpersonal stimuli (between people) or intrapersonal stimuli (within people). The black box model is related to the black box theory of behaviourism, where the focus is not set on the processes *inside* a consumer, but the *relation* between the stimuli and the response of the consumer.

The marketing stimuli are planned and processed by the companies, whereas the environmental stimulus are given by social factors, based on the economical, political and cultural circumstances of a society. The buyers black box contains the buyer characteristics and the decision process, which determines the buyers response.

The black box model considers the buyers response as a result of a conscious, rational decision process, in which it is assumed that the buyer has recognized the problem. However, in reality many decisions are not made in awareness of a determined problem by the consumer.

Information Search

Once the consumer has recognised a problem, they search for information on products and services that can solve that problem. Belch and Belch (2007) explain that consumers undertake both an internal (memory) and an external search.

Sources of information include:

- Personal sources
- Commercial sources
- Public sources
- Personal experience.

The relevant internal psychological process that is associated with information search is perception. Perception is defined as "the process by which an individual receives, selects, organises, and interprets information to create a meaningful picture of the world".

The Selective Perception Process

Stage Description:

- Selective exposure consumers select which promotional messages they will expose themselves to.
- Selective attention consumers select which promotional messages they will pay attention to.
- Selective comprehension consumer interpret messages in line with their beliefs, attitudes, motives and experiences.
- Selective retention consumers remember messages that are more meaningful or important to them.

The implications of this process help develop an effective promotional strategy, and select which sources of information are more effective for the brand.

Information Evaluation

At this time the consumer compares the brands and products that are in their evoked set. How can the marketing organization increase the likelihood that their brand is part of the consumer's evoked (consideration) set? Consumers evaluate alternatives in terms of the functional and psychological benefits that they offer. The marketing organization needs to understand what benefits consumers are seeking and therefore which attributes are most important in terms of making a decision. It also needs to check other brands of the customer's consideration set to prepare the right plan for its own brand.

Purchase Decision

Once the alternatives have been evaluated, the consumer is ready to make a purchase decision. Sometimes purchase intention does not result in an actual purchase. The marketing organization must facilitate the consumer to act on their purchase intention. The organization can use variety of techniques to achieve this. The provision of credit or payment terms may encourage purchase, or a sales promotion such as the opportunity to receive a premium or enter a competition may provide an incentive to buy now. The relevant internal psychological process that is associated with purchase decision is integration. Once the integration is achieved, the organization can influence the purchase decisions much more easily.

Postpurchase Evaluation

The EKB model was further developed by Rice (1993) which suggested there should be a feedback loop, Foxall (2005) further suggests the importance of the post purchase evaluation and that the post purchase evaluation is key due to its influences on future purchase patterns.

Internal Influences

Consumer behaviour is influenced by: demographics, psychographics (lifestyle), personality, motivation, knowledge, attitudes, beliefs, and feelings. Consumer behaviour concern with consumer need consumer actions in the direction of satisfying needs leads to his behaviour of every individuals depend on thinking

External Influences

Consumer behaviour is influenced by: culture, sub-culture, locality, royalty, ethnicity, family, social class, past experience reference groups, lifestyle, market mix factors.

Maximizing Yield from Value-creating Assets

Market segmentation is a concept in economics and marketing. A market segment is a sub-set of a market made up of people or organizations with one or more characteristics that cause them to demand similar product and/or services based on qualities of those products such as price or function. A true market segment meets all of the following criteria: it is distinct from other segments (different segments have different needs), it is homogeneous within the segment (exhibits common needs); it responds similarly to a market stimulus, and it can be reached by a market intervention.

The term is also used when consumers with identical product and/or service needs are divided up into groups so they can be charged different amounts. The people in a given segment are supposed to be similar in terms of criteria by which they are segmented and different from other segments in terms of these criteria.

These can broadly be viewed as 'positive' and 'negative' applications of the same idea, splitting up the market into smaller groups.

Examples:

- Gender
- Price
- Interests.

While there may be theoretically 'ideal' market segments, in reality every organization engaged in a market will develop different ways of imagining market segments, and create Product differentiation strategies to exploit these segments. The market segmentation and corresponding product differentiation strategy can give a firm a temporary commercial advantage.

Positioning

Once a market segment has been identified (via segmentation), and targeted (in which the viability of servicing the market intended), the segment is then subject to positioning. Positioning involves ascertaining how a product or a company is perceived in the minds of consumers.

This part of the segmentation process consists of drawing up a perceptual map, which highlights rival goods within one's industry according to perceived quality and price. After the perceptual map has been devised, a firm would consider the marketing communications mix best suited to the product in question.

Price Discrimination

Where a monopoly exists, the price of a product is likely to be higher than in a competitive market and the quantity sold less, generating monopoly profits for the seller. These profits can be increased further if the market can be segmented with different prices charged to different segments charging higher prices to those segments willing and able to pay more and charging less to those whose demand is price elastic.

The price discriminator might need to create rate fences that will prevent members of a higher price segment from purchasing at the prices available to members of a lower price segment. This behaviour is rational on the part of the monopolist, but is often seen by competition authorities as an abuse of a monopoly position, whether or not the monopoly itself is sanctioned. Examples of this exist in the transport industry (a plane or train journey to a particular destination at a particular time is a practical monopoly) where business class customers who can afford to pay may be charged prices many times higher than economy class customers for essentially the same service.

Selecting and Attracting the Right Customers

Taking on a new customer is a much bigger deal for a soloist than for a larger business. A new customer can have a major impact on your business and your life. You'll probably be working closely with your new customer, sometimes for a long period of time.

Therefore, to build a successful solo business, it's important to clearly articulate who your ideal customers are and to leave enough room in your schedule to work with them.

Here is a short exercise to try when you next plan or review your sales and marketing activities. It will help to sanity-check your strategy and to focus on the kind of customer relationships you most want to attract.

" A new customer can have a major impact on your business and your life. "

Sort your current customer list, or last year's customer schedule, into three groups according to how they fit these three descriptions.

"A" customers are your ideal target customers.

These are the people who most need what you have to offer. They are the ones who you most like to work with as they generate the most revenue or profit, present the best chance of repeat business or referrals. These can be in the form of high-profile assignments which enable you to stretch and learn. Basically they provide criteria that are important to you. This is the group you will be actively marketing to.

"B" customers are not your ideal target customers but offer the prospect of solid bread-and-butter work.

You might decide to take on a "B" customer if the job looks reasonably straightforward, the customer is willing to pay a fair fee, the customer seems organised, committed and easy to work with and/or you can easily fit in the work. This is a group that may be attracted by some elements of your marketing strategy, but who you do not chase after directly.

"C" customers are the ones that your business could do without.

For example, if you are a specialist in a particular area, you may want to refer requests for other kinds of work on to someone else. This list may also include those who are difficult to deal with, late paying their bills or possess some other negative quality.

What kind of picture emerges from your list? Are you working mostly with "A" and "B" customers or are there too many "Cs" in there? What thoughts has this inspired and what actions could you take to change the way you filter prospective customer relationships? Drop us a comment and let us know.

Choosing the right customers is important to the growth of a solo business so it's worth taking the time to do an exercise like this regularly. As a result, you will be happier and more focussed, both you and your customers will have clearer expectations and you will be able to get the very best from one another.

What is Customer Loyalty?

Customer loyalty is all about attracting the right customer, getting them to buy, buy often, buy in higher quantities and bring you even more customers. However, that focus is not how you build customer loyalty.

The term *customer loyalty* is used to describe the behaviour of repeat customers, as well as those that offer good ratings, reviews, or testimonials. Some customers do a particular company a great service by offering favourable word of mouth publicity regarding a product, telling friends and family, thus adding them to the number of loyal customers. However, customer loyalty includes much more. It is a process, a program, or a group of programs geared toward keeping a client happy so he or she will provide more business.

Customer loyalty can be achieved in some cases by offering a quality product with a firm guarantee. Customer loyalty is also achieved through free offers, coupons, low interest rates on financing, high value trade-ins, extended warranties, rebates, and other rewards and incentive programs. The ultimate goal of customer loyalty programs is happy customers who will return to purchase again and persuade others to use that company's products or services. This equates to profitability, as well as happy stakeholders.

Customer loyalty may be a one-time program or incentive, or an ongoing group of programs to entice consumers. Buy-one-get-one-free programs are very popular, as are purchases that come with rebates or free gifts. Another good incentive for achieving customer loyalty is offering a risk free trial period for a product or service. Also known as *brand name loyalty*, these types of incentives are meant to ensure that customers will return, not only to buy the same product again and again, but also to try other products or services offered by the company.

Excellent customer service is another key element in gaining customer loyalty. If a client has a problem, the company should do whatever it takes to make things right. If a product is faulty, it should be replaced or the customer's money should be refunded. This should be standard procedure for any reputable business, but those who wish to develop customer loyalty on a large-scale basis may also go above and beyond the standard. They may offer even more by way of free gifts or discounts to appease the customer.

You build loyalty by...

- keeping touch with customers using email marketing, thank you cards and more.
- treating your team well so they treat your customers well.
- showing that you care and remembering what they like and don't like.
- You build it by rewarding them for choosing you over your competitors.
- You build it by truly giving a damn about them and figuring out how to make them more success, happy and joyful.

In short, you build customer loyalty by *treating people how they want to be treated.* Does your marketing plan include strategies and tactics for customer loyalty & customer retention?

Inspire & Motivate People

You may or may not agree with Barack Obama's policies, but no one can deny that the inspiration he sparked in people helped him win the race to the White House in a historic & decisive manner.

People are emotional creatures. Not only is our decision-making influenced by what we feel, we get an energy boost from strong emotions.

When you're able to inspire and motivate people, particularly when they need it, you leave a mark. Want proof?

Rod Weckworth used inspiration as his secret weapon while at Rex Moore. He sent out a weekly newsletter called Rod's Ponders. It contained 7 inspirational quote of the days that all helped the reader feel good, inspired & got them thinking. His clients thanked him for it and asked him to continue. They also asked him to send it to a few friends of theirs. By the time he retired from Rex Moore in 1999, they were sending out 15,000 copies of Rod's Ponders every week.

Another example of providing inspiration & motivation are blogs that feature companies/people that are successful. For example, Mixergy.com is a website where Andrew Warner shares his interviews with people who have successfully built Internet businesses. In addition to educating people on how to build a good business, through his interviews, Andrew is exposing people to what success might look & feel like. When you see someone doing what you're trying to do and you see that they did become successful, you have hope that you too might be successful.

How Social Media Is Changing Customer Loyalty Programs

There is no denying the influence of social media on the way that we as human beings communicate on a daily basis. The impact of the digital age will be felt even more in the future if things continue on the same path that it is currently. Not only have we been put in contact with each other like we have never been before, businesses are making the most of social media networks as well. Since the majority of people in the country are constantly on social media sites at all hours of the day, companies realized that they had a whole new market to reach. But how would they do it without slameless promotion? With social media sites like Facebook, companies from every industry are gaining from a new-found connection with their customers. Since people are constantly updating their activity streams and current states of being, businesses are also able to update their clients and loyal customers with special discounts, offers, and marketing endeavours.

A really great thing about being able to do this is the fact that they can connect with their customers in a more timely manner. People are connected through sites like FourSquare, Twitter, and Facebook and enjoy the intimate bond that can be formed directly with owners and managers of businesses. Social media networks open the doors to new types of customer experiences by connecting you with them when they are a few feet away from their stores. Many companies have interactive collaborations with social networks in order to bring customers special discounts and notifications of new opportunities at any given moment. Many social media networks are accessible by such devices as the IPhone, Android, and the Blackberry, which give companies a 24 hour window for advertising to the countless masses.

Sites like Facebook, allow artists like Alicia Keys to reward the loyalty of their customers and fans by allowing them to listen her new album before anyone could even buy it. Not only does this give an exciting interactive experience for the fans, but it allows for new ways of self promotion in the music industry. Foursquare is the first choice in loyalty reward programs for many. They send out information to smart phones anywhere that people find themselves shopping. This means that not only the company sending the notification will have an increase in sales, but the location that the customer is pointed towards will also profit from this type of marketing. For companies that offer many common products to the masses, this means that they are able to maximize the exposure to their target audience like never before. For many customers, this type of marketing brings a new and innovative way to shop and be entertained in the modern age.

Social media is changing customer loyalty programs also by identifying problems through monitoring what people are saying about their brands. They also join the conversation to show that they are listening, to clear up miscommunications, or to add clarifications. As an example, Rackspace Cloud Sites have had problems where Robert Scoble acted as a channel of information to their customers on what is happening in real time. Instead of having to wait for quarterly reports to see where a company shines or is in need, they are now able to have instant response as to the impact of that particular promotional project or product. The amount of time and money wasted before is astronomical, and in retrospect, was a very unnecessary expenditure.

Having the ability to track their customer's behaviours and patterns in buying gives a company priceless information about the way to further market a particular angle. Sites like Zappos have been building more personal relationships with their customers by allowing their employees and executives to communicate directly with the public/ marketplace. If this is a sign of things to come, we have a lot to look forward to here soon.

Schedule Time

As we discussed in the lesson on proactively solving problems, time & sleep can really take a toll on relationships. The more time that passes with no communication, the more the relationship will fade away. This brings us to today's lesson: Schedule & make time for relationship maintenance. A major part of building relationships is being consistent. And to consistently do all the things we've talked about time this lesson takes time. The biggest reason people don't stay in touch is because something more urgent comes up.

The real trick is schedule time for relationships... from sending out thank you cards to making phone calls just to say hello. Keith Ferrazzi calls this pinging. I call it touching.

Call to Action

Pick a few few, maybe 3 or 4 of the techniques we've talked about so far and decide that you're going to really commit to them for the next year.

Think about how much time it will take to do each of the techniques you pick consistently. And then carve out that time in your schedule. If it will take you 30-minutes a day to write out 5 thank you cards, schedule the 30-minutes into your day and don't procrastinate on it.

Just do it. Get in a routine and turn it into a habit.

Setup Early Warning Systems That Alert You When Communication Stops Happening.

Lack of communication is the biggest problem that plagues most doomed relationships whether they are personal or professional. Identifying when a lack of communication is occurring can save problems from escalating. If you use your cell phone as your primary phone, SkyDeck.com can help you identify people you haven't connected with in some time. Another good practice is to keep notes of your conversations & activities relating to someone in your CRM system. These systems can sometimes help you identify which contacts haven't been touched in 30 days, which may be a red flag.

Call to Action

Identify 10 people you haven't spoken with in a month. Call them just to say hello.

Figure out a way to automatically alert you when you're loosing touch with your friends & clients. I introduced a couple ways in above.

Show Changes You've Made

When you make a change based on a complaint or a suggestion, tell them you made changes. This gets them to feel like they are in control. This will encourage them start to emotionally take ownership of your brand and what it stands for.

Call to Action

- Identify one thing that you improved in your business based on customer feedback. (If you cannot identify one thing you've improve by listening to your customers, you're not listening hard enough.)
- Find a way to communicate that you've made this change. Email is a good way. If you're able to pin point who all suggested this improvement, find a way to recognize and thank them.

Walk into the Lion's Den & Apologize

No one is perfect. Sometimes we'll mess up... we'll drop the ball. In these cases, as my friend Greg Roeszler says, try just walking into the lion's den and apologizing... and try to figure out how to make it right. Often, the problem isn't as big as you're making it out to be in your head. And if you messed up a while back, they probably don't even remember why they were mad at you... a benefit of the great eraser. This is a great way to win back lost clients.

Call to Action

- Identify 10 clients/friends that you've lost in the last 3 years because you dropped the ball or messed up somehow.
- Decide what the best way to communicate with them is (call vs personal meetup) and go own up to your part of what when wrong. Humility is true demonstration of personal strength.
- Track how many clients you're able to win back.

Solicit Complaints Regularly

What's the easiest way to identify problems early? Ask! Ask early & ask often.

While at Rex Moore, Rod Weckworth asked for feedback soon after a project got started. In the beginning he focused on how the paperwork process went, how they were doing so far, etc. The client feels involved with your company and it's decision making process. And if there was a problem, it was caught early and fixed before it escalated into a serious relationship-killer.

Call to Action

- How soon can you ask your client for feedback? Look at your project cycle and identify logical places to ask whether things are going as the clients expected it.
- Systematize feedback gathering. Make it part of the official procedures so it's done consistently. There various ways to ask. Here are a few ways you can use:
    - Phone call
    - Email survey via ListenUp component of ConstantContant
    - Fax
    - Snail Mail
- For non-client relationships, routinely asking if everything is okay could quickly get annoying. So instead of asking, you should

consider being tuned in to changes in behaviour and language. These can usually clue you in when things are not going right.

Proactively Solve Problems

In the past few lesson's we've discussed various ways we cause people to remember & recognize us by giving them what they they find valuable. But sometimes, all your efforts and energy can go to waste if a problems comes in an damages/kills your connection.

That's what we'll be talking about in the next few lessons: How to prevent long-term damage to your relationships.

Relationships are prone to damage. The usual culprits are time & sleep, both of which are connected.

Time & The Procrastination Effect

Time is like fire. As the saying goes: "You can use it to cook food or burn down your house."

If a customer has a problem and you handle it promptly with grace & make them happy, you'll probably have a customer for life. If a customer has a problem and you put off dealing with it for a week, you'll have an unhappy customer who will tell 20 people about their regretful decision of doing business with you.

What's worse is that as time passes, the gravity around problem seem to grow exponentially. If a company hasn't responded to a problem within a couple weeks, the phone will seem awfully heavy to the people in the company. Chances are strong that they won't respond to the customer with the problem and will hope that the problem goes away. The same happens with non-client relationships. If someone calls, and you don't respond within a reasonable amount of time, you'll mostly like not respond at all as more time passes on. I call this the *procrastination effect*: More time delay between when a problem arises & when it is resolved = decreased likelihood of a positive outcome + decreased likelihood that the problem will ever be resolved.

We'll look at how to not let the procrastination effect kill your valuable relationships in a minute, but first, let's explore the second main culprit: Sleep!

Sleep, The Great Eraser

Sleep is often called the great eraser because it's natures way of repairing our brain. In the process, it causes memories to fade, which is why you don't remember everything that you learned in the 5th grade.

Here's a scenario for you: You have a client or friend that you have a really good time working with or hanging out with. For some odd reason (maybe the project finished up or they moved out of town) you two stop talking for a few months or years.

When you meet them again, you can feel that things are not the same anymore. *Has this ever happened with you?* What changed? The good memories of working together/having fun together are not as fresh as they used to be. The Great Eraser has dulled the vibrant memories of the past.

Call to Action

In today's lesson, I want you to reflect on the relationships/clients you've lost in the last 2-3 years, how you might have caught problems early and how you might have fixed it once you realized that the relationship was in trouble.

These will help you implement the second major lesson Rod Weckworth taught me: "Make (client) your boss and show them they are very important to you." So go ahead, take out your notebook and write out your thoughts on the friends/clients you lost, how you might have caught problems early and how you might have fixed/prevent them.

Here's a few ideas to seed your list of how to fix/prevent them:

- Solicit complaints regularly
- Apologizing
- Show the changes you've made
- Setup systems to alert you to problems
- Automate tasks when appropriate
- Schedule time.

We'll discuss these and expand upon the above suggestions in the next lessons. Now start on your list of how to fix/prevent damage to your relationships.

Invite People to Events

My friend Ilya Miro invites people to events... whether it's a skiing trip up to Lake Tahoe or an exclusive business mixer or his Black Belt test/demonstration. These types of invites show that he is thinking of you... and if you take him up on the offer, the time spent together invariably leads to strengthening the bond. It also presents a great opportunity to introduce them to other people you know.

Call to Action

When you're going to an event where you know a few people, invite someone you want to build a better relationship with. At the event, spend time with them and introduce them to people you think they would get along with. For maximum effect, introduce them to a potential client, partner, employer or employee.

Guaranteeing customer value and product quality.

Warranty

In business and legal transactions, a warranty is an assurance by one party to the other party that specific facts or conditions are true or will happen; the other party is permitted to rely on that assurance and seek some type of remedy if it is not true or followed.

In real estate transactions, a general warranty deed is a promise that the buyer's title to a parcel of land will be defended. A limited warranty deed, on the other hand, is a promise that the title will be defended against a limited set of claims which is usually claims arising from incumberances executed by the grantor. Thus, a general warranty deed binds the grantor to defend the title against all claims even those arising from previous owners; whereas, a limited warranty deed typically only binds the grantor to defend the title against claims arising from when the grantor held title to the property. A limited warranty deed is the deed of choice for banks when selling foreclosed properties.

A warranty may be express or implied depending on what you bought.

Implied Warranty

An implied warranty is one that arises from the nature of the transaction, and the inherent understanding by the buyer, rather than from the express representations of the seller.

The warranty of merchantability is implied, unless expressly disclaimed by name, or the sale is identified with the phrase "as is" or "with all faults." To be "merchantable", the goods must reasonably conform to an ordinary buyer's expectations, i.e., they are what they say they are. For example, a fruit that looks and smells good but has hidden defects would violate the implied warranty of merchantability if its quality does not meet the standards for such fruit "as passes ordinarily in the trade". In Massachusetts consumer protection law, it is illegal to disclaim this warranty on household goods sold to consumers etc.

The warranty of fitness for a particular purpose is implied when a buyer relies upon the seller to select the goods to fit a specific request. For example, this warranty is violated when a buyer asks a mechanic to provide snow tires and receives tires that are unsafe to use in snow. This implied warranty can also be expressly disclaimed by name, thereby shifting the risk of unfitness back to the buyer.

Lifetime Warranty

A lifetime warranty is usually a guarantee on the lifetime of the product on the market rather than the lifetime of the consumer (the exact meaning should be defined in the actual warranty documentation). If a product has been discontinued and is no longer available, the warranty may last a limited period longer. For example, the Cisco Limited Lifetime Warranty currently lasts for five years after the product has been discontinued.

Second-hand Product Warranty

The importance of the used/second-hand product market as a fraction of the total market (new + second-hand) has been growing significantly since the beginning of the twenty-first century. Second-hand products include products that have previously been used by an end user/consumer. Users change their products even if they are still in good condition. Some products such as computers and mobile phones have a short lifetime and technologies of these products are released to the market every day. As a result, the sale of new products is often tied to a trade-in, resulting in a market for second-hand products. For instance, in France, used car unit sales increased from 4.7 million to 5.4 million between 1990 and 2005, at the same time as new car sales declined from 2.3 million to 2.07 million units.

Breach of Warranty

A warranty is violated when the promise is broken; when goods are not as should be expected, at the time the sale occurs, whether or not the defect is apparent. The seller should honor the warranty by making a timely refund or a replacement. The date of delivery starts the time under the statute of limitations for starting a court complaint for breach of warranty if the seller refuses to honor the warranty. This period is often overlooked where there is an "extended warranty" in which a seller or manufacturer contracts to provide the additional service of replacing or repairing goods that fail within the extended period. However, if the goods were defective at the time of sale, and the relevant statute of limitations has not expired, then existence or duration of any "extended warranty" is secondary: there was a breach of a primary warranty for which the seller may be liable.

It could be an unfair and deceptive business practice (a statutory type of fraud) to attempt to avoid liability for breach of a primary warranty by claiming expiration of the irrelevant extended warranty. A statute of limitations on a contract claim may be shorter (or longer) than that of a tort claim, and some breach of warranty cases are filed late and are characterized as a fraud or other related tort.

For example, a consumer buys an item that was discovered to be broken or missing pieces before it was even taken out of the package. This is a defective product and can be returned to the seller for refund or replacement, regardless of what the seller's "returns policy" might state (with limited exceptions for second-hand or "as is" sales), even if the problem wasn't discovered until after the "extended warranty" expired. Similarly, if the product fails prematurely, it may have been defective when it was sold and could then be returned for a refund or replacement. If the seller dishonors the warranty, then a contract claim can be started in court.

U.S.A & Canada

In retail business, a warranty (or "extended warranty") commonly refers to a guarantee of the reliability of a product under conditions of ordinary use. It is called "extended" warranty because it covers defects that could arise some time after the date of sale. Should the product malfunction within a stipulated amount of time after the purchase, the manufacturer or distributor is typically required to provide the customer with a replacement, repair, or refund. Such warranties usually do not cover "acts of God", owner abuse, malicious destruction, commercial use, or anything, for that matter, outside of a mechanical failure incurred with normal personal usage. Most warranties exclude parts that normally wear out, and supplies that must be periodically replaced as they are normally used up (e.g., tires and lubrication on a vehicle). An extended warranty may be included in the purchase price, or optionally extended for an additional fee, and may have yearly extensions as well as ambiguous terms like "lifetimes" of the product.

- *A manufacturer or distributor may be required to carry reserve funds on its financial balance sheet to cover potential services or refunds that may arise for any products still covered "under warranty".*

Third-party warranty providers offer optional "extended warranty" agreements for a multitude of products, considered a contract of insurance for that product. Third parties are sold through a range of smaller, self-insured companies as well as larger, well known store chains, such as Best Buy and Circuit City. As with other types of insurance, the companies are gambling that the products will be reliable, that the warranty will be forgotten, or that any claims made can be handled inexpensively. Some third party companies provide their own support such as JTF Business Systems; these companies will remove the defective part and send it back to the manufacturer for replacement.

Extended warranties are not usually provided through the manufacturer but are extended through independent administrators. In some circumstances it may work to the consumer's benefit having an assurance to the product from a company outside of place of purchase and/or service. For instance, when an auto warranty is provided through a car dealership, it's usually a sub-contracted warranty (often from the retailer with the lowest offer), where vehicle repairs are negotiated to a lower rate, often compromising the service, labour and parts to a lower standard. Many times these types of warranties require an unexpected out-of-pocket expense at the time of repair, such as:-unexpected services provided outside of the warranty terms-uncovered parts and labour rates-paying the full balance while a reimbursement is arranged through dealership/warranty claims offices. Some mechanics and dealer service Centres might put off, or defer the needed repair until the dealership's warranty has expired so that their (in-house) warranty will no longer be bound to cover the cost of repair, or so that the ordinary (higher) shop rate will apply.

- Most U.S. consumers with a combined total asset value of $4800+ (standard electronics, luxury electronics, antiques and collectibles, furnishings, automobile, home, etc.) or consumers averaging a combined household income of less than $122,000 per year, have 86% more likeliness of increasing the market value of their product, home, or vehicle, and are likely to triple their savings (cost of warranty extension vs. cost of proper service and repair on property exceeding $4800 in value) when owning a federally bonded and insured warranty. ~drp.report2007

Legal Aspects of Warranties and Disclaimers

In the United States, the rights and remedies of buyers and sellers of goods are governed by the Article 2 of Uniform Commercial Code (UCC) as it has been adopted with variations from state to state. The UCC governs both express and implied warranties. It also covers the extent to which sellers may disclaim certain types of warranties (e.g., warranty of merchantability or fitness for a particular purpose, or even disclaim all warranties in the case of goods sold "as is."

Whereas in the U.S. warranties are generally provided in writing subject to control of the laws, in other countries warranties may be governed by specific statutes. For example, a country's law may provide that goods are assured by the seller for a period of 12 months and may provide other specific rights and remedies in the event of a product failure. However, even in the U.S. there are specific laws that may provide warranties or warranty-like assurances to buyers. For example, many states have statutory warranties on new home construction, and many have so-called "lemon laws" governing new motor vehicles with repeated defects.....

"Representations and Warranties"

In complex commercial transactions, buyers and sellers may make specific representations and warranties to each other. In common parlance, these are known as "reps and warranties." These are statements by which one party gives certain assurances to the other, and on which the other party may rely. In this context, a representation is commonly a declaration of a specific fact that can be verified to be true or not, e.g., "seller represents that it is a corporation duly organized and validly existing under the laws of the state of Delaware." Here, a warranty may be more of an assurance, e.g. "supplier warrants that all of its employees working on this project will be subject to confidentiality agreements that include the ability of supplier to seek injunctive relief for breach."

Often there are specific remedies or consequences specified if the representations and warranties are not accurate or are not fulfilled. For example, a seller may represent and warrant that it has full ownership title in the item being sold, and that there is no legal impediment to the seller proceeding with the transaction. Should it turn out that the seller did not have complete title or was subject to another agreement that restricted the sale, and should these facts impact the buyer's ownership or cause it expense, the buyer would have remedies under the agreement to seek relief from the seller. Parties to these transactions typically seek representations and warranties to cover issues over which they are concerned. Because of the consequences of making representations and warranties, parties will typically try to limit the extent of any that they make. The tension between these two points of view will help to shape the negotiations between the parties as to the terms and conditions of the deal.

Car Warranty

A new car factory warranty extends from a minimal 1 year, more common 3 year and extended 5 years. While some car manufacturer warranties have gone as far as 10 years. Crate Engine manufacturers also give warranties based on the manufacturers' and workmanship warranties.

Some companies also offer *extended warranties* or *used car warranties* for vehicles up to 12 years old. The term *extended warranty*. Non-manufacturer based warranties are technically called *motor vehicle service agreements* or *service contracts.*

Home Warranty

A Home Warranty protects against the high costs of home and appliance repair by offering home warranty coverage for houses, town homes, condominiums, mobile homes, and new construction homes. When a problem occurs with a covered appliance or mechanical system such as an air conditioning unit or furnace, a service technician repairs or replaces it. The homeowner pays for a service call fee and the home warranty company pays the balance for the repair or replacement of the covered item.

Consumer Protection

Consumer protection laws designed to ensure fair trade competition and the free flow of truthful information in the marketplace. The laws are designed to prevent businesses that engage in fraud or specified unfair practices from gaining an advantage over competitors and may provide additional protection for the weak and those unable to take care of themselves. Consumer Protection laws are a form of government regulation which aim to protect the rights of consumers. For example, a government may require businesses to disclose detailed information about products—particularly in areas where safety or public health is an issue, such as food. Consumer protection is linked to the idea of "consumer rights" (that consumers have various rights as consumers), and to the formation of consumer organizations which help consumers make better choices in the marketplace.

Consumer is defined as someone who acquires goods or services for direct use or ownership rather than for resale or use in production and manufacturing.

Consumer interests can also be protected by promoting competition in the markets which directly and indirectly serve consumers, consistent with economic efficiency, but this topic is treated in Competition law.

Consumer protection can also be asserted via non-government organizations and individuals as consumer activism.

Consumer Law

"MODU" or "consumer law" is considered an area of law that regulates private law relationships between individual consumers and the businesses that sell those goods and services. Consumer protection covers a wide range of topics, including but not necessarily limited to product liability, privacy rights, unfair business practices, fraud, misrepresentation, and other consumer/business interactions.

Such laws deal with credit repair, debt repair, product safety, service and sales contracts, bill collector regulation, pricing, utility turnoffs, consolidation, personal loans that may lead to bankruptcy and much more.

Meaning

A minister of the federal cabinet is responsible for consumer rights and protection (*Verbraucherschutzminister*). In the current cabinet of Angela Merkel, this is Ilse Aigner.

When issuing public warnings about products and services, the issuing authority has to take into account that this affects the supplier's constitutionally protected economic liberty (article 12 Basic Law, see Bundesverwaltungsgericht (Federal Administrative Court)Case 3 C 34.84, 71 BVerwGE 183).

Republic of China (Taiwan)

Consumer Protection Law in the Republic of China (Taiwan) is the national special law which specifically protects the interests and safety of end-user using the products or services provided by business operators. Consumer Protection Commission of Executive Yuan serves as an ombudsman supervising, coordinating, reporting any unsafe products/services and periodically reviewing the legislation.

United Kingdom

The United Kingdom, as member state of the European Union, is bound by the consumer protection directives of the EU. Domestic (UK) laws originated within the ambit of contract and tort but, with the influence of EU law, it is emerging as an independent area of law. In many circumstances, where domestic law is in question, the matter judicially treated as tort, contract, restitution or even criminal law.

Consumer Protection issues are dealt with when complaints are made to the Director-General of Fair Trade. The Office of Fair Trading will then investigate, impose an injunction or take the matter to litigation. However, consumers cannot directly complain to the OFT. Complaints need to be made to Consumer Direct who will provide legal advice to complainants, or re-direct the individual complaint to Trading Standards for investigation. Due to restrictions within the Enterprise Act 2002, individual complainants are unable to be told whether their case is being investigated or not.

In very rare cases, Consumer Direct may direct a very large number of complaints to the OFT to be considered as a systemic complaint. The OFT can also be engaged by consumer groups e.g. The Consumers Association or the statutory consumer protection body-Consumer Focus-via a super complaint.

The OFT rarely prosecute companies, however, preferring a light touch regulation approach. Consumer complaints against companies are not published, but investigation work, undertakings and enforcements are located at. Many of the consumer protection laws e.g. Distance Selling Regulations 2000 or Unfair Terms in Consumer Contracts Regulations 1999 are actually UK implementations of EU directives. The OFT is one of the bodies responsible for enforcing these rules. This leads to a problem in that these examples of legislation are clearly designed to deal with individual complaints but the OFT will only deal with systemic complaints and will ignore individual complainants redirecting them back to Consumer Direct.

The Office of Fair Trading also acts as the UK's official consumer and competition watchdog, with a remit to make markets work well for consumers, and at a local, municipal level by Trading Standards departments. General consumer advice can be obtained from Consumer Direct or via a local branch of the Citizen's Advice Bureau.

Other Commonwealth Countries

In Australia the corresponding agency is the Australian Competition and Consumer Commission or the individual State Consumer Affairs agencies. The Australian Securities and Investments Commission has responsibility for consumer protection regulation of financial services and products.

In New Zealand, the corresponding agency is the Ministry of Consumer Affairs and the New Zealand Commerce Commission.

In India, the relevant agency is the National Consumer Disputes Commission and the Ministry of Consumer Affairs. Also organisations like Akosha.com and Mouthshut.com play a vital role in helping consumers articulate their concerns and resolves their problems as well.

United States

In the United States a variety of laws at both the federal and state levels regulate consumer affairs. Among them are the federal Fair Debt Collection Practices Act, the Fair Credit Reporting Act, Truth in Lending Act, Fair Credit Billing Act, and the Gramm-Leach-Bliley Act. Federal consumer protection laws are mainly enforced by the Federal Trade Commission and the U.S. Department of Justice.

At the state level, many states have a Department of Consumer Affairs devoted to regulating certain industries and protecting consumers who use goods and services from those industries.

For example, in the U.S. state of California, the California Department of Consumer Affairs regulates about 2.3 million professionals in over 230 different professions, through its forty regulatory entities. In addition, California encourages its consumers to act as private attorneys general through the liberal provisions of its Consumers Legal Remedies Act, Cal. Civil Code § 1750 *et seq.* California has the strongest consumer protection laws of any US state, partly because of rigorous advocacy and lobbying by groups such as Utility Consumers' Action Network, Consumer Federation of California and Privacy Rights Clearinghouse.

Other states have been the leaders in specific aspects of consumer protection. For example Florida, Delaware and Minnesota have legislated requirements that contracts be written at reasonable readability levels as a large proportion of contracts cannot be understood by most consumers who sign them.

Competition Law

Competition law, known in the United States as antitrust law, is law that promotes or maintains market competition by regulating anti-competitive conduct.

The history of competition law reaches back to the Roman Empire. The business practices of market traders, guilds and governments have always been subject to scrutiny, and sometimes severe sanctions. Since the 20th century, competition law has become global. The two largest and most influential systems of competition regulation are United States antitrust law and European Union competition law. National and regional competition authorities across the world have formed international support and enforcement networks. Modern competition law has historically evolved on a country level to promote and maintain competition in markets principally within the territorial boundaries of nation-states. Yet, at present most regimes allows for extraterritorial jurisdiction in antitrust cases based on so-called effects doctrine.

The protection of international competition is governed by international competition agreements. In 1945, during the negotiations preceding the adoption of the General Agreement on Tariffs and Trade (GATT) in 1947, limited international competition obligations were proposed within the *Charter for an International Trade Organisation.* These obligations were not included in GATT, but in 1994, with the conclusion of the Uruguay Round of GATT Multilateral Negotiations, the World Trade Organization (WTO) was created. The *Agreement Establishing the WTO* included a range of limited provisions on various cross-border competition issues on a sector specific basis.

Principle

Competition law, or antitrust law, has three main elements:

- prohibiting agreements or practices that restrict free trading and competition between business. This includes in particular the repression of free trade caused by cartels.
- banning abusive behaviour by a firm dominating a market, or anti-competitive practices that tend to lead to such a dominant position. Practices controlled in this way may include predatory pricing, tying, price gouging, refusal to deal, and many others.
- supervising the mergers and acquisitions of large corporations, including some joint ventures. Transactions that are considered to threaten the competitive process can be prohibited altogether, or approved subject to "remedies" such as an obligation to divest part of the merged business or to offer licenses or access to facilities to enable other businesses to continue competing.

Substance and practice of competition law varies from jurisdiction to jurisdiction. Protecting the interests of consumers (consumer welfare) and ensuring that entrepreneurs have an opportunity to compete in the market economy are often treated as important objectives. Competition law is closely connected with law on deregulation of access to markets, state aids and subsidies, the privatization of state owned assets and the establishment of independent sector regulators, among other market-oriented supply-side policies. In recent decades, competition law has been viewed as a way to provide better public services. Robert Bork has argued that competition laws can produce adverse effects when they reduce competition by protecting inefficient competitors and when costs of legal intervention are greater than benefits for the consumers.

Ideas about competitive law were published during the 18th century with such works as Adam Smith's The Wealth of Nations. Different terms were used to describe this area of the law, including "restrictive practices", "the law of monopolies", "combination acts" and the "restraint of trade".

Roman Legislation

An early example of competition law is the *Lex Julia de Annona,* enacted during the Roman Republic around 50 BC. To protect the grain trade, heavy fines were imposed on anyone directly, deliberately and insidiously stopping supply ships. Under Diocletian in 301 AD an edict imposed the death penalty for anyone violating a tariff system, for example by buying up, concealing or contriving the scarcity of everyday goods. More legislation came under the Constitution of Zeno of 483 AD, which can be traced into Florentine Municipal laws of 1322 and 1325. This provided for confiscation of property and banishment for any trade combination or joint action of monopolies private *or* granted by the Emperor. Zeno rescinded all previously granted exclusive rights. Justinian I subsequently introduced legislation to pay officials to manage state monopolies. As Europe slipped into the Dark Ages, so did the records of law making until the Middle Ages brought greater expansion of trade in the time of *lex mercatoria.*

Middle Ages

Legislation in England to control monopolies and restrictive practices were in force well before the Norman Conquest. The Domesday Book recorded that "foresteel" (i.e. forestalling, the practice of buying up goods before they reach market and then inflating the prices) was one of three forfeitures that King Edward the Confessor could carry out through England. But concern for fair prices also led to attempts to directly regulate the market. Under Henry III an act was passed in 1266 to fix bread and ale prices in correspondence with grain prices laid down by the assizes. Penalties for breach included amercements, pillory and tumbrel. A 14th century statute labeled forestallers as "oppressors of the poor and the community at large and enemies of the whole country." Under King Edward III the Statute of Labourers of 1349 fixed wages of artificers and workmen and decreed that foodstuffs should be sold at reasonable prices. On top of existing penalties, the statute stated that overcharging merchants must pay the injured party double the sum he received, an idea that has been replicated in punitive treble damages under US antitrust law. Also under Edward III, the following statutory provision outlawed trade combination.

> *"...we have ordained and established, that no merchant or other shall make Confederacy, Conspiracy, Coin, Imagination, or Murmur, or Evil Device in any point that may turn to the Impeachment, Disturbance, Defeating or Decay of the said Staples, or of anything that to them pertaineth, or may pertain."*

Examples of legislation in mainland Europe include the *constitutiones juris metallici* by Wenceslaus II of Bohemia between 1283 and 1305, condemning combination of ore traders increasing prices; the Municipal Statutes of Florence in 1322 and 1325 followed Zeno's legislation against state monopolies; and under Emperor Charles V in the Holy Roman Empire a law was passed "to prevent losses resulting from monopolies and improper contracts which many merchants and artisans made in the Netherlands." In 1553 King Henry VIII reintroduced tariffs for foodstuffs, designed to stabilize prices, in the face of fluctuations in supply from overseas. So the legislation read here that whereas,

> *"it is very hard and difficult to put certain prices to any such things... [it is necessary because] prices of such victuals be many times enhanced and raised by the Greedy Covetousness and Appetites of the Owners of such Victuals, by occasion of ingrossing and regrating the same, more than upon any reasonable or just ground or cause, to the great damage and impoverishing of the King's subjects."*

Around this time organizations representing various tradesmen and handicrafts people, known as guilds had been developing, and enjoyed many concessions and exemptions from the laws against monopolies. The privileges conferred were not abolished until the Municipal Corporations Act 1835..

Renaissance Developments

Europe around the 16th century was changing quickly. The new world had just been opened up, overseas trade and plunder was pouring wealth through the international economy and attitudes among businessmen were shifting. In 1561 a system of Industrial Monopoly Licenses, similar to modern patents had been introduced into England. But by the reign of Queen Elizabeth I, the system was reputedly much abused and used merely to preserve privileges, encouraging nothing new in the way of innovation or manufacture. When a protest was made in the House of Commons and a Bill was introduced, the Queen convinced the protesters to challenge the case in the courts. This was the catalyst for the Case of Monopolies or *Darcy v. Allin.* The plaintiff, an officer of the Queen's household, had been granted the sole right of making playing cards and claimed damages for the defendant's infringement of this right. The court found the grant void and that three characteristics of monopoly were (1) price increases (2) quality decrease (3) the tendency to reduce artificers to idleness and beggary. This put a temporary end to complaints about monopoly, until King James I began to grant them again. In 1623 Parliament passed the Statute of Monopolies, which for the most part excluded patent rights from its prohibitions, as well as guilds. From King Charles I, through the civil war and to King Charles II, monopolies continued, especially useful for raising revenue. Then in 1684, in *East India Company v. Sandys* it was decided that exclusive rights to trade only outside the realm were legitimate, on the grounds that only large and powerful concerns could trade in the conditions prevailing overseas. In 1710 to deal with high coal prices caused by a Newcastle Coal Monopoly the New Law was passed. Its provisions stated that "all and every contract or contracts, Covenants and Agreements, whether the same be in writing or not in writing... are hereby declared to be illegal." When Adam Smith wrote the *Wealth of Nations* in 1776 he was somewhat cynical of the possibility for change.

"To expect indeed that freedom of trade should ever be entirely restored in Great Britain is as absurd as to expect that Oceana or Utopia should ever be established in it. Not only the prejudices of the public, but what is more unconquerable, the private interests of many individuals irresistibly oppose it. The Member of Parliament who supports any proposal for strengthening this Monopoly is seen to acquire not only the reputation for understanding trade, but great popularity and influence with an order of men whose members and wealth render them of great importance."

Restraint of Trade

The English law of restraint of trade is the direct predecessor to modern competition law. Its current use is small, given modern and economically oriented statutes in most common law countries. Its approach was based on the two concepts of prohibiting agreements that ran counter to public policy, unless the reasonableness of an agreement could be shown. A restraint of trade is simply some kind of agreed provision that is designed to restrain another's trade. For example, in *Nordenfelt v. Maxim, Nordenfelt Gun Co.* a Swedish arms inventor promised on sale of his business to an American gun maker that he "would not make guns or ammunition anywhere in the world, and would not compete with Maxim in any way."

To be consider whether or not there is a restraint of trade in the first place, both parties must have provided valuable consideration for their agreement. In *Dyer's* case a dyer had given a bond not to exercise his trade in the same town as the plaintiff for six months but the plaintiff had promised nothing in return. On hearing the plaintiff's attempt to enforce this restraint, Hull J exclaimed, "per Dieu, if the plaintiff were here, he should go to prison until he had paid a fine to the King."

The common law has evolved to reflect changing business conditions. So in the 1613 case of *Rogers v. Parry* a court held that a joiner who promised not to trade from his house for 21 years could have this bond enforced against him since the time and place was certain. It was also held that a man cannot bind himself to not use his trade generally by Chief Justice Coke. This was followed in *Broad v. Jolyffe* and *Mitchell v. Reynolds* where Lord Macclesfield asked, "What does it signify to a tradesman in London what another does in Newcastle?" In times of such slow communications, commerce around the country it seemed axiomatic that a general restraint served no legitimate purpose for one's business and ought to be void. But already in 1880 in *Roussillon v. Roussillon* Lord Justice Fry stated that a restraint unlimited in space need not be void, since the real question was whether it went further than necessary for the promise's protection. So in the *Nordenfelt* case Lord Macnaughton ruled that while one could validly promise to "not make guns or ammunition anywhere in the world" it was an unreasonable restraint to "not compete with Maxim in any way." This approach in England was confirmed by the House of Lords in *Mason v. The Provident Supply and Clothing Co.*

Today

Modern competition law begins with the United States legislation of the Sherman Act of 1890 and the Clayton Act of 1914. While other, particularly European, countries also had some form of regulation on monopolies and cartels, the US codification of the common law position on restraint of trade had a widespread effect on subsequent competition law development. Both after World War II and after the fall of the Berlin wall, competition law has gone through phases of renewed attention and legislative updates around the world.

The two largest and most influential systems of competition regulation are United States antitrust law and European Community competition law. National and regional competition authorities across the world have formed international support and enforcement networks.

United States Antitrust

The American term antitrust arose not because the US statutes had anything to do with ordinary trust law, but because the large American corporations used trusts to conceal the nature of their business arrangements. Big trusts became synonymous with big monopolies. The perceived threat to democracy and the free market these trusts represented led to the Sherman and Clayton Acts. These laws, in part, codified past American and English common law of restraints of trade. Senator Hoar, an author of the Sherman Act said in a debate, "We have affirmed the old doctrine of the common law in regard to all inter-state and international commercial transactions and have clothed the United States courts with authority to enforce that doctrine by injunction." Evidence of the common law basis of the Sherman and Clayton acts is found in the *Standard Oil* case, where Chief Justice White explicitly linked the Sherman Act with the common law and 16th century English statutes on engrossing. The Act's wording also reflects common law. The first two sections read as follows,

"Section 1. Every contract, combination in the form of trust or otherwise, or conspiracy, in restraint of trade or commerce among the several States, or with foreign nations, is declared to be illegal. Every person who shall make any contract or engage in any combination or conspiracy hereby declared to be illegal shall be deemed guilty of a felony, and, on conviction thereof, shall be punished by fine....

Section 2. Every person who shall monopolize, or attempt to monopolize, or combine or conspire with any other person or persons, to monopolize any part of the trade or commerce among the several States, or with foreign nations, shall be deemed guilty of a felony, and, on conviction thereof, shall be punished by fine...."

The Sherman Act did not have the immediate effects its authors intended, though Republican President Theodore Roosevelt's federal government sued 45 companies, and William Taft used it against 75. The Clayton Act of 1914 was passed to supplement the Sherman Act. Specific categories of abusive conduct were listed, including price discrimination(section 2), exclusive dealings (section 3) and mergers which substantially lessen competition (section 7). Section 6 exempted trade unions from the law's operation. Both the Sherman and Clayton acts are now codified under Title 15 of the United States Code.

Since the mid-1970s, courts and enforcement officials generally have supported view that antitrust law policy should not follow social and political aims that undermine economic efficiency. The antitrust laws were minimalized in the mid-1980s under influence of Chicago school of economics and blamed for the loss of economic supremacy in the world.

European Union Law

In 1957 six Western European countries signed the Treaty of the European Community (EC Treaty or Treaty of Rome), which over the last fifty years has grown into a European Union of nearly half a billion citizens. The European Community is the name for the economic and social pillar of EU law, under which competition law falls. Healthy competition is seen as an essential element in the creation of a common market free from restraints on trade. The first provision is Article 81 EC, which deals with cartels and restrictive vertical agreements. Prohibited are:

> *"(1)...all agreements between undertakings, decisions by associations of undertakings and concerted practices which may affect trade between Member States and which have as their object or effect the prevention, restriction or distortion of competition within the common market..."*

Article 81 EC's goals are unclear. There are two main schools of thought. The predominant view is that only consumer welfare considerations are relevant there. However, a recent book argues that this position is erroneous and that other Member State and European Union public policy goals (such as public health and the environment) should also be considered there. If this argument is correct then it could have a profound effect on the outcome of cases as well as the Modernisation process as a whole.

Article 81(1) EC then gives examples of "hard core" restrictive practices such as price fixing or market sharing and 81(2) EC confirms that any agreements are automatically void. However, just like the Statute of Monopolies 1623, Article 81(3) EC creates exemptions, if the collusion is for distributional or technological innovation, gives consumers a "fair share" of the benefit and does not include unreasonable restraints (or disproportionate, in ECJ terminology) that risk eliminating competition anywhere.

Article 82 EC deals with monopolies, or more precisely firms who have a dominant market share and abuse that position. Unlike U.S.

Antitrust, EC law has never been used to punish the existence of dominant firms, but merely imposes a special responsibility to conduct oneself appropriately. Specific categories of abuse listed in Article 82 EC include price discrimination and exclusive dealing, much the same as sections 2 and 3 of the U.S. Clayton Act.

Also under Article 82 EC, the European Council was empowered to enact a regulation to control mergers between firms, currently the latest known by the abbreviation of Regulation 139/2004/EC. The general test is whether a concentration (i.e. merger or acquisition) with a community dimension (i.e. affects a number of EU member states) might significantly impede effective competition. Again, the similarity to the Clayton Act's substantial lessening of competition.

Finally, Articles 86 and 87 EC regulate the state's role in the market. Article 86(2) EC states clearly that nothing in the rules can be used to obstruct a member state's right to deliver public services, but that otherwise public enterprises must play by the same rules on collusion and abuse of dominance as everyone else. Article 87 EC, similar to Article 81 EC, lays down a general rule that the state may not aid or subsidize private parties in distortion of free competition, but then grants exceptions for things like charities, natural disasters or regional development.

Recognizing that existing remedies and sanctions may be insufficient to deter breaches of competition law, several EU Member States have followed the US example and introduced pecuniary penalties for executives, professional disqualification orders, and even jail sentences.

Indian Competition Law

The courts have harmonized such conflicts by giving higher weightage to either of two. The concerned chapter IV directs State in matter of concentration of wealth, welfare of consumers' vis-a-vis Fundamental Rights of a citizen (supplier of consumers). From this general mandate, government enacted MRTP Act, Consumer Protection Act, Competition Act, Company Act and few other Statutes.

International Enforcement

Competition law has already been substantially internationalized along the lines of the US model by nation states themselves, however the involvement of international organizations has been growing. Increasingly active at all international conferences are the United Nations Conference on Trade and Development (UNCTAD) and the

Organisation for Economic Co-operation and Development (OECD), which is prone to making neo-liberal recommendations about the total application of competition law for public and private industries. Office of Fair Trading Director and Professor Richard Whish wrote sceptically that it "seems unlikely at the current stage of its development that the WTO will metamorphose into a global competition authority." Despite that, at the ongoing Doha round of trade talks for the World Trade Organization, discussion includes the prospect of competition law enforcement moving up to a global level. While it is incapable of enforcement itself, the newly established International Competition Network (ICN) is a way for national authorities to coordinate their own enforcement activities.

It is unclear whether competition policy is a sensible role for government in developing, particularly low-income countries. In these countries the markets are usually very small and fragmented so that developing scale sufficient to raise competitiveness and engage in international markets is a major challenge. The bigger problem is however poor governance-in societies with widespread corruption, inadequate public finances, and weak judiciary and oversight institutions, competition policy may become another tool for capture by vested interests-becoming in itself a barrier to entry.

Theory

Classical Perspective

Under the doctrine of laissez-faire, antitrust is seen as unnecessary as competition is viewed as a long-term dynamic process where firms compete against each other for market dominance. In some markets a firm may successfully dominate, but it is because of superior skill or innovativeness. However, according to laissez-faire theorists, when it tries to raise prices to take advantage of its monopoly position it creates profitable opportunities for others to compete. A process of creative destruction begins which erodes the monopoly. Therefore, government should not try to break up monopoly but should allow the market to work.

The classical perspective on competition was that certain agreements and business practice could be an unreasonable restraint on the individual liberty of tradespeople to carry on their livelihoods. Restraints were judged as permissible or not by courts as new cases appeared and in the light of changing business circumstances. Hence the courts found specific categories of agreement, specific clauses, to fall foul of their doctrine on economic fairness, and they did not contrive an overarching conception of market power. Earlier theorists like Adam Smith rejected any monopoly power on this basis.

> *"A monopoly granted either to an individual or to a trading company has the same effect as a secret in trade or manufactures. The monopolists, by keeping the market constantly under-stocked, by never fully supplying the effectual demand, sell their commodities much above the natural price, and raise their emoluments, whether they consist in wages or profit, greatly above their natural rate."*

In *The Wealth of Nations* (1776) Adam Smith also pointed out the cartel problem, but did not advocate legal measures to combat them. "People of the same trade seldom meet together, even for merriment and diversion, but the conversation ends in a conspiracy against the public, or in some contrivance to raise prices. It is impossible indeed to prevent such meetings, by any law which either could be executed, or would be consistent with liberty and justice. But though the law cannot hinder people of the same trade from sometimes assembling together, it ought to do nothing to facilitate such assemblies; much less to render them necessary."

By the latter half of the 19th century it had become clear that large firms had become a fact of the market economy. John Stuart Mill's approach was laid down in his treatise *On Liberty* (1859).

> *"Again, trade is a social act. Whoever undertakes to sell any description of goods to the public, does what affects the interest of other persons, and of society in general; and thus his conduct, in principle, comes within the jurisdiction of society... both the cheapness and the good quality of commodities are most effectually provided for by leaving the producers and sellers perfectly free, under the sole check of equal freedom to the buyers for supplying themselves elsewhere. This is the so-called doctrine of Free Trade, which rests on grounds different from, though equally solid with, the principle of individual liberty asserted in this Essay. Restrictions on trade, or on production for purposes of trade, are indeed restraints; and all restraint, qua restraint, is an evil..."*

Neo-classical Synthesis

After Mill, there was a shift in economic theory, which emphasized a more precise and theoretical model of competition. A simple neo-classical model of free markets holds that production and distribution of goods and services in competitive free markets maximizes social welfare. This model assumes that new firms can freely enter markets and compete with existing firms, or to use legal language, there are no barriers to entry. By this term economists mean something very specific, that competitive free markets deliver allocative, productive and dynamic efficiency. Allocative efficiency is also known as Pareto efficiency after the Italian economist Vilfredo Pareto and means that resources in an economy over the long run will go precisely to those who are willing and able to pay for them. Because rational producers will keep producing and selling, and buyers will keep buying up to the last marginal unit of possible output – or alternatively rational producers will be reduce their output to the margin at which buyers will buy the same amount as produced – there is no waste, the greatest number wants of the greatest number of people become satisfied and utility is perfected because resources can no longer be reallocated to make anyone better off without making someone else worse off; society has achieved allocative efficiency. Productive efficiency simply means that society is making as much as it can. Free markets are meant to reward those who work hard, and therefore those who will put society's resources towards the frontier of its possible production. Dynamic efficiency refers to the idea that business which constantly competes must research, create and innovate to keep its share of consumers. This traces to Austrian-American political scientist Joseph Schumpeter's notion that a "perennial gale of creative destruction" is ever sweeping through capitalist economies, driving enterprise at the market's mercy. This led Schumpeter to argue that monopolies did not need to be broken up (as with Standard Oil) because the next gale of economic innovation would do the same.

Contrasting with the allocatively, productively and dynamically efficient market model are monopolies, oligopolies, and cartels. When only one or a few firms exist in the market, and there is no credible threat of the entry of competing firms, prices rise above the competitive level, to either a monopolistic or oligopolistic equilibrium price. Production is also decreased, further decreasing social welfare by creating a deadweight loss. Sources of this market power are said to include the existence of externalities, barriers to entry of the market, and the free rider problem. Markets may fail to be efficient for a variety of reasons, so the exception of competition law's intervention to the rule of *laissez faire* is justified if government failure can be avoided. Orthodox economists fully acknowledge that perfect competition is seldom observed in the real world, and so aim for what is called "workable competition". This follows the theory that if one cannot achieve the ideal, then go for the second best option by using the law to tame market operation where it can.

Chicago School

A group of economists and lawyers, who are largely associated with the University of Chicago, advocate an approach to competition law guided by the proposition that some actions that were originally considered to be anticompetitive could actually promote competition. The U.S. Supreme Court has used the Chicago School approach in several recent cases. One view of the Chicago School approach to antitrust is found in United States Circuit Court of Appeals Judge Richard Posner's books *Antitrust Law* and *Economic Analysis of Law*.

Robert Bork was highly critical of court decisions on United States antitrust law in a series of law review articles and his book *The Antitrust Paradox*. Bork argued that both the original intention of antitrust laws and economic efficiency was the pursuit *only* of consumer welfare, the protection of competition rather than competitors. Furthermore, only a few acts should be prohibited, namely cartels that fix prices and divide markets, mergers that create monopolies, and dominant firms pricing predatorily, while allowing such practices as vertical agreements and price discrimination on the grounds that it did not harm consumers. Running through the different critiques of US antitrust policy is the common theme that government interference in the operation of free markets does more harm than good. "The only cure for bad theory", writes Bork, "is better theory". The late Harvard Law School Professor Philip Areeda, who favours more aggressive antitrust policy, in at least one Supreme Court case challenged Robert Bork's preference for non-intervention.

Policy Developments

Anti-cartel enforcement is a key focus of competition law enforcement policy. In the United States, the Antitrust Criminal Penalty Enhancement and Reform Act of 2004 raised the maximum imprisonment term for price fixing from three to ten years, and the maximum fine from $10 to $100 million.

These actions complement the private enforcement which has always been an important feature of United States antitrust law. The United States Supreme Court summarized why Congress allows punitive damages in *Hawaii v. Standard Oil Co. of Cal.*:

> *"Every violation of the antitrust laws is a blow to the free-enterprise system envisaged by Congress. This*

system depends on strong competition for its health and vigor, and strong competition depends, in turn, on compliance with antitrust legislation. In enacting these laws, Congress had many means at its disposal to penalize violators. It could have, for example, required violators to compensate federal, state, and local governments for the estimated damage to their respective economies caused by the violations. But, this remedy was not selected. Instead, Congress chose to permit all persons to sue to recover three times their actual damages every time they were injured in their business or property by an antitrust violation."

In the EU, the Modernisation Regulation 1/2003 means that the European Commission is no longer the only body capable of public enforcement of European Community competition law. This was done in order to facilitate quicker resolution of competition-related inquiries. In 2005 the Commission issued a Green Paper on *Damages actions for the breach of the EC antitrust rules*, which suggested ways of making private damages claims against cartels easier. Antitrust administration and legislation can be seen as a balance between;

- guidelines which are clear and specific to the courts, regulators and business but leave little room for discretion that prevents the application of laws from resulting in unintended consequences.
- guidelines which are broad, hence allowing administrators to sway between improving economic outcomes versus succumbing to political policies to redistribute wealth.

Antitrust administration and legislation, in general is understood to serve the public interest which, is caught in the conflict between;

- promoting rivalry and economic efficiency
- economic performance of an industry and its competitiveness in the market
- and, as Bork has argued, between interests of competitors and those of consumers.

Practice

Collusion and Cartels

Dominance and Monopoly: When firms hold large market shares, consumers risk paying higher prices and getting lower quality products than compared to competitive markets. However, the existence of a very high market share does not always mean consumers are paying excessive prices since the threat of new entrants to the market can restrain a high-market-share firm's price increases. Competition law does not make merely having a monopoly illegal, but rather abusing the power that a monopoly may confer, for instance through exclusionary practices.

First it is necessary to determine whether a firm is dominant, or whether it behaves "to an appreciable extent independently of its competitors, customers and ultimately of its consumer." Under EU law, very large market shares raise a presumption that a firm is dominant, which may be rebuttable. If a firm has a dominant position, then there is "a special responsibility not to allow its conduct to impair competition on the common market". Similarly as with collusive conduct, market shares are determined with reference to the particular market in which the firm and product in question is sold. Then although the lists are seldom closed, certain categories of abusive conduct are usually prohibited under the country's legislation. For instance, limiting production at a shipping port by refusing to raise expenditure and update technology could be abusive. Tying one product into the sale of another can be considered abuse too, being restrictive of consumer choice and depriving competitors of outlets. This was the alleged case in *Microsoft v. Commission* leading to an eventual fine of €497 million for including its Windows Media Player with the Microsoft Windows platform. A refusal to supply a facility which is essential for all businesses attempting to compete to use can constitute an abuse. One example was in a case involving a medical company named *Commercial Solvents*. When it set up its own rival in the tuberculosis drugs market, Commercial Solvents were forced to continue supplying a company named Zoja with the raw materials for the drug. Zoja was the only market competitor, so without the court forcing supply, all competition would have been eliminated.

Forms of abuse relating directly to pricing include price exploitation. It is difficult to prove at what point a dominant firm's prices become "exploitative" and this category of abuse is rarely found. In one case however, a French funeral service was found to have demanded exploitative prices, and this was justified on the basis that prices of funeral services outside the region could be compared. A more tricky issue is predatory pricing. This is the practice of dropping prices of a product so much that in order one's smaller competitors cannot cover their costs and fall out of business. The Chicago School (economics) considers predatory pricing to be unlikely. However in *France Telecom*

SA v. Commission a broadband internet company was forced to pay €10.35 million for dropping its prices below its own production costs. It had "no interest in applying such prices except that of eliminating competitors" and was being cross-subsidized in order to capture the lion's share of a booming market.

One last category of pricing abuse is price discrimination. An example of this could be offering rebates to industrial customers who export your company's sugar, but not to customers who are selling their goods in the same market as you are in.

Mergers and Acquisitions

A merger or acquisition involves, from a competition law perspective, the concentration of economic power in the hands of fewer than before. This usually means that one firm buys out the shares of another. The reasons for oversight of economic concentrations by the state are the same as the reasons to restrict firms who abuse a position of dominance, only that regulation of mergers and acquisitions attempts to deal with the problem before it arises, *ex ante* prevention of market dominance.

In the United States merger regulation began under the Clayton Act, and in the European Union, under the Merger Regulation 139/2004 (known as the "ECMR"). Competition law requires that firms proposing to merge gain authorization from the relevant government authority, or simply go ahead but face the prospect of demerger should the concentration later be found to lessen competition.

The theory behind mergers is that transaction costs can be reduced compared to operating on an open market through bilateral contracts. Concentrations can increase economies of scale and scope. However often firms take advantage of their increase in market power, their increased market share and decreased number of competitors, which can adversely affect the deal that consumers get. Merger control is about predicting what the market might be like, not knowing and making a judgment. Hence the central provision under EU law asks whether a concentration *would* if it went ahead "significantly impede effective competition... in particular as a result of the creation or strengthening off a dominant position..." and the corresponding provision under US antitrust states similarly,

"No person shall acquire, directly or indirectly, the whole or any part of the stock or other share capital... of the assets of one or more persons engaged in commerce or in any activity affecting commerce, where... the effect of such acquisition, of such stocks or assets, or of the use of such stock by the voting or granting of proxies or otherwise, may be substantially to lessen competition, or to tend to create a monopoly.

What amounts to a substantial lessening of, or significant impediment to competition is usually answered through empirical study. The market shares of the merging companies can be assessed and added, although this kind of analysis only gives rise to presumptions, not conclusions. Something called the Herfindahl-Hirschman Index is used to calculate the "density" of the market, or what concentration exists. Aside from the maths, it is important to consider the product in question and the rate of technical innovation in the market. A further problem of collective dominance, or oligopoly through "economic links" can arise, whereby the new market becomes more conducive to collusion. It is relevant how transparent a market is, because a more concentrated structure could mean firms can coordinate their behaviour more easily, whether firms can deploy deterrents and whether firms are safe from a reaction by their competitors and consumers.

The entry of new firms to the market, and any barriers that they might encounter should be considered. If firms are shown to be creating an uncompetitive concentration, in the US they can still argue that they create efficiencies enough to outweigh any detriment, and similar reference to "technical and economic progress" is mentioned in Art. 2 of the ECMR. Another defence might be that a firm which is being taken over is about to fail or go insolvent, and taking it over leaves a no less competitive state than what would happen anyway. Mergers vertically in the market are rarely of concern, although in *AOL/Time Warner* the European Commission required that a joint venture with a competitor Bertelsmann be ceased beforehand. The EU authorities have also focused lately on the effect of conglomerate mergers, where companies acquire a large portfolio of related products, though without necessarily dominant shares in any individual market.

Public Sector Regulation

Public sector industries, or industries which are by their nature providing a public service, are involved in competition law in many ways similar to private companies. Under EC law, Articles 86 and 87 create exceptions for the assured achievement of public sector service provision. Many industries, such as railways, electricity, gas, water and media have their own independent sector regulators. These government agencies are charged with ensuring that private providers carry out certain public service duties in line of social welfare goals.

For instance, an electricity company may not be allowed to disconnect someone's supply merely because they have not paid their bills up to date, because that could leave a person in the dark and cold just because they are poor. Instead the electricity company would have to give the person a number of warnings and offer assistance until government welfare support kicks in.

Intellectual Property, Innovation and Competition

Intellectual property and competition have become increasingly intertwined. On the one hand, it is believed that promotion of innovation through enforcement of intellectual rights promotes competitiveness, while on the other the contrary may be the consequence. The question rests on whether it is legal to acquire monopoly through accumulation of intellectual property. In which case, the judgment needs to decide between giving preference to intellectual rights or towards promoting competitiveness

- Should antitrust laws accord special treatment to intellectual property
- Should intellectual rights be revoked or not granted when antitrust laws are violated.

Concerns also arise over anti-competitive effects and consequences due to

- Intellectual properties that are collaboratively designed with consequence of violating antitrust laws (intentionally or otherwise)
- and the further effects on competition when such properties are accepted into industry standards
- Cross-licensing of intellectual property.
- Bundling of intellectual rights to long term business transactions or agreements to extend the market exclusiveness of intellectual rights beyond their statutory duration.
- Trade secrets, if remain undecipherable, having an eternal length of life.

Some scholars suggest that a prize instead of patent would solve the problem of deadweight lose, when innovators got their reward from the prize, provided by the government or non-profit organization, rather than directly selling to the market, see Millennium Prize Problems.

However innovators may accept the prize only when it is at least as much as how much they earn from patent, which is a question difficult to determine.

Customer Defection Management – Measuring the Salesperson's Efforts

Everyone knows that customer retention is important to the success of your dealership. I also know that you are probably making a pretty significant investment in processes, procedures and technology designed to make sure your hard-earned customers remain your customers. There is no arguing the importance of customer retention. Conquering new customers with expensive advertising is not nearly as beneficial as keeping the customers you already have. Also, everyone knows that the good grosses are in repeat customers, not the customers that have to be won with the bid process.

I know you measure customer retention, like everything else that is important to the success of your dealership; it must be measured to be managed. But, how often do we measure the customer retention effectiveness of the individuals in our organizations?

Question: Who in the dealership has the most influence with your customers? You may answer, "Depends on the customers' needs." In the service department it is probably the service advisor, the estimator in the body shop, parts counter person in parts and of course you, the dealer, reigns supreme in the skills required to convince the customer that your dealership is where they want, along with their family and friends, to spend their automotive dollars.

Granted, this is somewhat subjective and you may have a different view. But I submit to you that the salesperson has the most influence with their individual customers. Or better said, they should have the most influence. In my opinion, salespeople are the front line in the battle for customer retention. The process of selling and delivering a vehicle requires that the salesperson establish rapport and trust and they have demonstrated that they have a good understanding of what it takes to satisfy their customer. Hopefully you already give your salespeople incentive to keep their delivery customers happy and coming back to you for the "between deliveries" activity.

It goes without saying that getting customers back into your dealership between vehicle purchases means service visits. The thing is if they are going to another service department the chances are there is a showroom attached to it and, well, something bad could happen there. Anyway, there is much more at stake than delivery grosses. Even more to the point, as it gets harder and harder to maintain unit volumes and variable operation grosses, service absorption is often the difference between every day being a scramble to stay alive or having the financial wherewithal to maintain and improve position in your market.

This month's DMS report is a basic report, generated from the service history database that provides us with the only true measure of how well your salespeople are performing their customer defection duties. What we want is a simple list of the salesperson deliveries that tells us if their customers are returning to your service department. Run the report for your DMS and make your analysis. If you don't like what you see you might consider revamping your salesperson's pay plans by including an element related to this metric. It does not have to be a commission component.

Using this retention metric as a qualifier for attaining professional or executive level could be effective as well. Please understand that either way I am not suggesting that you increase your pay out as a percent of gross. Instead consider a realignment of the elements that produce the payout to direct the salesperson's efforts while at the same time keep the payout at the optimum level. Good luck and have fun.

For ADP Elite Users

Using ADP's Reflection and from the service application function prompt, select RPX. Choose the HISTORY file and select the appropriate items from the listed fields. Please note if you cannot find the SALESPERSON fields, call support and they will add it for you. For a complete report I like to include basic customer and vehicle information and the date and type of repair or maintenance performed over at least a six-month date range. *Submitted by Jim Skeans of Jim Skeans Consulting Group LLC*

For ADP w.e.b.Suite 1000 Users

In the Report Writer application, select Service from the Design a New Report screen. Choose the Service Customer Vehicle Records file and name the report when prompted. Select the appropriate items from the Available Data Fields. This would probably include items like salesperson, customer and vehicle information, delivery date, and the date of their last visit to service. Next you could filter or sort the report different ways before printing, saving or exporting the report to MS Excel. *Submitted by Matt Parsons of ADP Dealer Service*

For ACS Customers

The Report Generator is available via each major ACCESS application: Accounting, Parts & Service, and ACSFirst. It is also available via a standalone program if needed.

Upon accessing, the user is prompted to select a report. If the desired report is not available, the user has the option to create a new or edit an existing report. The data is organized into sections (customers, parts inventory, parts invoices, service invoices, deals, etc.).

The Customers tab would be selected in order to create a report containing customer number, first name, and last name. In addition, the VIN and Service Tracking Last Visit Date are accessible via the Deal tab.

Once all fields have been selected, the report is created by selecting an order, current or historical data (current for this example), and the type of report desired, standard text or export to a spreadsheet. *Submitted by Allison Burnett of ACS*

For AutoMate Users

Using AMPS, from the Service Merchandising menu, select Option 20, Report Selection. Select # 1 – Recent Service Visit Report, and input desired date range. You have filtering options such as year, make, salesperson, service advisor, etc., and the option to choose a Detail of History or Summary Report. You can also omit stock vehicles and/or specific labour operations. Sort options are by vehicle ID, customer name, date or service advisor. *Submitted by Scott Berdar of Auto/Mate Dealership Systems*

For AutoSoft International Users

ASI has the ability to generate this report using the Report Generator option. Users have a separate icon on their screen to access the ASI Report Generator. If this icon does not exist they can call the support line and an associate will help them put it on their desktop, as well as create the desired report. Simply check the desired fields to build the report. ASI also has another option which works very well to achieve customer retention with the use of our CSI reporting. This gives the user the ability to print CSI sheets for each customer visiting the service department. This sheet includes name, address, phone number, year, make, model, repair information, and other information, as well as the salesperson. These sheets are then distributed to the salesperson to contact the customer personally, allowing for more accurate reporting on how the service department experience is and also developing a long lasting relationship with the customer. This option is found from the ASI Main Menu, CSI/SSI and then pull CSI data, choose working day and print report. *Submitted by Jim Auld of AutoSoft International*

For Dubuque Data Services Users

Dubuque Data Services provides a user accessible custom report module but most of our clients prefer that we create the report for them, as this is a no0charge service. Our support team will create a report designed to output a customer unit that was sold by a salesperson who has returned to have their unit service by the dealership. The report can show the name, the last time the customer was in for service, the type of work they had done and also the salesperson who sold the unit. This report is customizable to include additional information. *Submitted by Reuel B. Persaud, of Dubuque Data Services*

For Reynolds & Reynolds ERA Users

Using Query Builder and from the service application, select the AA.SER.CUST file. Choose the items dialogue box and select the criteria for date range, labour type, etc. Press the output button and chose the fields you want for the analysis. Don't forget to select the PC/Process in the output area and take note of the folder where the Excel worksheet will be stored. *Submitted by Jim Skeans of Jim Skeans Consulting Group LLC*

Jim Skeans is the president of Jim Skeans Consulting Group LLC and has been in the automobile business for more than 25 years. Jim is a former senior consultant for an international automotive consulting group and has served in all of the traditional dealership management and staff positions as well as director position with a large national dealership group.

Customer Defection can be Stopped: 5 Key Factors

"Reducing customer defections by just 5 %, can increase overall profits by 30%."-Fred Reicheld-"The Loyalty Effect" Great-but most businesses cannot be in control of their future cash flow. Here's why.

Factor 1: According to the 2009 Leaky Bucket Survey from the Restaurant Marketing Group, the industry "Leaky Bucket®" average in 2009 was 36%, up 7% from 2008. This means that in 2009, 36% of past six month users are unsure of returning to a brand! Whilst customers leave for reasons the business cannot control (i.e. moving, death), the majority of customers leave for reasons that aretotally within the control of the restaurant. All businesses have defections-you will be surprised how large the %, and how few know it.

Factor 2: A dissatisfied customer can efficiently trash talk your business to more people, more quickly via new tools like social media. Pete Blackshore's new book sums it up in the title "*Satisfied Customers Tell 3 friends, Angry Customers Tell 3,000*"

Factor 3: Jill Griffen in her book "*Customer Loyalty*" states that the typical business only hears complaints from about 4% of its dissatisfied customers. The remaining 96% go away and 91% never return-so the restaurant won't know it has a problem until it's too late to do anything about it

Factor 4: More alarmingly, a 2008 Gartner study showed that whilst 95% of companies collected feedback (the good news), only 50% alert staff to these findings, only 30% make decisions based on these findings, 10% deploy and improve, and only 5% inform the customer. Why bother collecting anything if no action is taken? Could it be the wrong questions are asked, at the wrong time without analytics?

Factor 5: The ubiquitous coupon is bad news. Not only has it helped lead to the average company investing six times as much in acquiring customers than it does in retaining existing ones-but it simply trains the customer to wait for the next offer. (A Stewart-Fortune Magazine ed. 132). In addition, the full cost impact of discounting, especially when everyone else is doing it, is unlikely to yield a positive return.

So we have the perfect storm-customers who leave, for reasons within our control, who can quickly destroy a reputation-yet the mechanism we choose to employ to stop this, is badly chosen and poorly executed. Today's restaurant operations are hurt, not so much by low acquisition of new customers, but by the defections of their original customer base.

Current customer feedback is the way to go but only if the feedback is scored, anonymous, on premise, in real-time at the point of experience. Forget customer comment cards, social media and review sites, mystery shops, and post purchase surveys. Anything answered after the event is less accurate and less in volume.

I can't remember what I had for breakfast today yet am supposed to be able to recall how a meal was the day before! Twitter and Yelp are just fine for telling a story, but not the basis by which a business makes decisions. And please, please let the user determine if he wants to tell you who he is (or not!)-the more you force him to give up personal details, the more reluctant he is to help. But there is light-let's look to the now. Wouldn't it be profitable if feedback could be gathered, analysed, and acted upon when the customer is still on site, OR the experience still fresh in their memories? Not only would the problem be fixed before it affected others and lead to 'I'm never coming back here again'-but maybe the customer who gave the feedback gets to see the business make the improvement-that's a story you want them to broadcast.

Now you have engaged customers who tell everyone in their networks (for free), and you have a management team that intelligently addresses what needs fixing without the guesswork.

New technologies now available that are cloud based, with no capital needed (for hardware, software, gadgets or widgets), means that the cost per data point of obtaining actionable feedback can be substantially decreased and makes redundant the paper based comment card system. Use of the customer's mobile phone as the input device means fewer errors, provides engagement and differentiation. So now you can have the technology, the application, the analytics and the price point to help solve the biggest issue in restaurant strategy today-customer defection. It's in the palm of your hand.

Ensuring a Customer-focused Corporate Culture

Organizational culture is the workplace environment formulated from the interaction of the employees in the workplace. Organizational culture is defined by all of the life experiences, strengths, weaknesses, education, upbringing, and so forth of the employees. While executive leaders play a large role in defining organizational culture by their actions and leadership, all employees contribute to the organizational culture.

Cultivating a Customer-Focused Corporate Culture

Businesses are increasingly adopting customer-focused business processes to gain competitive advantage. Especially prevalent in industries where product offerings and price no longer provide sufficient differentiation, this new focus offers a myriad of benefits. Customer experience is the battleground, and you can't win with a culture that doesn't truly embrace the concept.

Corporate culture, as any business textbook will tell you, is tricky to define and trickier still to change. Culture can neither be simply imposed on a business nor created by flicking a switch. However, the following key steps can help put your business on the path toward a customer-focused culture.

Cement Your Customer Relationships

To build your business around customers, you need to understand them, so create a regular dialogue. Don't send an annual survey to see if they're satisfied with your products, contact Centre or delivery performance. Talk to them regularly at key points in your relationship with them — when they've made a purchase, called your contact Centre or canceled an order. If you arm yourself with the tools to better understand your customers, you will be better able to act in their best interests.

Talking to customers at regular intervals is not simply about monitoring progress; it is a core part of becoming a business that listens to its customers.

If you don't listen to them, you cannot possibly be focused on them. Listening is only the start. You must act upon what they tell you. Following up an interaction with a survey is a great start, but if your customer tells you they had a poor experience, then you must do something about it. A simple "Thank you for your input" adds insult to injury. Create a process through which you can share feedback with the right people in your organization and put things right.

Involve the Crew

You can't impose a change in culture by sending an email saying "We are now a customer-focused organization." Well, you can try, but the result will be eye-rolling and mockery, not a newly customer-focused culture.

Your employees possess great insight into your customer base and how you treat them. Tap this knowledge base to better understand employee views. Don't limit your outreach to customer-facing staff. A customer-focused culture is not just about providing better customer service at the front line; it is about infusing all your actions as a business with a sense of how the customer is affected by those actions (or lack of them).

Customer feedback is not always welcomed by employees, so get buy-in from them. Too often feedback is understood to be a euphemism for "complaints" and creates only fear and disengagement. When listening to the Voice of the Customer, remember to include and share the positive feedback. While acting on negative feedback may strengthen customer engagement, sharing and acting on positive feedback will strengthen employee engagement. Use feedback as a carrot, not a stick, and feedback will become a welcome motivator that underpins your culture.

Rebuild Your Processes

Evangelizing is just one step in developing a new corporate culture. To engage employees, you must make changes and demonstrate what you're doing. Where customers and employees are telling you that you could be doing something better, take action, and tell them you've taken action. By asking for feedback, you're setting up a level of expectation that you need to meet; otherwise the process is destined to fail. Corporate culture is a long-term consideration, and demonstrating that you're truly investing in change will help to drive further change and engage your employees in the process. The changes you make may be internal or external. For example, feedback may identify a new business process that makes sense to internal stakeholders but confuses or frustrates customers. Alternatively, you may find that some employees don't feel equipped to resolve certain customer queries, which you can address through tailored training and coaching. Share the changes you make with the appropriate audience. The first changes may be hard, but they will speak volumes and start to build a culture which embraces improvement.

Check Your Measurements

Whatever metrics you use to measure success in your business, a handful of them will already be customer-focused. Customer satisfaction, complaint levels and first-call resolution are all commonly used to monitor the way in which companies handle their customers. However, your customer and employee feedback may uncover more intelligent ways to understand customer relationships. Learn how your customers judge their relationship with you, rather than the other way round. For example, they may be less interested in how long your call Centre takes to answer the phone, and more keen to know that the person they speak to can really help them. If the metric matters to your customer, it matters to you.

Whatever metrics you settle on, make them accessible and use them to create common goals. You don't have to share every piece of data with every person in the company, but share the right data with the right people. Use your intranet, reporting dashboards or a portal to show them how their actions affect the customer experience, even if they don't see or talk to customers on a daily basis. If you're basing metrics on feedback data that you're regularly collecting, then your data will always be changing. Show people what's changing and give them the tools they need to check on the data so that it becomes part of their day.

Share Responsibility and Construct a Common Goal

Involvement and engagement build and solidify corporate culture. When employees can identify and resolve failures, they contribute to that culture and help it to become entrenched. Just as change must be demonstrated, so must employees be empowered to take action where necessary in order to be part of building the culture.

The customer must not be seen purely as the domain of the customer service team, so it is crucial to have buy-in from the top level of your business. Not only must executives take the issues seriously, but they must be seen to take it seriously. Some companies have sped the process along by tying financial rewards to the new customer-focused metrics, and having senior executives, as well as front line staff rewarded on the same numbers. Few things say "commitment" like senior people pegging their success on the same figures as the rest of the business.

Changing a corporate culture cannot and should not be an immediate process, and neither can it be a half-hearted one. Businesses that truly dedicate themselves to building a customer-focused culture can be stronger competitively — and provide better places to work.

Eight Traits of a Healthy Organizational Culture

Developed by the Institute for Business, Technology, and Ethics (IBTE)

Any good organization must have an inspiring, shared mission at its core—and it must have capable leadership in place and in development. Assuming these two factors are present, the following eight traits define a healthy corporate or organizational culture.

1. Openness and humility from top to bottom of the organization

   Arrogance kills off learning and growth by blinding us to our own weaknesses. Strength comes out of receptivity and the willingness to learn from others

2. An environment of accountability and personal responsibility

   Denial, blame, and excuses harden relationships and intensify conflict. Successful teams hold each other accountable and willingly accept personal responsibility.

3. Freedom for risk-taking within appropriate limits

   Both extremes—an excessive, reckless risk-taking and a stifling, fearful control—threaten any organization. Freedom to risk new ideas flourishes best within appropriate limits.

4. A fierce commitment to "do it right"

   Mediocrity is easy; excellence is hard work, and there are many temptations for shortcuts. A search for excellence always inspires both inside and outside an organization.

5. A willingness to tolerate and learn from mistakes

   Punishing honest mistakes stifles creativity. Learning from mistakes encourages healthy experimentation and converts negatives into positives.

6. Unquestioned integrity and consistency

   Dishonesty and inconsistency undermine trust. Organizations and relationships thrive on clarity, transparency, honesty, and reliable follow-through.

7. A pursuit of collaboration, integration, and holistic thinking

   Turf wars and narrow thinking are deadly. Drawing together the best ideas and practices, integrating the best people into collaborative teams, multiplies organizational strength.

8. Courage and persistence in the face of difficulty

   The playing field is not always level, or life fair, but healthy cultures remain both realistic about the challenges they face and unintimidated and undeterred by difficulty.

Chapter 8

Strategic Management System

Overview

NASA consists of NASA Headquarters, nine Centres, the Jet Propulsion Laboratory (operated under contract to NASA by the California Institute of Technology), and several ancillary installations and offices in the United States and abroad. As a result of the Agency's decentralized operations, NASA's organization has evolved into a two-tiered structure of Agencywide management: (a) Agency management, including the Administrator, officials within the Office of the Administrator, and Functional Offices; and (b) Enterprise management, including Enterprise Associate Administrators and Centre Directors. The implementation of NASA programs and aeronautical and space/ Earth science and technology research occurs primarily at the Centres.

The success of NASA's missions relies in part on the Agency's four Uquot; Crosscutting Processes. Uquot; These processes are the way we perform our mission. All activity within NASA is contained within one or more of these four processes: provide aerospace products and capabilities, generate knowledge, communicate knowledge, and manage strategically. Policies and procedural guidelines governing these Crosscutting Processes will be found in their respective NPD's and NPG's. NASA's strategic management system is a set of ongoing and interlinked activities that includes strategic planning, implementation performance planning, and performance evaluation.

Strategic Planning

Strategic Planning establishes the direction for all Agency efforts and forms the basis for strategic and tactical decisionmaking, resource allocation, and capital investment. It does so in the context of the

Agency's vision, mission, goals, objectives, values, and policies, as well as external and internal environments. The Strategic Planning process requires alignment among NASA's Strategic Plan, the Enterprise Strategic Plans, programs, and institutional capabilities.

Implementation: Performance and Budget Planning

The implementation planning process produces annual budget formulation guidance and performance plans to achieve the goals and objectives identified during the Strategic Planning process. It is a cyclical process that is ongoing throughout the development of NASA's Strategic Plan and Enterprise Strategic Plans, capital investment plans, and Agency budgets and forms the basis for performance evaluation.

Performance Evaluation and Reporting

NASA's progress in achieving the objectives of its Strategic Plan is routinely evaluated by both internal and external organizations. The Government Performance and Results Act (GPRA) of 1993) requires Federal agencies to submit annual performance plans following the transmittal to Congress of the President's budget. NASA's performance report will reflect the performance goals against which the Agency expects its effectiveness to be measured in any given fiscal year.

Because investments in research and development can yield results 5, 10, and 20 years in the future, NASA's annual performance measures must incorporate measures of both output and outcome, addressing a longer term view than fiscal year by fiscal year. NASA will continue to rely on its internal management councils, its advisory committees, and the National Research Council for assistance in evaluating its performance over extended periods of time.

The performance evaluation process allows NASA to identify potential opportunities for improvement in program execution and process management and to ensure safety and health, efficiency, and effectiveness. Performance evaluation can also yield information that may indicate a need to change the Agency's long-term strategies or near-term objectives. NASA will report publicly on the results of its performance evaluations to the Administration and Congress in an annual performance report.

Roles and Responsibilities

Organizational Overview

NASA's organizational structure encompasses corporate, Agencywide management and the management of NASA's Strategic

Enterprises. Strategic Enterprise management includes the management of NASA's Centres as well as programs and projects. A number of management councils and boards coordinate Agency planning.

Agency Management

Agency management is responsible for Agency leadership, the development of NASA's strategy, and the integrated management of the Strategic Enterprises. It is the external focal point for NASA communication and accountability, serving as the principal interface with the Administration, Congress, and oversight agencies. Agency management integrates the NASA budget, determines long-term institutional investment strategy, sets NASA policy and standards, and ensures Agency functional management.

Agency management defines the Strategic Enterprises and is responsible for reviewing requirements, allocating resources, assessing performance, and setting investment goals across the Enterprises. Executive management authority for the Agency resides with the Administrator, Deputy Administrator, and Associate Deputy Administrator, advised and supported by the staff officials of the Office of the Administrator and the senior-level councils and boards chartered to perform Agency-level integration.

NASA Administrator

The Administrator serves as NASA's chief executive officer, accountable to the President for the leadership necessary to achieve the Agency's mission. This leadership requires articulating the Agency's vision, setting its programmatic and budget priorities and internal policies, and assessing Agency performance. Senior staff officials within the Office of the Administrator include the Deputy Administrator, Associate Deputy Administrator, Chief Engineer, Chief Information Officer, and Chief Scientist.

Senior Management Council

NASA's Senior Management Council is chaired by the Administrator and consists of Associate Administrators, Officials-in-Charge of Headquarters offices, and Centre Directors. This council advises the Administrator on the institutional health of the Agency and the status of its programs and plans and serves as a forum for the discussion of issues affecting Agency management. The council reviews the Agency and Enterprise Strategic Plans, Centre Implementation Plans, and Functional Leadership Plans, and it recommends approval or redirection by the Administrator.

Program Management Council (PMC)

The PMC reviews the readiness of programs in formulation to proceed to implementation according to criteria established through the approval process. The PMC will also review the implementation of selected Enterprise programs and projects, as defined in the Program Commitment Agreement, and functional initiatives referred to it by the Capital Investment Council and requiring Program Commitment Agreements. The review of some programs may be delegated to Centre Program Management Councils. The PMC's formal review process evaluates cost, schedule, technical content, performance, and safety to ensure that NASA meets its programmatic commitments.

Capital Investment Council (CIC)

The CIC examines Agencywide capital investments and policy issues. This includes the balance among Enterprise program investments, crosscutting technology investments, and institutional investments. The CIC ensures an Agency perspective for all large, long-term investments that enable the Agency and the Strategic Enterprises to execute their programs. Investment areas include:

a. Facilities
b. Environmental Management
c. Information Technology
d. Science
e. Technology
f. Human Resources
g. Safety and Occupational Health
h. Other designated investments.

The CIC is the principal advisory group to the Administrator in resolving issues, prioritizing activities (capital investments, Functional Office initiatives, and programs), and balancing resources among the Strategic Enterprises.

The CIC's advice to the Administrator is a significant element of the Agency's detailed implementation planning process and during the budget development process. The council resolves or recommends options to the Administrator on issues among the Enterprises, Functional Offices, and Centres, or combinations thereof, in terms of Agency investment in assets or functional capabilities. The council also reviews major Functional Office initiatives and reviews and recommends budget guidance initiating each annual budget cycle. When these reviews are required, the council will consider, among other criteria, the cumulative effect a proposed initiative will have on Agency resources. The Administrative Issues Board provides support for this review activity.

Significant augmentation of a Centre of Excellence facility, human resource levels and skill mix, and proposals to change or designate new Centres of Excellence are all Agency investment decisions, on which the CIC makes formal recommendations to the Administrator.

Other Councils of the Office of the Administrator

The Administrator also has chartered the following councils, which are chaired by individuals from the Office of the Administrator or the Chief Financial Officer (CFO).

Science Council

The Science Council, chaired by the Chief Scientist, coordinates NASA's science activities, promotes public communication, and ensures the quality of the Agency's science program. This council advises the Administrator on all aspects of science related to NASA's flight and ground programs.

The Science Council serves as a forum for reviewing Agency policies, practices, and issues as they relate to science activities; communicating and discussing interdisciplinary science goals and the national and international policies that guide their development; and integrating science plans. The council also participates in the Agency's process of developing recommendations for Agency-level science priorities and budgets. It shares information about operational areas of the Agency's Strategic Enterprises as they relate to the quality and content of the science program.

Technology Leadership Council

The Technology Leadership Council, chaired by the Associate Administrator for Aero-Space Technology, advises the Administrator on all material aspects of technology related to NASA's flight and ground programs.

It coordinates NASA's technology activities, including advanced research and development, across Enterprises and promotes public communication of NASA's technology programs. The Technology Leadership Council also serves as a forum for reviewing Agency policies, practices, and issues as they relate to technology activities, communicating and discussing technology goals and the national policies that guide their development, and integrating technology plans. The council participates in the Agency's process of developing recommendations for technology priorities across Enterprise budgets for technology and supports the CIC with recommendations for Centre of Excellence designation.

Engineering Management Council

The Engineering Management Council, chaired by the Chief Engineer, is a forum for assessing and improving Agency engineering practices, policies, training and certification standards, procedures, and capabilities. When requested by the chair of the PMC or the Chief Engineer, this council conducts or supports independent technical reviews of NASA programs and technology/advanced development activities.

Space Operations Council

The Space Operations Council, chaired by the Chief Engineer, serves as a forum for assessing and improving Agency space operations policies, practices, standards, procedures, and capabilities, while providing Agencywide policy guidance for activities associated with NASA operations. This council also provides policy guidance and recommends issue resolution to the NASA space operations management organization that provides operational mission support to all NASA Enterprises.

Space Transportation Council

The Space Transportation Council, chaired by the Chief Engineer, advises the Administrator and coordinates all aspects of space transportation investments related to NASA's flight and ground technology programs.

The council serves as a forum for establishing and reviewing Agency and interagency policies, practices, and issues related to space transportation requirements and technology development. The council also defines an investment plan necessary for space transportation technology development and system upgrades and participates in the Agency process of developing recommendations for transportation technology priorities and advanced development programs across the individual Enterprises.

Information Technology Investment Council

The Information Technology Investment Council, chaired by the Chief Information Officer, is responsible for establishing Agency-level information technology policies, plans, and standards. This council approves NASA's information technology plans and conducts reviews of proposed major information technology investments required to accomplish these plans. The council also serves as the supporting panel for information technology and provides recommendations on proposed information technology investments to the CIC. With the support of this council, the Chief Information Officer provides leadership and advice to the Administrator and other senior officials for information technology plans, policies, and standards, as well as for assessing returns on information technology investments in terms of mission outcomes or support.

Information Technology Security (ITS) Council

The ITS Council, co-chaired by the Chief Information Officer and the Chief Infrastructure Assurance Officer (currently the Associate Administrator for Management Systems), is responsible for the coordination of Agency unclassified and classified ITS efforts. With the support of this council, the Chief Information Officer and the Associate Administrator for Management Systems provide support and advice to the Administrator and other senior officials for ITS.

Chief Financial Officer Council

The Chief Financial Officer Council, chaired by the CFO, is responsible for improving financial and resource management, strengthening communications, improving coordination, and promoting professional development. The council advises and coordinates the activities of the Agency on such matters as the development and implementation of financial and budget systems, the improvement of the quality of financial and resources information, financial data and information standards, management controls, professional development standards, and any other matters that will facilitate financial and resources management excellence.

Internal Senior Management Boards

To coordinate and support Agency wide management in certain key areas, NASA has established internal Senior Management Boards, which are chaired by one of NASA's Associate Administrators or, in selected cases, by a designated senior Agency official. These boards include, but are not limited to:

a. Administrative Issues Board

b. Agency Performance Review Board

c. Chief Information Officer Representatives Board

d. Environmental Management Board
e. Equal Employment Opportunity Board
f. Facilities Review Board
g. Flight Assignment Board
h. Integrated Financial Management Board
i. Medical Policy Board
j. Occupational Health and Safety Executive Board
k. Space Station Utilization Board.

Enterprise Management

NASA has established the four Strategic Enterprises to function in primary business areas for implementing NASA's mission and serving customers. Each Enterprise has a unique set of strategic goals, objectives, and implementing strategies that address the requirements of the Agency's primary customers.

Enterprise Associate Administrators/Institutional Program Officers

The Enterprise Associate Administrators are accountable for delivering program results to the NASA Administrator. As such, they serve as the stewards, advocates, and chief executives of their respective Enterprises, setting Enterprise priorities and strategies for achieving them. In addition, the Strategic Enterprises provide program definition (requirements, opportunities for cross-program efficiency, and synergy). They are responsible for the safety and human health of their Enterprise's activities, integrated Enterprise budget development, program resource allocation, performance assessment, policies and standards, and the implementation of NASA policies.

The Enterprise Associate Administrator is the senior official in the Enterprise with principal responsibility for developing long-term strategy and ensuring that the necessary capabilities are in place to meet both the near-term program objectives and the longer term goals.

As the Enterprise leader, the Associate Administrator determines what the Enterprise does and why, with a specific focus on the requirements of external customers. In this context, the Enterprise Associate Administrators are responsible for:

a. Developing Enterprise strategy, policy, and standards that fulfill the Agency's goals and objectives
b. Formulating program requirements and objectives

c. Providing advocacy for the Enterprise
d. Providing external/customer interfaces
e. Allocating resources for the full cost of each program, including personnel and facilities, within the context of Agency strategic determinations
f. Assessing program performance
g. Selecting projects
h. Serving as the NASA "internal customer"
i. Making Lead Centre assignments for the Administrator's approval
j. Overseeing Enterprise education and public Outreach
k. Coordinating interactions between the Office of Management and Budget and NASA's Office of the Chief Financial Officer
l. Coordinating interactions between Congress and NASA's Office of Legislative Affairs
m. Coordinating all international partnership arrangements with the Office of External Relations.

The Associate Administrators for Space Science, Earth Science, and Life and Microgravity Sciences and Applications have oversight of NASA's scientific research programs. These Associate Administrators' responsibilities in science research include strategic planning, implementation and performance planning, the selection of missions and investigations, and the ongoing evaluation of research activities.

The Associate Administrator for Life and Microgravity Sciences and Applications is also responsible for all Agency health activities. Enterprise Associate Administrators are responsible for managing program initiation, formulation and integration, science management, and program oversight and performance assessment. The Centres are responsible for program implementation on behalf of their respective Enterprise Associate Administrator.

When a Strategic Enterprise consists of multiple Headquarters organizations, a Lead Associate Administrator is appointed who is responsible for setting policy and requirements guidance for that Enterprise. The Associate Administrator for Space Flight is the Lead Associate Administrator for the Human Exploration and Development of Space (HEDS) Enterprise and is responsible for an integrated human exploration and development of space strategy. The Associate Administrator for Life and Microgravity Sciences and Applications reports to the NASA Administrator and is a key member of the HEDS

Enterprise. In this instance, the Associate Administrator is not an Enterprise Associate Administrator, but has the full responsibilities of an Enterprise Associate Administrator for programmatic activities in the areas of life sciences, agency health activities, microgravity sciences, and associated space product and commercial development.

To ensure alignment between programs and institutional capabilities, the Administrator will normally designate the Enterprise Associate Administrator for the predominant activity at each Centre that Centre's Institutional Program Officer. As an Institutional Program Officer, the Associate Administrator is responsible for ensuring that the Centre has the capability to meet its programmatic and functional commitments, as well as long-term mission responsibilities, in a safe and effective manner.

The Institutional Program Officer/Associate Administrator is also responsible for implementation, conformance, and the assurance of safe and efficient functional operations. Enterprise Associate Administrators serving as Institutional Program Officers must have a broader perspective than their individual Strategic Enterprises.

In this management capacity, the Institutional Program Officer works with the Centres, other Enterprise Associate Administrators, and Functional Offices to:

a. Provide safe and healthful workplaces and environmentally sound work processes
b. Plan long-term institutional strategies
c. Determine institutional and infrastructure investment requirements
d. Pursue integration and synergies, crosscutting strategies, and investments across multiple Centres
e. Approve institutional budgets proposed by the Centre
f. Develop a long-term institutional investment strategy
g. Determine major adjustments to and trade-offs among the programs and institutions within overall budget availability
h. Assess the performance of the Centre in meeting its mission and Centre of Excellence responsibilities
i. Review Functional Office initiatives, as a member of the Administrative Issues Board.

Each Institutional Program Officer also ensures a broad perspective by providing the opportunity for all the Enterprises that have work at the Centre to participate in institutional decision processes. These processes encompass policy decisions, allocation of common resources, approval of the Centre's institutional operations budgets, and recommendations on proposed capital investments, including determining fund sources.

Centres and Centre Directors

NASA's Centres are responsible for the safety and occupational health of their workforce and for the safe implementation of the Agency plans, programs, and activities of the Strategic Enterprises. Centres of Excellence and Centre missions are two key concepts in the management of NASA. NASA's Centre Directors are responsible for program management and execution. They determine how Enterprise programs and central services will be implemented. Centre Directors manage the institution (including capability development and maintenance), manage multi-Enterprise resources, implement functional leadership and central service activities, and implement NASA, Strategic Enterprise, and Agency-level functional policies.

In collaboration with Agency-level Functional Offices, the Centre Directors will establish oversight and evaluations of Centre functions through self-assessments, ISO 9000 audits, performance metrics, or other requirements identified.

The Centre Directors serve as both members of the Senior Management Council and as heads of their respective Centres. In this latter role, they have primary management responsibility in three areas: program management (determining how programs are accomplished), institutional infrastructure (maintaining and enhancing both human and physical resources), and the assurance of the Agency's capabilities in assigned Centres of Excellence.

Centre Missions

Centre missions identify the primary area of concentration of each Centre's capabilities. A Centre mission is a long-term responsibility. The Centre Directors are responsible for building and maintaining human and physical resources to support their Centres' missions. Enterprise program and project assignments are based on mission designations. The Administrator assigns the Centre missions. In implementing its mission, the Centre may capitalize on capabilities residing at supporting Centres or outside of NASA, as necessary, to provide the cost-effective implementation of its mission. Designated Centre Mission Areas and Centres of Excellence are listed in Appendix A.

Lead Centre Directors for Programs

Each NASA program involving more than one Centre is assigned to a Lead Centre for implementation. NASA program Lead Centre assignments are selected by the Enterprise Associate Administrator and approved by the Administrator. In making such assignments, the Enterprise Associate Administrators will consider Centre mission and Centre of Excellence responsibilities. (Lead Centre designations for NASA's current programs are listed in Appendix C.) Lead Centre Directors have full program management responsibility and authority. They are fully accountable for ensuring that assigned programs are managed to agreed-on schedule milestones, budget guidelines, technical requirements, and all safety and reliability standards.

The Enterprise Associate Administrators must configure each program so that it can be efficiently and effectively accomplished within the framework of Lead Centre assignments and funding allocations. The level and number of Enterprise Associate Administrator—controlled requirements must be consistent with safety, mission success, customer expectations, and statutory and regulatory requirements. The Lead Centre Directors, in turn, establish supporting assignments for other Centres (Supporting Centres), considering Centre mission and Centre of Excellence responsibilities. The Centre Directors delegate management responsibility to the Program Managers who report to them.

Centres of Excellence

Centre of Excellence designation represents exceptional Agency capabilities in certain areas of science, engineering, or technology. These capabilities include personnel, facilities, and tools and may reside at more than one NASA Centre. The exceptional capabilities a Centre of Excellence represents are expected to serve the needs of the Enterprises as well as NASA's strategic objectives, and they are the responsibility of the Centre Director.

A NASA Centre designated as a Centre of Excellence is responsible for planning and, as permitted by available resources, maintaining or augmenting the personnel skills, facilities, and tools required to sustain its area of excellence. A Centre of Excellence's implementation plan must be prepared at the Centre and approved by that Centre's Enterprise Associate Administrator/Institutional Program Officer. It will include strategies for advocating, coordinating, collaborating among, and, where cost-effective, consolidating Agency capabilities supporting a particular Centre of Excellence designation. Agency investment decisions in such areas as facilities development, human resource levels, and skill mix will consider and support such consolidations.

The Institutional Program Officer is responsible for ensuring the viability of the Centres of Excellence in keeping with NASA's Strategic Plan. Normally, Centre of Excellence issues, including plans to cover resource shortfalls, will be resolved at the Strategic Enterprise/ Institutional Program Office level.

However, significant adjustments in Centre of Excellence assignments, personnel levels or skills, facilities, funding, and tools are all Agency investment decisions to be recommended to the Administrator by the CIC, supported for this purpose by the Technology Leadership Council.

Proposals to change or to designate new Centres of Excellence will be based on annual assessments conducted by the Centre Director, as well as on reviews involving corresponding external expertise, which must be conducted every 3 years. Criteria used in assessments and reviews of Centres of Excellence will include record of performance, competitiveness with external sources of equivalent capabilities, adequacy of resources, and extent of support for NASA's Enterprises and strategic objectives.

Program and Project Managers

The Program Manager ensures the most expeditious and cost-effective implementation approach for a program, consistent with safety and taking into account Centre of Excellence capabilities and Centre mission assignments. Program Managers are selected by, and report to, the Lead Centre Director. If more than one project exists within a program, they are managed by Project Managers who report to the Program Manager. Project Managers are selected by the responsible Centre Director. For programs and projects covered under NPD 7120.4 and NPG 7120.5, refer to these documents for the detailed responsibilities and procedures for specific program and project managers.

Centre Scientists

While overall science management and direction resides with the science Enterprise Associate Administrators, as discussed in section 2.3.1, flight and ground systems development and operations management responsibilities are delegated to the Centres.

NASA's Centre scientists provide enabling support to the broader space research community by serving as project scientists and operating unique Centre facilities.

In addition, Centre scientists may compete with external researchers for funding to conduct original research of their own (including instrument development) that also maintains their scientific currency. Agency policies and guidelines for science program management are provided in NPD 1080 and NPG 1080, currently under development.

Functional Management

The Headquarters Functional Office Associate Administrators and Officials-in-Charge are the Administrator's principal advisors for their areas of responsibility. They establish plans to improve functional performance across the Agency, disseminate internal Agency policies, and, in collaboration with the Enterprise Associate Administrators and Centre Directors, maintain sufficient insight into Enterprise and Institutional Program Office activities to ensure that they are conducted in accordance with all statutory, regulatory, and fiduciary responsibilities. In addition, these officials advise the Administrator and senior managers of potential efficiencies and required compliance to be gained by implementing proposed functional initiatives.

Headquarters Functional Offices include the Offices of the Chief Financial Officer, Chief Engineer, Chief Information Officer, and Chief Scientist, as well as Headquarters Operations, Equal Opportunity Programs, Human Resources and Education, General Counsel, Procurement, External Relations, Management Systems, Small and Disadvantaged Business Utilization, Legislative Affairs, Public Affairs, Safety and Mission Assurance, and Policy and Plans. The Associate Administrator for Management Systems serves as the Agency's Chief Infrastructure Assurance Officer.

Functional Office activities fall into any or all of three major categories: functional leadership, staff to the Administrator, and central services across the Agency. The Office of Headquarters Operations will be responsible for matters pertaining to the planning, execution, and evaluation of the management of the Headquarters institution.

As functional leaders, Functional Office Associate Administrators and Officials-in-Charge focus on improving processes, stimulating efficiency in the performance of activities related to the programs, and providing consistency, when consistency serves Agency management objectives, across the Strategic Enterprises. They oversee the performance of their particular functions across all of the Centres, as well as provide liaison to external organizations performing similar functions and stakeholders who establish Government wide policy and requirements.

Central services for specific functional activities are offered to gain efficiencies and to eliminate redundancy across the Agency. The decision to provide a function centrally (for example, Agency wide payroll processing) is made by the Administrator, on the CIC's recommendation, on a case-by-case basis showing a clear benefit to the Agency.

A Functional Office or Strategic Enterprise may provide central services. Such services include staff support, training, internal communications, and consolidated mainframe computing operations. The CIC will recommend a control mechanism (such as a memorandum of understanding) for the service provision. Once established, the service provision will be evaluated annually as part of the budget process and continued on the basis of cost-effective support to Agency customer requirements.

Principal Centres may be established to lead particular functional leadership operations. The Functional Office selects the Centre that can best execute the function on behalf of NASA and submits that selection, with the concurrence of the Institutional Program Office Associate Administrator and the Associate Administrator for Headquarters Operations, to the Deputy Administrator for approval. Delegations of authority to conduct these responsibilities are negotiated and documented with memoranda of understanding, signed by the Functional Office Associate Administrator or Official-in-Charge, the Institutional Program Office Associate Administrator, the Associate Administrator for Headquarters Operations, and the Centre Director. The memoranda of understanding must contain provisions for direction and funding flow, as well as performance review.

The Principal Centre Director, in turn, may establish supporting assignments for other Centres (Supporting Centres) considering their particular functional capability.

The memoranda of understanding must stipulate that budget processes will follow guidance provided by the Headquarters Office of the Chief Financial Officer and Office of Headquarters Operations. (Principal Centre designations for NASA's current programs and processes are listed in Appendix B.)

Crosscutting Process Management

NASA recognizes that the broad application of certain operating principles can enhance the returns on its work toward diverse programmatic and functional objectives. As a framework for operating in accordance with these principles, NASA has grouped the following major activities into four "Crosscutting Processes":

a. Manage Strategically
b. Provide Aerospace Products and Capabilities
c. Generate Knowledge
d. Communicate Knowledge.

The Administrator assigns stewardship responsibilities for the Crosscutting Processes. These responsibilities have been assigned to:

- Associate Administrator for Policy and Plans—Manage Strategically
- Chief Engineer—Provide Aerospace Products and Capabilities
- Chief Scientist—Generate Knowledge
- Chief Scientist—Communicate Knowledge.

Manage Strategically

No NASA organization can succeed for long unless NASA succeeds. Inter organization coordination and collaboration are essential to defining common strategic goals and operating principles, implementation planning, and achieving mission success. To bring about Agency wide coordination and collaboration among all of its organizational units, the Agency designed the Strategic Management System that is described in this NASA Procedures and Guidelines directive (NPG 1000.2).

The stewardship of NASA's strategic management process is the responsibility of the Office of Policy and Plans. The process is implemented by all NASA organizations as indicated in this directive (NPG 1000.2).

The scope of NASA's commitment to managing strategically is far-reaching and all-inclusive. The process includes the roles and responsibilities of Agency and Enterprise management as well as Functional Offices.

The Office of Policy and Plans is responsible for scheduling and coordinating an orderly, well-documented, and inclusive Agency process to update every 3 years the Agency's Strategic Plan and, as needed, its strategic management guidelines (NPG 1000.2). This office also collaborates with the Office of the Chief Financial Officer to define and apply assessment tools to evaluate its performance.

Provide Aerospace Products and Capabilities

NASA conducts aerospace programs to provide aeronautical and space technology to researchers, industry, and the general public. Provide Aerospace Products and Capabilities is NASA's process for delivering systems (for example, aeronautics, space and ground), technologies, data, and operational services to NASA customers. Management policies, procedures, and guidelines for the formulation, approval, implementation, and evaluation of NASA programs and projects are provided in NPD 7120.4 and NPG 7120.5.

Generate Knowledge

NASA conducts and supports basic and applied research to extend the boundaries of knowledge of science, technology, and engineering, to capture new knowledge in useful and transferable media, and to share new knowledge with customers.

This Crosscutting Process provides a framework for ensuring that the research is consistent with the Agency's strategic plans and that the quality of the research is maintained to the highest standards. Directives and guidelines for the Generate Knowledge process will be in NPD 1080.x and NPG 1080.x.

Communicate Knowledge

The Communicate Knowledge process coordinates, integrates, disseminates, and shares consistent information and experiences about the content, relevance, results, applications, and excitement of NASA's mission of research, development, education, and exploration. This process will be described in greater detail in NPD 1090.x and NPG 1090.x.

NASA and Its Employees: Mutual Responsibilities

The success of NASA's strategic plans, performance plans, and Strategic Management System, depends on the active support of all Agency employees. NASA management conducts the Agency's planning activities in an inclusive, open, and well-documented manner.

All employees, including managers and executives, are responsible for familiarizing themselves with their respective Agency, Enterprise, Functional Office, and Centre plans. NASA makes an investment with each employee. Employee development is an essential form of capital investment for the Agency.

Office of Inspector General

NASA's Office of Inspector General (OIG) is an independent organization with responsibility to detect fraud, waste, abuse, and mismanagement, while promoting economy, efficiency, and effectiveness in the Agency's programs and operations. The OIG conducts audits, criminal investigations, inspections, and assessments. The OIG staffs are located at NASA Headquarters, all NASA Centres, the Jet Propulsion Laboratory, and some ancillary offices. Additional information about OIG activities can be found in NPD 9800.1.

Strategic Planning

NASA's purpose as an Agency of the U.S. Government is defined by its enabling statute, the National Aeronautics and Space Act of 1958, as amended. This and other Federal statutes and regulations elaborate on the kinds of programs Congress and the President have directed NASA to carry out, as well as the regulations that govern how NASA manages the national resources entrusted to it by the American people.

Not long after it was established, the Agency undertook the first in a series of long-range plans to ensure that it used those resources effectively, not only to meet current expectations, but also in anticipation of future needs. These long-range plans evolved into the NASA Strategic Plan.

The Government Performance and Results Act of 1993

In 1993, Congress passed the Government Performance and Results Act (GPRA) to "improve the confidence of the American people in the capability of the Federal Government, by systematically holding Federal agencies accountable for achieving program results... [by] setting program goals, measuring program performance against those goals, and reporting publicly on their progress." GPRA requires the following of Federal agencies (including NASA):

a. Develop periodic Agency strategic plans, setting forth NASA's mission, long-term goals, and associated resource requirements. The Strategic Plan is to "cover a period of not less than 5 years forward from the fiscal year in which it was submitted." Updated Strategic Plans must be submitted every 3 years.
b. Prepare and submit to the President and Congress annual performance plans that establish performance goals, measurable objectives, and associated resources required to achieve long-term goals.

c. Submit annual performance reports that "set forth the performance indicators established in the Agency performance plan... along with the actual program performance achieved." When performance goals have not been achieved, explanations should be provided, along with plans for meeting the unattained goals, or reasons for revising performance goals.

NASA Strategic Planning Requirements

In response to GPRA, the Strategic Plans developed for the Agency and the Strategic Enterprises will contain:

a. A comprehensive mission statement covering NASA's major functions and operations
b. General goals and objectives, including outcome-related goals and objectives, for major functions and operations
c. A description of how the goals and objectives are to be achieved
d. An identification of those key factors, external to the Agency and beyond its control, that could significantly affect the achievement of the general goals and objectives
e. The program evaluations used in establishing or revising general goals and objectives.

NASA's Strategic Plan

NASA's Strategic Plan articulates the Agency's vision, mission, goals, and objectives, as well as Agency wide strategies for achieving them. In so doing, it gives direction to the work of all NASA organizations and employees. Strategic planning is a continuous process. NASA's Strategic Plan is fully reviewed and updated at least every 3 years. Interim adjustments may be made as needed, in parallel with the annual performance planning process.

Enterprise Strategic Plans

Enterprise Strategic Plans will elaborate on their respective missions and goals, in alignment with NASA's Strategic Plan, with detailed objectives, implementing strategies, and brief descriptions of their principal programs and/or processes. They must be signed by their respective Enterprise Associate Administrators. Enterprise Strategic Plans will be reviewed by the Office of Policy and Plans for consistency with NASA's Strategic Plan and other Enterprise Strategic Plans. Enterprise Strategic Plans are reviewed by the Senior Management Council and approved by the Administrator. To ensure that they remain current, Enterprise plans will be reviewed and updated as part of any update to the NASA Strategic Plan, but in any event, not less than every 3 years.

Capital Investment Planning

NASA has established an Agency wide capital investment planning process because the size, scope, time horizon, and technical nature of these investments are critical to long-term Agency viability. In addition, such investments must be balanced across NASA organizations and prioritized on an Agency wide basis, consistent with external financial constraints and partnership opportunities. This planning process also supports NASA compliance with related Federal guidance on capital/ asset investments (Office of Management and Budget.

Capital investment planning represents a key activity in the strategic management process and an important element of NASA's 5-year financial planning and budget activities. NASA's Capital Investment Council (CIC) advises the Administrator during preparation of the Agency's Program Operating Plan (POP) guidance at the beginning of the implementation planning process and during the annual budget development process. The council meets as often as the chair deems appropriate. Its meetings will examine interrelated Agency wide issues, such as information technology and security, critical infrastructure protection, human resources, technical capabilities, high-risk generic technologies, Functional Office initiatives, and facilities.

The CIC ensures the integration of Enterprise, Centre of Excellence, and other investment plans; it reviews and recommends investments and provides guidance to NASA entities for subsequent implementation. The council also examines such proposals as Agency-level downsizing or restructuring. The implementation planning process produces annual budget formulation guidance and performance plans to achieve the goals and objectives identified during the Strategic Planning process. It is a cyclical process that is ongoing throughout the development of NASA's Strategic Plan and Enterprise Strategic Plans, capital investment plans, and Agency budgets and forms the basis for performance evaluation.

Functional Office Planning

The Functional Offices formulate Functional Leadership Plans, with Enterprise support, to implement the Agency's Strategic Plan, improve Agency management, and respond to new external direction. A Functional Leadership Plan establishes the overall purpose and direction of functional activities, including goals, objectives, and performance metrics or indicators used to assess success. It is based on the Enterprise Strategic Plans, self-assessments, and externally mandated requirements. Each plan must include a general description of proposed and statutorily required functional initiatives deemed necessary to implement the Agency Strategic Plan and statutory mandates. The Senior Management Council must receive a presentation of and concur with the Functional Leadership Plans, and then the Administrator must approve them. The plans are updated, reviewed, and approved again as required by the Administrator.

Following presentation to and concurrence with the Functional Leadership Plans by the Senior Management Council and approval by the Administrator, decision and guidance are to be documented for inclusion in the NASA POP guidance and, in the case of new policies, for formal coordination and dissemination. The Functional Offices also ensure that the appropriate metrics or performance indicators are developed to evaluate function performance.

Implementation Planning

Performance and Budget Planning Process

Implementation planning ensures that the detailed planning, resources, and performance expectations are aligned to support the achievement of the NASA and Enterprise Strategic Plans. Implementation planning is based on the previous cycle of NASA and Enterprise Strategic Plans, capital investment planning, the 5-year Agency budget, and the results of the ongoing performance evaluation process. Essential elements of implementation planning include program planning to establish technical, schedule, and cost, as well as performance criteria at all management levels. NASA's budget planning process is the vehicle for integrating these implementation plans.

Five-Year Budget Planning Overview

NASA's budget planning is an ongoing process that incorporates a detailed analysis of current requirements with outyear projections of funding needs. Each budget cycle is initiated by guidance from OMB that includes planning estimates, as well as policy guidance for the preparation of the Agency's budget request. This broad guidance uses the 5-year runout of the President's budget request for NASA before Congress at the time, and it updates the total to reflect further economic policy or program decisions that may have been made.

Agency guidance for allocations among the Strategic Enterprises, priorities for decisionmaking and trade-offs, and any broad strategy issues are developed to initiate both the internal planning and budget processes. The Administrator issues this guidance, with full participation and advice of the CIC, through the Agency CFO. The CFO and Comptroller then integrate the Administrator's guidance with more detailed programmatic and funding guidance provided by the Strategic Enterprises and the Functional Offices. The multi year budget estimates, program assumptions, and strategic direction establish a baseline for planning and budget formulation activities and are distributed as guidelines to the NASA Centres.

Responding to Program Operating Plan (POP) guidance from the CFO, the Centres assess their program planning and develop integrated resource requirements with the assistance of their respective Institutional Program Offices. They review these requirements with the Lead Centres and incorporate Lead Centre decisions. The Lead Centres submit integrated resource recommendations to their Enterprise Associate Administrators and Institutional Program Officers for integration into the Agency's annual submission of its 5-year budget. Coordination among the Strategic Enterprises and the Functional Offices enables a comprehensive Agency budget submission that is reflected in Program Commitment Agreements, Program and Project Plans, and institutional planning.

As the budget formulation process proceeds, decisions must be made about activities that have been formulated—for example, whether they can be afforded within the guideline level and those that will be proposed as over-guideline activities. Each Strategic Enterprise must justify the relevance of the requested programs to the NASA and Enterprise Strategic Plans. New initiative candidates must be prioritized. The approval of such initiatives for inclusion in the Agency budget generally is subject to their having reached an appropriate stage of maturity in the formulation processes outlined in NPG 7120.5, as applicable. In their capacity as principal advisors to the Administrator in their respective subject areas, the Chief Scientist, Chief Information Officer, and Chief Engineer will review the Agency budget proposals and evaluate them for science, information systems, and engineering merit.

The final budget request transmitted to OMB reflects this decision process for the entire Agency. The budget process will be compatible with NASA's Strategic Plan. The content of the budget request describes the way in which the Administrator plans to achieve progress toward meeting the goals and objectives that appear in the NASA Strategic Plan within the multi year funding allowance available. The Administrator approves the final 5-year budget submittal.

Performance Planning

GPRA requires the submission of an Agency Performance Plan, following the transmittal to Congress of the President's budget. This annual Performance Plan sets out measurable goals that define what will be accomplished during a fiscal year. The goals should reflect a level of accomplishment commensurate with the resources requested and subsequently funded. For a fiscal year, at least two iterations of NASA's annual Performance Plan are prepared: an initial plan (submitted along with the NASA budget request to OMB) and a final plan that reflects budget, policy, and programmatic decisions and is consistent with the President's budget.

A final plan revised to reflect congressional action on an agency's budget request is not required by GPRA, but may be submitted by NASA, if necessary, early in the new fiscal year.

Developing and Issuing Guidance

The development of implementation guidelines flows from the approval of the Agency and Enterprise Strategic Plans and approved Functional Leadership Plans. Annually, the NASA Administrator issues guidance to the Enterprise Associate Administrators and the Functional Office Associate Administrators and Officials-in-Charge, consistent with those plans. The Strategic Enterprises and Functional Offices, in turn, translate the Administrator's guidance into a set of technical, managerial, and budgetary guidelines.

Agency Guidance

The Administrator's guidance initiates the implementation planning cycle. This guidance is developed taking into account the results of the prior-year planning cycle, new guidance from OMB, and any significant changes in the Agency's external and/or internal environment. The NASA Administrator's guidance will also be influenced by policy and budget recommendations to the President from the National Science and Technology Council and preliminary discussions with Congress. In developing NASA's POP guidance, the Administrator establishes first-order priorities for program content, also giving consideration to information received from senior management.

On behalf of the Administrator, the NASA Office of the Chief Financial Officer (CFO) integrates the budget guidance from OMB, the Administrator's guidance, the specific programmatic guidance from the Enterprises, institutional guidance from the Institutional Program Offices, and guidance from Functional Offices into the integrated NASA

POP guidance. The resulting POP guidance will contain directions for preparing and submitting budget and Performance Plan data, including formats and due dates. This guidance reflects prior-year budget plans and capital investment decisions documented by the CIC. It also includes additional guidance for potential new initiatives, an investment profile for ongoing programs, performance goals, and associated metrics.

Performance and Budget Decisionmaking Process

Enterprise Decisionmaking

The Strategic Enterprises integrate program planning and resource planning during the budget process. The Enterprises make a series of preliminary program decisions in response to changes in funding, new program emphases, and ongoing performance—decisions that are reflected in the POP guidance to the Centres. Once the Enterprise offices have received their Centres' budget requirements in response to the POP call, they work with their Lead Centres to balance anticipated resources with activities identified during implementation planning. This will entail integration and adjustment of Centre implementation plans with Enterprise customer requirements and expected resources.

The Institutional Program Offices are responsible for forwarding funding requirements and corresponding implementation plans from the Centres to the appropriate Functional Offices. This assists the Functional Offices in identifying needs for conflicts of a functional or institutional nature. The Functional Offices are responsible for advising and making recommendations to the Institutional Program Offices on the Centre budget submissions. Functional Office reviews may also be used to develop associated performance measures or indicators. Enterprise Associate Administrators then reallocate resources among programs and revise performance requirements as necessary to establish performance baselines. This integrated package of performance objectives and resource requirements is subsequently provided to the Administrator, through the Office of the Chief Financial Officer.

Functional Office Implementation Planning

Functional Office implementation planning defines activities required to implement the Functional Leadership Plans. In collaboration with the Strategic Enterprises and Centres, the Functional Offices ensure that Agency activities are conducted in accordance with all statutory and regulatory requirements and fiduciary responsibilities.

Functional Office initiatives are efforts developed or sponsored by Functional Offices to meet new requirements, improve a current process or procedure, adapt to externally imposed mandates, or recognize evolving functional standards or trends. Such initiatives can reasonably be expected to have a significant Agency wide impact on personnel, resources, or organizations outside the Functional Office developing or sponsoring the initiative. Because the cumulative impact of functional initiatives on the Agency's program and institutional resources may be substantial, proposed functional initiatives require thorough Agency discussion and review prior to approval. The heads of Functional Offices developing initiatives likely to have a significant Agency wide impact on personnel, resources, or organizations outside the originating Functional Office must meet with the affected organization(s) to determine whether agreement on the initiative's implementation can be reached. If the affected organizations reach agreement, which must have the documented concurrence of the cognizant Institutional Program Officers and/or Officials-in-Charge, implementation shall proceed in accordance with the agreement.

If agreement is not reached, the Functional Office shall prepare a statement of need, along with an estimate of the costs and a projection of the benefits of the initiative, and submit this statement to the CIC for review. The Administrative Issues Board serves as staff to the CIC for these reviews and may, for significant initiatives, request a more detailed implementation plan, including, as appropriate, the scope, resource requirements (human, financial, and physical), a schedule, the impact on the Centres and Enterprises, the potential impact on other proposed or ongoing activities, and the expected return on investment. The Administrative Issues Board may also ask those Enterprises or Centres that do not agree to the initiative's implementation for their analyses of the impacts on resources, operations, or other Enterprise- or Centre-related activities.

The CIC ensures the integration of requirements with the support of the Administrative Issues Board. The CIC also prioritizes funding to be included in the budget guidance during the annual budget development and review cycle. If the CIC supports the initiative, the CIC will recommend the proposal to the Administrator for approval and integration into NASA's budget request. The CIC may recommend to the Administrator that the proposing office create a Program Commitment Agreement, which will define the Program Management Council's review requirements. Program Commitment Agreements will be signed by the proposing office Associate Administrator or Official-in-Charge and the Administrator after formulation and prior to implementation. If the CIC does not support the initiative, the proposing Associate Administrator or Official-in-Charge may appeal directly to the Administrator. Required initiatives originating from external requirements or from the Administrator's direction shall be reviewed by the CIC, with support from the Administrative Issues Board, for impact and implementation issues only.

Agency Performance Plan and Budget Submission

NASA's annual Performance Plan integrates the performance plans provided by the Agency's Strategic Enterprises. Consistent with GPRA requirements, this plan includes:

a. Performance goals
b. Level of performance to be achieved during the budget year
c. Specific nonprogrammatic actions planned within the time frame and fiscal scope of the proposed budget
d. Performance indicators to measure or otherwise evaluate Agency performance.

The annual goals, performance objectives, and associated information included in this plan will be grouped by Strategic Enterprise and Crosscutting Process. Crosscutting Process performance targets and indicators must be developed and updated, if necessary, in parallel with the other performance planning activities of the Agency.

The Office of the Chief Financial Officer coordinates the integration of the Agency Performance Plan, the Enterprise Strategic Plans, and the Functional Leadership Plans with the Agency's 5-year budget. Each Enterprise or Functional Office, as appropriate, presents its recommended resources and Performance Plan targets to the CIC. The CIC supports this decision process as the principal advisory group to the Administrator in resolving Agency issues, prioritizing activities (programs, capital investments, and Functional Office initiatives), and distributing resources among the Enterprises.

The CIC develops an integrated recommendation, which is then provided to the Administrator and the Senior Management Council. The Administrator's decisions, taking into account NASA's current Strategic Plan, form the basis of the Agency's 5-year budget request and Performance Plan that are to be submitted to OMB.

All program planning for the upcoming fiscal year is updated or revalidated following the submission of the Agency budget to OMB. The Enterprises work with their Lead Centres to balance anticipated resources with program and institutional planning. This may entail the adjustment of Centre Implementation Plans, Program Commitment Agreements, and Program and Project Plans as necessary.

Centre Implementation Planning

Centre implementation planning integrates programmatic direction, resources availability, functional needs, and institutional capabilities to achieve strategic plans. The Centre Implementation Plans define the relationship of the Agency and Enterprise strategic plans to the Centres' missions, Centre of Excellence responsibilities, program-specific assignments, and support activities. These plans also ensure alignment of the institutional, program, and functional activities at the Centres with the Enterprise (Lead Centre, Supporting Centre) and functional (Principal Centre) assignments. The Centre Implementation Plans should be consistent with corresponding Centre Program and Project Plans and coordinated during preparation with the appropriate Functional Offices. The plans must be updated as necessary to reflect current budget and program realities.

Institutional Program Offices are responsible for approving the Centre Implementation Plans, with the concurrence of all Enterprise Associate Administrators associated with the Centre. The Enterprise Associate Administrators approve the performance and budget decisions of their respective Centres, ensuring that the Centre Implementation Plans support the Enterprise Strategic Plan and budget in force at the time they are issued. The Senior Management Council reviews the Centre Implementation Plans annually.

Management and Employee Performance Planning

Enterprise Associate Administrator Performance Plans

Each Enterprise Associate Administrator's Performance Plan is executed annually, for the upcoming year, as a documented agreement between the Administrator and the respective Enterprise Associate Administrator. This planning requirement also applies to the Associate Administrator for the Office of Life and Microgravity Sciences and Applications.

Functional Office Associate Administrator and Official-in-Charge Performance Plans

A Performance Plan for each Functional Office Associate Administrator and Official-in-Charge is also executed annually, for the upcoming year, as a documented agreement between the Administrator and the respective Functional Office Associate Administrator or Official-in-Charge.

Centre Director Performance Plans

Each Centre Director's Performance Plan is to be executed annually as a documented agreement between Enterprise Associate Administrators/ Institutional Program Officers and their respective Centre Directors. This plan will include performance goals and indicators for the Centre. Concurrence of other Headquarters officials may be required if the scope of the plan is broad and as agreed between the Centre Director and the Enterprise Associate Administrator.

Individual Performance Plans

All civil service NASA employees, including managers and executives, will have personal annual performance plans developed with their supervisors. These plans will not only be consistent with all pertinent NASA directives, but also explicitly support the overall strategic goals of the Agency. The performance plans will serve as the reference documents for the annual performance appraisals of all employees, managers, and executives.

Implementation in the Operating Year

Preparation and Transmission of an Operating Plan

As a part of the budget planning cycle, and in anticipation of receiving new obligational authority from congressionally enacted appropriations, the Agency prepares a draft of a detailed operating plan. This draft documents programmatic changes that have occurred since the submission of the President's budget, and it identifies any associated changes in the resources required to implement the program for the upcoming fiscal year.

After Congress enacts the Agency's appropriation for the operating year, the draft operating plan is modified to reflect any congressionally directed changes contained in the appropriations or authorization bills. This initial operating plan is then signed by the Administrator after clearance from OMB and sent to NASA's congressional committees.

Appropriations or Authorization Impact on the Performance Plan

In the event that NASA's appropriations and authorization bills require changes to the programs or program funding that, in turn, require changes to the performance targets included in the final Performance Plan for the operating year, NASA will revise the plan to reflect those changes. The revised final Performance Plan must be cleared by the Executive Office of the President prior to transmittal to Congress, after which program planning that is affected during this budget deliberation and approval process is updated.

Operating Plan Adjustments

As necessary during the period of the appropriation's availability for obligation, NASA provides notice to the Executive Office of the President and Congress of material changes in program plans and funding allocations. These notifications enable NASA to keep all parties appropriately advised of new developments and receive in return their advice and consent.

Performance Evaluation

Performance Evaluation Process

Whether NASA is successful in carrying out its missions is determined by the Agency's ability to meet or surpass the goals outlined in its strategic and performance plans. NASA uses objective and verifiable performance metrics, regular management insight and review processes, or comparable tools to assess its performance at all levels—Agency, Strategic Enterprises, Functional Offices, Centres, Crosscutting Processes, programs and projects, and the individual employee. Each level participates in setting performance targets, evaluating performance against those targets, and reporting the results. If performance measures are carefully and thoughtfully chosen and applied, the annual performance evaluation becomes one of our most important ways of identifying problem areas and opportunities for better management and greater organizational effectiveness.

Agency Annual GPRA Performance Report and other External Reporting Requirements

The external reporting required by NASA's performance evaluation process is extensive. The underlying principle is that the public and elected Federal officials are entitled to assurances that appropriations requested and received have been, and will continue to be, spent judiciously, efficiently, and effectively for approved goals and missions. Accordingly, the NASA annual Performance Report on its fiscal operations of the past fiscal year includes considerable discussion of plans accomplished and results achieved. In addition, of course, the annual budget formulation and justification process requires the linkage of performance plans to requested budgets, as well as justification for the acquisition of capital assets. Information developed for NASA's performance-reporting obligations may be used as well to comply with additional reporting requirements, such as the Chief Financial Officers Act, the Federal Managers Financial Integrity Act, and the Administrator's Performance Report to the President.

External Reviews

Much of NASA's success in carrying out its missions results from its close working relationships with researchers in universities and other nongovernment organizations, including the National Research Council's Space Studies Board and Aeronautics and Space Engineering Board, and with industry. All of these relationships contribute to planning and evaluating NASA's exploration of space while keeping the United States on the forefront of aerospace technologies.

These diverse communities understand the varied nature of NASA's challenges and are well positioned to assess its progress in meeting them. NASA also maintains a broad and diverse system of advisory committees under the Federal Advisory Committee Act, which includes the NASA Advisory Council and its subcommittees and the Aerospace Safety Advisory Panel, created by Congress. The Agency uses these advisory groups to obtain external input to its strategies and performance planning and evaluation activities.

Some other Federal agencies (such as the Environmental Protection Agency, the General Accounting Office, the Occupational Safety and Health Administration, and the Small Business Administration) are entrusted by Congress to assure that certain governmental activities comply with Federal laws and regulations for which those agencies have primary jurisdiction.

Independent Validation of Performance Measures

NASA's performance measures will be subjected to independent validation by organizations, including the General Accounting Office, NASA's Office of Inspector General, and other cognizant entities. Periodic independent audits may also be conducted by outside registrars to achieve ISO 9001 certification for NASA's principal processes.

Education, Training, and Rewards in Strategic Management

The Office of Human Resources and Education develops Agency policy for employee training pertaining to the general principles of strategic management, GPRA, NASA's strategic management process, the NASA Strategic Plan, performance planning and measurement, and the importance of all employees to NASA's success. This office also develops Agency-level policy and guidance regarding awards and other forms of recognition that foster and reward exceptional employee achievements and contributions toward the accomplishment of NASA's strategic mission and performance targets.

Bibliography

Adler, N.J.: *International Dimensions of Organizational Behavior*, PWS-Kent Publishing Company, Boston, 1991.

Bardsley, N., Cubitt: *Assessing Experimental Marketing*, Princeton, Princeton University Press, 2009.

Benería, Lourdes. *Gender, Development, and Globalization, Economics as if All People Mattered,* New York and London, Routledge, 2003.

Cakar, F. and Bititci, U.S.: *Human Resource Management as a Strategic Input to Manufacturing,* Aalborg, Denmark, 2001.

Commons, J. R., *Institutional Economics-Its Place in Political Economy*, The University of Wisconsin Press, Madison, Wisconsin, 1934.

Desmond, Glenn, and John A, Marcell, *Handbook of Small Business Valuation Formulas and Rules of Thumb,* Valuation Press, 1993.

Dunfee, T. : *That Bind: A Social Contracts Approach to Business Ethics,* Boston, HBS HBS Harvard Business School, 1999.

Elliot, Richard and Larry Percy: *Strategic Brand Management*, Oxford University Press, Delhi, 2007.

Fleetwood, S. & Hesketh, A.: *Understanding the Performance of Human Resources*, Cambridge University Press, Cambridge, 2009.

Fruhan, W. E.: *Financial Strategy, Studies in the Creation, Transfer and Destruction of Shareholder Value*. Homewood, 1979.

Goodall, Steve: *Developing Environmental Education in the Curriculum*, London, David Fulton Publishers, 1994.

Granger, Clive W. J.: *Empirical Marketing in Economics, Specification and Evaluation*, London, Cambridge University Press, 1999.

Haines, S. G.: *The Systems Thinking Approach to Strategic Planning and Management*, St. Lucie Press, Delray Beach, FL, 2000.

Hayek, F. A. *Individualism and Economic Order*, The University of Chicago Press, Chicago, 1948.

Jack Murrin, *Valuation: Measuring and Managing the Value of Companies,* New York, Wiley, 1994.

Janis, I. L., & Mann, L.: *Decision Making, A Psychological Analysis of Conflict, Choice and Commitment*. New York, Free Press, 1977.

Kapferer, J : *Strategic Brand Management : Creating and Sustaining Brand Equity Long Term*, Kogan Page India, Delhi, 2009.

Keith Davis : *Business and Society.-Corporate Strategy, Public Policy, and Ethics,* New York, McGraw-Hill, 1992.

Lindblom, C. E.: *A Strategy of Decision: Policy Evaluation as a Social Process*, New York, The Free Press, 1970.

Lindblom, C. E.: *A Strategy of Decision: Policy Evaluation as a Social Process*, New York, The Free Press, 1970.

Magnussen, L., *Evolutionary and Neo-Schumpeterian Approaches to Economics*, Kluwer, Boston, 1994.

Manuel, G. Velasquez : *Business Ethics Concepts and Cases,* Delhi, Pearson Education, 2002.

Pareek, Saroj : *Strategic Brand Management : Research Theory and Practice,* Shree Niwas Publications, Delhi, 2012.

Patel, Vinod N. and Sandeep Sharma: *Brand Management and Consumer Marketing,* Oxford Book Company, Delhi, 2011.

Robbins, P. : *Greening the Corporations: Management Strategy and the Environmental Challenge* , London: Earthscan, 2001.

Russell Parr, *Valuation of Intellectual Property and Intangible Assets,* New York: Wiley, 1994.

Salancik, G. R.: *The External Control of Organizations, A Resource Dependence Perspective*, New York, 1978.

Schumpeter, J. A., *The Theory of Economic Development*, Harvard University Press,Cambridge, Massachusetts, 1934.

Tietenberg, Tom, *Environmental Economics and Policy,* New York, HarperCollins, 1994

Tim Koller, and Jack Murrin, *Valuation: Measuring and Managing the Value of Companies,* New York, Wiley, 1994.

Weber, M.: *The Theory of Social and Economic Organizations*, New York, Oxford University Press, 1947.

Weber, M.: *The Theory of Social and Economic Organizations*, New York, Oxford University Press, 1947.

Woodward, J.: *The Oxford Handbook of Philosophy of Economics*, New York, Oxford University Press, 2009.

Yegge, Wilbur M., *A Basic Guide for Valuing a Company*, New York, Wiley, 1996.

Zipp, Alan S., *Business Valuation Methods* New York, American Institute of Certified Public Accountants, 1990.

Index

❑❑❑